Arndt Brendecke, Peter Vogt (Eds.)
The End of Fortuna and the Rise of Modernity

The End of Fortuna and the Rise of Modernity

Edited by
Arndt Brendecke and Peter Vogt

DE GRUYTER
OLDENBOURG

ISBN 978-3-11-066019-7
e-ISBN (PDF) 978-3-11-045504-5
e-ISBN (EPUB) 978-3-11-045259-4

Library of Congress Cataloging-in-Publication Data
A CIP catalog record for this book has been applied for at the Library of Congress.

Bibliografische Information der Deutschen Nationalbibliothek
The Deutsche Nationalbibliothek lists this publication in the Deutsche Nationalbibliografie;
detailed bibliographic data are available on the Internet at http://dnb.dnb.de.

© 2019 Walter de Gruyter GmbH, Berlin/Boston
This volume is text- and page-identical with the hardback published in 2017.
Typesetting: bsix information exchange GmbH, Braunschweig
Printing and binding: CPI books GmbH, Leck
♾ printed on acid free paper
Printed in Germany

www.degruyter.com

Content

Brendecke/Vogt
Introduction
The Late Fortuna and the Rise of Modernity —— 1

Susanne Reichlin
The Relationship between Regularity and Irregularity in Middle High German Poems on Fortuna —— 15

Burkhardt Wolf
Fortuna's Sea Change
Renaissance Poetics of Contingency —— 47

Nicolette Mout
Justus Lipsius (1547–1606): Fortune and War —— 63

Müller/Gruber
Fortuna Revalued
On the Goddess's Sexualisation in the Renaissance —— 82

José M. González García
Fortuna in Seventeenth Century Spain
Literature, Politics and the Visual Arts —— 108

Peter Vogt
The Death of Fortuna and the Rise of Modernity
Prolegomena to any Future Theory of Modernity —— 125

Franziska Rehlinghaus
Farewell to Fortuna – Turning towards Fatum
The Transformation of Fate Conceptions in the Seventeenth and Eighteenth Centuries —— 151

Kristiina Savin
Fortuna in Early Modern Sweden
The Heyday and Decline of a Commonplace Concept —— 175

Florence Buttay
La Fortune victime des Lumières ?
Remarques sur les transformations de Fortune aux
XVIIe et XVIIIe siècles —— **192**

List of Illustrations —— **211**

Index of Persons —— **215**

Arndt Brendecke/Peter Vogt
The Late Fortuna and the Rise of Modernity

1 Fortuna's Transformations

Fortuna, the goddess of chance and luck, should actually no longer have had a place in the Christian mediaeval period, at least if Christianity had abided by the condemnation of Fortuna in late antiquity by the church father Augustine. As Walter Haug – in a reference to Matthew 10:29 – aptly put it, Fortuna would have "no place [in a world] in which not a single sparrow falls to earth without the will of God."[1] But Fortuna possessed a fascinating ability to transform, allowing her to survive the transition of the ages and live on until the threshold of modernity.[2] An ancient goddess, known as Tyche or Fortuna, thus became a persistent motive in the Christian mediaeval period.[3] This transformation was possible on the basis of Stoic-Neoplatonic traditions which maintained their influence within Christianity. They see Fortuna and chance (*casus*) as the expression of a hidden order, i.e. based on causes that exist but remain unknown to us.[4] While Boethius, in *De consulatione philosophiae* (524 CE), was not entirely able to resolve the fundamental contradiction between the omniscience and providence of God and the actions of an apparently arbitrary Fortuna, he did manage to exploit it for Christian didactic purposes. This Boethian Fortuna, namely, was able to demonstrate to the individual Christian the unpredictable vicissitudes of worldly existence. She taught him or her to place little value on earthly life and to treasure the safe ground of faith. This Christian mediaeval Fortuna appeared with increasing frequency from the twelfth century onwards:

---

[1] Haug, Walter, "O Fortuna. Eine historisch-semantische Skizze zur Einführung", in: Walter Haug and Burghart Wachinger (eds.), *Fortuna*. Tübingen 1995, 1–22, 1.
[2] Meyer-Landrut, Ehrengard, *Fortuna. Die Göttin des Glücks im Wandel der Zeiten*, Munich, Berlin 1997.
[3] Frakes, Jerold C., *The Fate of Fortune in the Early Middle Ages. The Boethian Tradition*, Leiden, New York, Copenhagen, Cologne 1998, 29–30.
[4] Even in the early work of Augustine, in *Contra Academicos* (AD 386), the argument can clearly be found that that which we call Fortuna could be directed by a system of order to which we have no access ("etenim fortasse quae vulgo fortuna nominatur, occulto quodam ordine regitur"). Later, in *De civitate Dei* (AD 415) and in the *Retractationes* (AD 426/427), an explicit criticism of *Contra Academicos*, Augustine rejects his earlier position as an illegitimate obligation to ancient thought. See Markschies, Christoph, "'Providence leaves no real room to fortuna'. Vom Zufall bei Augustinus" in: Hartmut Böhme, Werner Röcke and Ulrike Stephan (eds.): *Contingentia. Transformationen des Zufalls*, Berlin, Boston 2016, 39–49, 43.

as an assistant of the Christian God, she no longer stood for pure arbitrariness, but rather for the decrepitude of all that is worldly. The wheel now became her primary attribute: its rotation demonstrated a drastic change in fortune, which did, however, follow a certain regular pattern. But the depiction of kings being cast down and peasants raised up was in fact a representation of a phenomenon that was virtually non-existent in estates-based society, namely social mobility between the estates and a rotation of social roles.[5] Fortuna's actions could thus lead to abrupt change in individual cases, but what seemed unjust in an single case was actually subject to a balancing logic overall.

The Renaissance formed a very different concept of the increasingly popular Fortuna. She was considered to be fundamentally unpredictable, but also potentially open to influence, either through *fortitudo* or *prudentia*, thus reviving and renewing ancient ideas on the subject. The former was also based on authors such as Terence ("fortis fortuna adiuvat"), but primarily on Cicero with his concept of a *vir virtutis*,[6] while the latter drew its legitimacy from Seneca and Stoicism. Cicero had argued that Fortuna could be set on a favourable course through *fortitudo*. The Stoic tradition, in contrast, emphasised that one should make oneself independent of her whims through *prudentia* and the calmness of one's own soul (*tranquillitas animi*). One should allow oneself to be corrupted neither by misfortune nor by unexpected luck, which Fortuna also constantly promised to deliver. The one tradition thus aims for a self-awareness able to win the benevolence of Fortuna, climaxing in the topos of *virtù vince fortuna*. The other, Stoic tradition aims for an inner countenance which minimises the effect of worldly vicissitudes. Both have been well researched, as the Renaissance Fortuna has attracted generations of historians. They have followed the transformation of the goddess into a topos, thereby always remaining aware of her role as a highly significant marker of the epochal transition of European forms of thought.[7] For with Fortuna's help, a new relationship of the individual to history can be marked out, thus enabling us to follow the two great epochal trends of the early modern period, namely the development of a new under-

---

[5] Haug, Walter, "O Fortuna", 7; Müller, Jan-Dirk, "Die Fortuna des Fortunatus. Zur Auflösung mittelalterlicher Sinndeutung des Sinnlosen", in: Walter Haug and Burghart Wachinger (eds.), *Fortuna*, 216–238, 218.

[6] Cicero, *Tusculanae Disputationes*, lib. II, cap. 18, par. 43; Vogt, Peter, "Virtù vince fortuna. Aufstieg, Wandel und späte Blüte eines frühneuzeitlichen Topos", in: Hartmut Böhme, Werner Röcke and Ulrike Stephan (eds.), *Contingentia*, 81–82.

[7] Haug, Walter, "O Fortuna", 21; Politis, Cordula, *The Individualization of Fortune in the Sixteenth-Century Novels of Jörg Wickram. The Beginnings of the Modern Narrative in German Literature*, Lewiston, N.Y. 2007, 1.

standing of historical time (and open future) and the constitution of a self-consciously acting subject.

The history of Fortuna shows that this transformation occurred neither quickly nor in linear fashion. A single moment cannot be determined in which, as Jacob Burckhardt illustratively put it, the veil was lifted under which the mediaeval period had lain "dreaming or half-awake".[8] In fact, the opposite is more the case, namely that there was a long period of overlap between late mediaeval-Christian and proto-modern views of mankind and history. Fortuna was party to neither one nor the other. In fact, she was quite the opposite, contributing to the practical mediation between the fundamental contradictions which persisted for an extended period of time. For pointing out these contradictions meant admitting that the success and failure, the luck and misfortune of a person could be ascribed neither entirely to providence nor entirely to his or her own achievements and virtues, and above all meant emphasising that it was indeterminable in a very significant way which of these factors was most decisive. The motif of Fortuna, therefore, continued to appear during the Renaissance as a quasi-divine power, while also representing a deficiency, namely human inability to predict and plan the courses of their lives and courses of action, i.e. the lack of ability both to dispose over oneself and to decipher the mechanisms of history in their entirety.

The lessons to be learned from this varied and transformed considerably during the Renaissance. In Dante's *Divina Commedia* (ca. 1307–1321) as well as in Petrarca's *De remediis utriusque fortunae* (1366), Fortuna initially remained a figure who acted mostly within the confines of God's providence. For the individual, this meant that it appeared to be neither virtuous nor promising to rebel against Fortuna, i.e. to question God's providence.[9] In historical-philosophical terms, this raised serious questions: if Fortuna's actions did indeed follow a (hitherto) hidden plan, then this plan must eventually be able to be deciphered.[10] Fortuna, however, historically distributed luck whimsically and unequally. The Renaissance experience of a rather increasing amplitude in the vi-

---

[8] Jacob Burckhardt, *Die Cultur der Renaissance in Italien. Ein Versuch.* 2nd Edition, Leipzig 1869, 104.
[9] Particularly Petrarca's concept of Fortuna is subject to varying interpretations. Cf. on the one hand Heitmann, Klaus, *Fortuna und Virtus. Eine Studie zu Petrarcas Lebensweisheit*, Cologne, Graz 1958, 84; on the other hand: Keßler, Eckhard, *Petrarca und die Geschichte. Geschichtsschreibung, Rhetorik, Philosophie im Übergang von Mittelalter zur Neuzeit*, Munich 1978, 141–158.
[10] Wootton, David, "From Fortune to Feedback. Contingency and the Birth of Modern Political Science", in: I. Shapiro and S. Bedi (eds.), *Political Contingency. Studying the Unexpected, the Accidental and the Unforeseen*, New York 2007, 21–53, 22.

cissitudes of luck and misfortune, rise and fall, poverty and wealth, historical success and failure, led to a need for new models both of history and of human control over it. Both emerged in places where such vicissitudes could be most directly observed and indeed experienced, namely at the courts and in the city republics of Italy. There, the motif of Fortuna experienced a new blossoming: strokes of fate became a literary theme, and even, to a certain extent, a structural element of biographical narrative, such as in Boccaccio's *De casibus virorum illustrium* written around 1360.

But how should one brace oneself for these whims of Fortuna? In the works of many authors, including Boccaccio, the dominant argument is a moralising one which insists that pride and greed must be avoided, as they provoke a punishment which corrects the will to advance if it is driven by sinful motives. An actual transformed relationship between *virtus* and Fortuna did not appear until the quattrocento: many authors then began to portray Fortuna as a power which could be controlled through *virtù*, although the extent of this control remained a matter of contention. Leon Battista Alberti highlighted the fact that individuals and peoples were the architects of their own fortune. One's own *virtù* was thereby marked as a determining factor to which Fortuna potentially adhered.[11] The ancient argument now reappeared that fortune favoured the bold and strong. "Audentis fortuna iuvat", Virgil wrote.[12] Aeneas Silvius Piccolomini went a step further in his *Somnium de fortuna* (1444): here, it is the victorious Alfonso V of Aragon entering Naples who grabs Fortuna by the scruff of the neck and subjugates her.[13]

Fortuna was now literally being brought down to earth and luck was becoming potentially controllable. This subjugation topos had notable gender connotations, for men were now conceptualising the goddess as a women. This was most clearly formulated by Machiavelli, who famously wrote that Fortuna is "a woman". In order to subjugate her, according to Machiavelli, it is necessary "to beat her and strike her down. And one also sees that she lets herself be won more by the impetuous than by those who proceed coldly. And so always, as a woman, she is the friend of the young, since they are less cautious, more ferocious, and command her with more audacity."[14]

---

[11] Vogt, "Virtù", 90–91.
[12] Aeneis X.284, Vogt, "Virtù", 81.
[13] Wolkan, Rudolf (ed.), *Die Briefe des Eneas Silvius Piccolomini. I. Abteilung. Briefe aus der Laienzeit (1431–1445). Band 1: Privatbriefe*, Vienna 1909, 350.
[14] "perché la fortuna è donna, e è necessario, volendola tenere sotto, batterla e urtarla; e si vede che la si lascia piú vincere da questi, che da quelli che freddamente procedano e però sempre, come donna, è amica de' giovani, perché sono meno respettivi, piú feroci e con piú audacia la comandano.", Machiavelli, Il Principe, XXV, here quoted after: Edizione Nazionale

This Fortuna can not only be defeated by a masculine connoted *virtù*: she now becomes observable as well, namely as *occasio*.[15] A subject is now assumed who observes the passage of time, continually calculates his chances and attempts "to make" his luck, whether this be through a spirited action or through a carefully considered investment.

As modern as both this image of a man of action making his own luck and that of a clever agent calculating his chances are, they are constantly put into perspective by contemporaries. Machiavelli, for example, cautions that control over our actions is only half based on *virtù*, with the other half remaining the domain of Fortuna.[16] Francesco Guicciardini even returns to a more pessimistic estimation of the possibilities for action situated within an individual's power. This noticeable "loss of faith in the power of virtù"[17] was interpreted by Felix Gilbert as a symptom of the decline of republican city culture. The topos of *virtù vince fortuna* lost credibility, and Fortuna once again gained the upper hand, rising to become a "ruler of world history", as Gilbert suggested.[18]

It is at this point that the present volume begins, taking the fact that we know disproportionately little about the late blooming of Fortuna following the Renaissance as its point of departure. It also raises questions concerning the significance of the subsequent end of Fortuna, i.e. her significance for the epochal transition to the early modern period. In doing so, as the contributions to the volume clearly show, a wide spectrum of scenarios and concepts come to the fore, including vernacular traditions, confessional differences and complementary concepts, such as those of luck, fate and contingency.[19] Before introducing this spectrum of topics through a summary of the individual contributions, however, we consider it necessary to mention several more general aspects of the question regarding the epochal transition.

---

delle Opere di Niccolò Machiavelli, vol. I/1, a cura di Mario Martelli, corredo filologico a cura di Nicoletta Marcelli, 310.
15 Vogt, "Virtù", 91–92.
16 Ibid., 93–94.
17 Skinner, Quentin, *The Foundations of Modern Political Thought. Volume 1: The Renaissance*, Cambridge, London, New York 1978, 187.
18 Gilbert, Felix, *Machiavelli and Guicciardini. Politics and History in Sixteenth-Century Florence*, Princeton 1965, 269–270.
19 For the transformation of Fortuna into the concept of fate see: Münkler, Herfried, *Machiavelli. Die Begründung des politischen Denkens der Neuzeit aus der Krise der Republik Florenz*, Frankfurt am Main 1982, 300; further: Frick, Werner, *Providenz und Kontingenz. Untersuchungen zur Schicksalssemantik im deutschen und europäischen Roman des 17. und 18. Jahrhunderts*, Teil 1, Tübingen 1988; Rehlinghaus, Franziska, *Die Semantik des Schicksals. Zur Relevanz des Unverfügbaren zwischen Aufklärung und Erstem Weltkrieg*, Göttingen 2015.

2 The Late Fortuna – a Rise of Modernity?

We assume that the end of Fortuna is significant for the transition to modernity. For the improbable did in fact occur: Fortuna actually died. This happened in the wake of a late blossoming of the motif found in French and Dutch Stoicism, English literature of the Elizabethan Age, the Spanish literature of the *Siglo de Oro* and German baroque poetry. But the manifold references to Fortuna, which appeared to be equally natural for Quevedo or Calderón de la Barca, for Shakespeare or Marlowe, for Lipsius, Opitz or Fleming, are entirely absent in the works of authors such as Descartes, Galilei, Calvin and Pascal. While there are still some allusions to Fortuna to be found after the seventeenth century, the motif now seems to have become empty, with an autonomous will of Fortuna no longer being acceptable. Wherever one still finds the word or the motif, it can be harmlessly replaced with "chance", "luck" or "misfortune". In the eighteenth and nineteenth centuries, the term was further vulgarised, with Fortuna being used to advertise for lotteries. From the perspective of Fortuna's very long history, the question arises as to what caused her "death", and also which transformations characterise the views of history and mankind to emerge once Fortuna has been removed.

Without wishing to steal thunder from the following contributions, almost all of which both address the late forms of reference to Fortuna and formulate their own hypotheses to explain her end, introductory remarks will be made here concerning long-term transformations which seemed to rob Fortuna of the air she breathed.

Unsurprisingly, no single cause can be identified for the demise of Fortuna. We must accept that a cluster of factors is responsible, the exact make-up of which varies according to the respective cultural context and historical moment. It is relatively easy, for example, to identify Neostoicism or Calvinism as important factors. Lipsius devalued Fortuna, considering instead *fatum* and *providentia* to be of significance.[20] And in Calvinism, there was no longer a legitimate place for Fortuna or luck or chance, since success was to be seen as a blessing from God, and its opposite as his punishment.[21] These two factors alone, however, cannot explain why Fortuna lost significance throughout all of Europe, despite there being slight delays in the phases of this process. In order to arrive at an explanation for this, transformations in the history of ideas must

---

[20] Vogt, "Virtù", 100–101; Wilfried Barner, "Die gezähmte Fortuna. Stoizistische Modelle nach 1600", in: W. Haug / B. Wachinger (eds.), *Fortuna*, Tübingen 1995, 311–343; Cf. also the contribution by Nicolette Mout in this volume.
[21] Novak, Maximilian E., *Defoe and the Nature of Man*, Oxford 1963, 7.

be abstracted from and our view must be directed towards structural changes found in the society, economy and semantics of the sixteenth and seventeenth centuries. It then becomes clear that the locations and moments of dramatic experiences of contingency shifted. It was no longer the political vicissitudes of Italian city republics that provided the blueprints for the question of one's rise and fall, but rather the early absolutist courts with their factions and their peculiar *malice*,[22] civil and trading towns with their specific organisational, investment and insurance forms, and new, long wars, which affected many more people both directly and indirectly.

These growing and often new spaces of experience posed challenges to the management of contingency that the Fortuna motif was no longer able to meet in the medium term. With respect to the impact of the Reformation and of urban, competitive society, Eric Voegelin boldly retraced one of these processes:

> By the nineteenth century the biological formula of the survival of the fittest had replaced the Renaissance speculation on the 'fortuna secunda et adversa', and the survival of the fittest implies the plebeian assumption that the survivor is the better man.[23]

More recent research has shown that in the field of trade, semantic shifts devaluing Fortuna occurred much earlier. She especially lost her suitability in situations in which it was necessary to cover contingency in contracts and to take it into account economically. In such contexts, it seemed advisable to define the possible effects of accidental occurrences and thus to limit the damage sustained. This was possible by distinguishing between the primary (and unavoidable) uncertainty of a ship's voyage, for example, and the secondary uncertainty, which would consist of uncertainty regarding the possible consequences of a shipwreck. Fortuna, as a goddess *entirely* responsible for bestowing luck or misfortune, was not suitable to frame this distinction. While she was able to occupy a place in stories about the participating traders or sailors for several more centuries, she was no longer present in their contracts and books, or only in a very different form. The word indeed appeared as early as the thirteenth century

---

22 Vogt, Peter, *Kontingenz und Zufall. Eine Begriffs- und Ideengeschichte*, Berlin 2011, 596.
23 Eric Voegelin, David L. Morse u. William M. Thompson (eds.), *History of Political Ideas. Vol. IV: Renaissance and Reformation. Edited with an Introduction by David L. Morse and William M. Thompson*, Columbia, London 1998, 48. For the emergence of a bourgeois adventure ideology, see Nerlich, Michael, *Ideology of Adventure. Studies in Modern Consciousness*, 1100 – 1750, Minneapolis 1987.

in the form of *fortuna maris*, but was revealingly limited to the primary uncertainty, i.e. to certain accidental occurrences while the ship was at sea.[24] Although one was unavoidably prone to the primary risks of storm and shipwreck when putting to sea, one could at least avert the secondary uncertainties by planning in advance who was to be liable for which share of a partial or complete loss, and then if necessary insuring against this possible loss or minimising risk by spreading one's own investment over several ships. For this distinction between (unavoidable) natural risks on the one hand and (insurable) resulting costs on the other, there was a need not only for new terms, such as that of risk (*risco*), which can be found from the thirteenth century onwards, but also for new practices. In the field of trade, these meant that it became less frequent for the merchants financing the venture to travel themselves, instead having others carry out the voyage.[25] The provider of capital, and this is of decisive importance for us, was thus able to elude the power of Fortuna. Storms could no longer harm him physically, and were he to fall into poverty, this could only be because he had insured his ventures poorly or calculated incorrectly. Particularly in the field of trade, a second and powerful semantic shift thus took place. While Fortuna did experience a late blossoming there, especially in Venice, on which Burkhardt Wolf in particular goes into detail in this volume, she ceases to be a quasi-divine figure, instead becoming a linguistic metaphor for economic success. From then on, one was able to "make one's own luck", with expressions such as *to make a fortune* becoming increasingly common. They testify to a new subject-object relationship in which the individual merchant or adventurer "makes" Fortuna – and no longer vice versa. In Edmund Spenser's *The Faerie Queene* (1596), one even finds the verb form *to fortunize*.[26]

Comparable strategies can be observed in many sections of society at this time. While it was always acknowledged that there was a certain proportion of the indeterminable over which Fortuna ruled, noticeable efforts were being made to limit this share in any undertaking. Machiavelli himself describes in *Il*

---

24 Scheller, Benjamin, "Risiko – Kontingenz, Semantik und Fernhandel im Mittelmeerraum des Hoch- und Spätmittelalters", in: F. Becker, B. Scheller and U. Schneider (eds.): Die Ungewissheit des Zukünftigen. Kontingenz in der Geschichte, Frankfurt am Main 2016, 185–210, 193; Boiteux, Louis A., *La fortune de mer. Le besoin de sécurité et les débuts de l'assurance maritime*, Paris 1968; Cf. the contribution by Burkhardt Wolf in this volume.
25 For this purpose, an ad hoc consortium (*commenda*) was founded, in which the so-called *commendator* provided the capital and the *tractator* either simply ran the venture or added his own additional capital. Cf. Scheller, "Risiko – Kontingenz", 190–191.
26 Edmund Spenser, *The Second part of The faerie queene*, London 1596, VI, IX, Gg6v. On Fortuna in the work of Spenser, see the excellent study: Steppat, Michael, *Chances of Mischief. Variations of Fortune in Spenser*, Cologne, Vienna 1990.

Principe such a limitation strategy. Tellingly, Fortuna does not appear here as a woman to be subjugated, but rather as a river. The passage reads:

> I compare her [Fortuna] to one of those dangerous rivers that, when they become enraged, flood the plains, destroy trees and buildings [...] but this does not mean that, when the river is not in flood, men are unable to take precautions, by means of dykes and dams, so that the streams, when they swell once again, either remain within their riverbeds or their force is no longer as unbridled and devastating.[27]

It is thus quite literally possible to limit the terrain upon which Fortuna rages, hence allowing a limitation of her ability to affect the biography of a person or the political and economical stability of a municipal society. In this case, too, there is a basis in real life for this imagery, as Machiavelli, along with Leonardo da Vinci, was involved in the ultimately unsuccessful project of diverting the Arno River.[28]

Such strategies for limiting Fortuna naturally point to the coming of the modern age, with its desire for rationality and planning. But overemphasising this point would be to overlook the long-persisting coexistence of planning practices alongside a stubborn rear guard of Fortuna references. They run parallel, with Fortuna references fulfilling at least two functions well into the seventeenth century. On the one hand, they allow a continuation of Christian-moral didactics, with Fortuna still appearing as an assistant of God who primarily punishes pride. In certain genres of literature, this role remained so dominant that the Antwerp lexicographer Laurentius Beyerlinck even went as far as to define God himself as "Fortuna apud christianos".[29]

On the other hand, a quick reference to Fortuna allowed all elements which refused to submit to planning to be categorised rather elegantly into one sphere. The common feature of these two late forms of the Fortuna motif is that Fortuna functions as a placeholder, on the one hand – with a long tradition – for divine providence, and on the other for contingency. For both of these ideas, however, more appropriate terms and figures were increasingly becoming available, fi-

---

[27] "E assomiglio quella a uno di questi fiumi rovinosi, che, quando s'adirano, allagano e' piani, ruinano li arberi e li edifizii, [...]. e benché sieno cosí fatti, non resta però che li òmini, quando sono tempi quieti, non vi potessino fare provvedimenti e con ripari e argini, in modo que, crescendo poi, o andrebbono per uno canale, o l'impeto loro non sarebbe né sí licenzioso né sí dannoso." Vgl Machiavelli, *Il Principe*, XXV, here quoted after: Edizione Nazionale delle Opere di Niccolò Machiavelli, vol. I/1, a cura di Mario Martelli, corredo filologico a cura di Nicoletta Marcelli, 302–303.
[28] Masters, Roger D., *Fortune is a River. Leonardo Da Vinci and Niccolò Machiavelli's Magnificent Dream to Change the Course of Florentine History*, New York, London, Toronto u. a. 1998.
[29] Kirchner, Gottfried, *Fortuna in Dichtung und Emblematik des Barock. Tradition und Bedeutungswandel eines Motivs*, Stuttgart 1970, 117; Frick, *Providenz und Kontingenz*, 99.

nally substituting Fortuna once interest in her intrinsic ambivalence had disappeared. This is easily recognisable in areas, for example, where the remaining elements of uncertainty, which could have been attributed to Fortuna, were economised, as it was then no longer acceptable for these elements to be ambivalent, wild and arbitrary. Neither mercantile calculation nor its ethics, and the claim to social participation and leadership based upon them, could have any long-term interest in defining success as a product of random acts on the part of Fortuna. The terrain of her activity was thus not only reduced as much as possible and limited through planning and calculation, but also the concept of Fortuna was split: the products of this split were risk on the one hand[30], chance and luck on the other, but certainly no longer a figure who was able to unite the two sides, luck and misfortune, substantially.

3 The Contributions to this Volume

The articles collected in this volume have arisen from lectures presented in March 2015 upon invitation from the research centre "Fundamente der Moderne" of the Ludwig Maximilians University Munich. They cover a wide chronological spectrum that traces the transformations of the Fortuna motif from the High Middle Ages into the eighteenth century. In spatial terms, the focus of the articles reflects the great variety of an international conference which attempted to represent the European linguistic world as comprehensively as possible. With only one exception, it was possible to gather all lectures from the conference together in this volume. The following section will briefly summarise these contributions and outline the relationships between them:

The fundamental point of departure for the work of Susanne Reichlin is an objection to the schematic contrasting of the mediaeval and early modern Fortunas which has long dominated research on the topic. The specific objects of her investigation are the Middle High German *Sangsprüche* emerging between the late thirteenth and the early fourteenth centuries. The late mediaeval vernacular texts interpreted by Reichlin always speak of Fortuna, *saelde* and *gelücke* in an ambiguous manner which is not compatible with the image of a *single* homogeneous mediaeval Fortuna, a Fortuna who acts exclusively in the service of divine providence. In accordance with this, Reichlin sees in the late mediaeval texts which she interprets not so much the attempts of individual au-

---

30 For the concept of risk in the context of English economic and political theory, cf. Nacol, Emily C., *An Age of Risk. Politics and Economy in Early Modern Britain*, Princeton, Oxford 2016.

thors to find consistent theoretical answers to theological or metaphysical questions, but rather an "imaginary and ironic mode of coping with fortune" (page 46).

Burkhardt Wolf investigates the nautical connotations of Fortuna: from the interpretation of Tyche as the daughter of Oceanus in Hesiod's *Theogony* to Bernardo Falconi's sculpture at the entrance to the Canal Grande from 1678, which connects the political fate of the republic of Venice to the fortunes and dangers of marine trade and travel in a particularly striking manner. Wolf analyses the connection between his carefully chosen case studies and the developments in the field of insurance during the early modern period, and thus the accelerating transformation of a Fortuna previously considered unpredictable into the idea of risks, the assessment of which was of central importance for the emerging insurance business and the stock market: "Henceforth, one no longer dealt with Fortuna and her unfathomable temper, but rather with virtual realities, virtual values and virtual goods." (page 55) In conclusion, while Wolf does not speak of an "end" or even "death" of Fortuna, he does see her "demise" (pages 57, 62): "the notion of fortuna [...] was superseded by the estimations, calculations and pricings of modern risk management" (page 62).

Nicolette Mout, in her contribution, concentrates on the handling of Fortuna in the works of Justus Lipsius, particularly in his writings *De Constantia* (1584) and *Politica* (1589). Mout shows that Lipsius, entirely in accordance with his attempt to harmonise the teachings of the Stoa with those of Christianity, interprets Fortuna and Fatum as instances subject to divine providence. Mout places particular emphasis on Lipsius's work on the relationship between Fortuna and the incalculable intricacies of warfare and on the role of Fortuna for military strategy. While Fortuna disappears entirely from Lipsius's late writings on military theory and history, Mout demonstrates that the Stoic term *fatum* remains relevant even for these late works.

At the beginning of their article, Jürgen Müller and Bettina Gruber remind us of the early modern loss of significance of the mediaeval Fortuna with her wheel, going on to discuss the rise of Fortuna upon the sphere or even a globe. On the basis of an extensive discussion of literary and artistic representations of Fortuna from the late fifteenth century onwards, particularly in the works of Urs Graf, they reach the conclusion that the early modern Fortuna, who broke with long-standing iconological traditions, is to be seen as a "ground-breaking innovation in the self-perception of early modern societies" (page 83).

José González García addresses the presence of Fortuna in the Spanish literature and visual arts of the period from the middle of the fifteenth century until the middle of the seventeenth century. He first examines representations in which a connection between the reign of Charles V and Fortuna is established.

He then discusses the representation of Fortuna in the famous tapestry *Los Honores*, which was completed in 1523. At the end of his article, González García turns his attention to the Fortuna interpretation of Cervantes and sees in the pertinent exploits of Don Quijote an ambivalent view, since Fortuna is equated on the one hand with divine providence, while on the other hand, man is clearly declared to be the master of his own life and biography.

Peter Vogt, in the first section of his contribution, distinguishes between the phase of a "late blossoming" of Fortuna between 1580 and 1650 and a "subsequent decline of Fortuna" (page 125) beginning from the middle of the seventeenth century, which eventually led to a "death" of Fortuna around 1670. The premise of this argumentation and dating is a specific understanding of Fortuna. Vogt speaks of Fortuna "as a visual or textual representation of chance" (page 125). In this vein, Vogt argues that over a period of many centuries, "the most fundamental dimensions of human life" (page 126) were negotiated under the label "Fortuna". Vogt addresses the question of the historical causes of this development in the second section of his article. He discusses five *historical trends* of the early modern period and thus attempts to explain the findings presented in the first section. At the end of his contribution, Vogt argues in favour of two separate versions of modernity, versions between which he distinguishes based on their respective methods of dealing both practically and theoretically with the dimensions of uncertainty, ambiguity and chance connected with the term Fortuna.

At the beginning of her article, Franziska Rehlinghaus finds a fundamental "semantic transformation" (page 151) of Fortuna in the course of the late sixteenth and the seventeenth centuries, and connects this "agony" of Fortuna with the rise "of different forms of the concept of Fatum" (page 152). She then connects, in turn, the emergence of that concept of Fatum which attempted to reconcile *fatum* and *providentia* to the rise of a "mechanistic philosophy" (pages 152, 165 and 171) in the second half of the seventeenth century. In accordance with this, Rehlinghaus formulates her central theory as follows: "The concept of Fatum can thus be regarded as the missing link between a genuinely early modern interpretation of the world and a modern one" (page 152). For the relevance and reputation of Fortuna, the rise of the concept of Fatum had disastrous consequences. Fortuna, she argues, increasingly became an "absurdity" from the middle of the seventeenth century onwards: "Fortuna had to lose her place in a world that was no longer structured by anything but natural laws" (page 173).

Kristiina Savin, at the beginning of her contribution, reminds us of the theory proposed by the sociologist Anthony Giddens, who, in *The Consequences of Modernity*, described the replacement of the concept of Fortuna with that of risk as the constitutive signum of modernity. In the detailed examination of her sources from early modern Sweden, Savin arrives at a theory which is reminiscent of Rehlinghaus's argumentation: while Fortuna was increasingly vanishing from the theological discourse in the final decades of the seventeenth century, the term *fatum*, which Savin sees as being closely connected "with the mechanical view of the world and of nature that took hold around 1700" (page 183), gained in importance. A further cause of the demise of Fortuna lies for Savin in the "gradual move from orality to literacy" from the early eighteenth century onwards, along with a corresponding decline in rhetoric as an academic subject and an organ of cultural self-understanding: "Fortuna and a wide range of other classical Graeco-Roman personifications would probably be perceived as strange or comically pretentious in a modern text of highly literate culture" (page 188). This last argument leads Savin to arrive at a slightly different dating for the end of Fortuna than Vogt and Rehlinghaus: "It is probably no coincidence that the end of Fortuna falls in the period labelled *Sattelzeit* or *Schwellenzeit*, a transition from early modern to modern society with extensive significance for the vocabularies of European nations" (page 189).

Florence Buttay investigates the semantics of Fortuna and of *fortune* in the sense of money, property or wealth for the French-speaking world of the seventeenth and eighteenth centuries. Buttay does not consider it appropriate to speak of a "disparition" (page 192) of Fortuna during this period. Instead, Buttay finds a renewed transformation of Fortuna at the transition from the seventeenth century to the eighteenth century. As evidence to support this theory, she cites the burgeoning conjecture of the French term *fortune* at the beginning of the eighteenth century, which for Buttay demonstrates an "assimilation progressive de la Fortune à la richesse" (page 199). The stock market crash of 1720 in particular made this assimilation socially and culturally influential: "On peut donc dire que dans ce premier tiers du XVIIIe siècle, la Fortune se trouve étroitement liée aux expériences financières et aux ascensions sociales plus ou moins condamnables qu'elles promettent" (page 201). Here, Buttay contests the theory put forward by Yves Giraud, for whom the assimilation of Fortuna and *fortune* is an indication of the emaciation (*épuisement*) of the content traditionally designated by the term or allegory of Fortuna. Buttay's entire argumentation is based on a methodical premise which she explains in the concluding remarks of her article: Fortuna, she states, is not a substantial term, but rather a variable form which can serve various functions in different historical contexts. Since Fortuna never existed in a substantial sense, she can also never die: "En quelque sorte, Fortune ne peut pas mourir puisque Fortune, en elle-même, n'existe pas" (page 208). Nevertheless, Buttay also claims, following directly on from this theory, that the Fortuna who was inseparably connected in past times with the question of divine providence and was only discussed and able to be discussed in the context of this theme could indeed no longer be present in a society that had entirely disconnected itself from its Christian traditions. And therefore, even the article which, of all the contributions collected in this volume, speaks out most clearly against the theory of a possible end of Fortuna nevertheless seems to rehabilitate the idea within the framework of a contemporary diagnosis of present society.

The editors expressly wish to thank kindly the following people for their editorial support: Susanne Friedrich, Leonard Horsch and Hannes Ziegler, Isabel Sieger, Franz Huber, Florian Runschke and Liza Soutschek, and finally Linda Needham and Kerry Jago, as well as Bettina Neuhoff from the publishing house De Gruyter Oldenbourg.

Susanne Reichlin
The Relationship between Regularity and Irregularity in Middle High German Poems on Fortuna

1 Introduction

Boethius's *Consolatio* shaped Fortuna as a figure which links not only a theological, cosmological, moralistic and didactic discourse, but also different modes of representation, namely the voice of the personification (*prosopopoeia*[1]), her figurative description by different characters (dialogue) and the abstract philosophical discussion. The dialogue develops not one, but several verbal images of Fortuna: Fortuna as a blind (II 1p 33) and deaf figure (II 1c 5) and Fortuna crushing the mighty (II 1c 3); she is evoked as a donor who gives without obligation, but who has a right to reclaim everything (II 2p 3–21); she is compared to the sea (II 1p 54–55; 2p 26) and is also presented as a figure who turns a wheel (II 2p 29–33). Although Fortuna is vividly evoked as a personification, Philosophia at the same time questions her existence and unmasks her as a false pretence (II 1p 6–7, 31–32) or just a name (II 4p 8–9; 6p 62–70). Boethius thereby recalls antique textual and pictorial representations of Fortuna.[2] From its beginnings, the personification of Fortuna thus links text and image, and the popularity of Fortuna is undoubtedly to do with this media combination.

However, this has led to the supposition of a strong influence of pictorial and textual sources as well as of philosophical and literary texts in both Latin and the vernacular in the historical research. Pictorial documents of Fortuna are explained by philosophical texts and literary personification by miniatures, even when the temporal or geographical relations are not obvious. The pictorial representations of the wheel of fortune in combination with a standard refer-

---

[1] In the Second Book, the personification of Philosophia lends her voice to the personification of Fortuna (II 2p 1–2). We could therefore speak of a "second class" personification (II 3p 1–2). For an overview of the theoretical study on personifications in medieval literature, see Kiening, Christian, "Personifikation. Begegnungen mit dem Fremd-Vertrauten in mittelalterlicher Literatur", in: Helmut Brall / Barbara Haupt / Urban Küsters (eds.), *Personenbeziehungen in der mittelalterlichen Literatur*, Düsseldorf 1994, 347–387.
[2] Appuhn-Radtke, Sibylle, Art. "Fortuna", *Reallexikon der Kunstgeschichte* (2005), col. 271–401, 274–281; Courcelle, Pierre, *La consolation de philosophie dans la tradition littéraire*, Paris 1967, 127–134.

ence to the *Consolatio* have particularly shaped the idea which scholars have of the "medieval Fortuna":[3] The wheel stands for the arbitrary ascent and descent of man in worldly matters and reminds him – in a moral respect – of eternal Christian values and the vanity of worldly ambition. In a more metaphysical respect, the "medieval Fortuna" is said to raise the question of how the antique notion of an autonomous power of contingency can be integrated into a Christian world view, assuming the providence of the divine will.

In contrast to this idea of a global "medieval Fortuna", which not only looks alike in every medium, but also embodies the same concepts, I would like to take a closer look at the differences between pictorial and textual, philosophical and lyrical representations of Fortuna, thereby focusing on Middle High German poems about Fortuna.

---

[3] Patch, Howard R., *The Goddess Fortuna in Mediaeval Literature*, New York 1967, 152–159; Pickering, Frederik P. *Augustinus oder Boethius? Geschichtsschreibung und epische Dichtung im Mittelalter und in der Neuzeit*, Bd. 1: *Einführender Teil*, Berlin 1967, 21–25; Schilling, Michael, "Rota fortunae. Beziehungen zwischen Bild und Text in mittelalterlichen Handschriften", in: Wolfgang Harms / Peter L. Johnson (eds.), *Deutsche Literatur des Mittelalters. Hamburger Colloquium 1973*, Berlin 1975, 293–313, 296. This view of the medieval Fortuna was shaped by Alfred Doren, "Fortuna im Mittelalter und in der Renaissance", in: Ernst Cassirer / Fritz Saxl (eds.), *Vorträge der Bibliothek Warburg, Bd. 2, 1. Teil*, Leipzig 1922/23, 71–145, 76–86, whose study is – for his time – very impressive, although it needs to be reconsidered today. Doren follows the notion of the dark Middle Ages compared to the bright Renaissance and ignores all other notions of Fortuna (like the *fortuna caesarea*) which do not derive from Boethius, for which he has been criticised by modern scholars such as Schouwink, Wilfried, *Fortuna im Alexanderroman Rudolf von Ems. Studien zum Verhältnis von Fortuna und Virtus bei einem Autor der späten Stauferzeit*, Göppingen 1977, 25–28; for these, see Georg Steer, "Das Fortuna-Bild der 'Carmina Burana'-Handschrift Clm 4660. Eine Darstellung der 'fortuna caesarea' Kaiser Friedrichs II.?", in: Egon Kühebacher (ed.), *Literatur und bildende Kunst im Tiroler Mittelalter*, Innsbruck 1982, 183–207, 187–190; Schmidt-Wiegand, Ruth, "Fortuna Caesarea. Friedrich II u. Heinrich (VII) im Urteil zeitgenössischer Spruchdichter", in: Rüdiger Krohn et. al. (eds.), *Stauferzeit: Geschichte, Literatur, Kunst*, Stuttgart 1979, 195–205, 202–204. There are also several studies that do examine the distinctions between pictorial and textual representations of Fortuna closely, e.g. de Boor, Helmut, "Fortuna in mittelhochdeutscher Dichtung, insbesondere in der Crône Heinrichs von dem Türlin", in: Hans Fromm / Wolfgang Harms / Uwe Ruberg (eds.), *Verbum et signum. FS Friedrich Ohly. Bd. 2*, München 1975, 311–328; Kiefer, Frederick, "The Conflation of Fortuna and Occasio in Renaissance thought and iconography", *The Journal of Medieval and Renaissance Studies* 9 (1979), 1–27; Schilling, "Rota fortunae", or examine the specific traits of one media: Kitzinger, Ernst, "World Map and Fortune's Wheel: A Medieval Mosaic Floor in Turin", *Proceedings of the American Philosophical Society* 117 (1973), 344–373; Thürlemann, Felix, "Die Narrative Sequenz mit doppelter Figurenidentität. Zur Erzählstruktur der Rota Fortunae", in: Adolf Reinle / Peter Stotz / Ludwig Schmugge (eds.), *Variorum munera florum. Latinität als prägende Kraft mittelalterlicher Kultur. Festschrift für Hans F. Haefele zu seinem sechzigsten Geburtstag*, Sigmaringen 1985, 141–156.

These poems date from the late thirteenth and early fourteenth centuries and belong to the *Sangsprüche*, a lyric genre "of gnomic, monostanzaic songs. This genre coexisted with *Minnesang* (courtly love singing) at the German-speaking courts as a form of popular entertainment".[4] The genre was developed around 1200 by Walther von der Vogelweide, who addresses not only moral and didactic questions, but also political ones. Some stanzas are teaching extracts of courtly and Christian ethics. Others take sides in political disputes or reflect on the position of the poets, who depend of the favour of patrons and therefore have to flatter them. The songs are short and concise, but at the same time highly dependent on repetition, since a small group of motifs and commonplace figures are used repeatedly. The status of these texts with regard to their historical significance is thus hard to determine. On the one hand, the poems seem independent of specific historic events, repeating old and common knowledge. On the other hand, due to the repetition, the poets can also alter the traditional motifs and adapt them to new ways of thinking.

This also applies to the songs addressing Fortuna: they pick up the traditional interpretation of Fortuna as an allegory for the arbitrariness of success and wealth and the transience and vanity of earthly goods. They thereby develop new verbal images for the effects of fortune and chance. They pick up different traditions representing Fortuna and conflate traits and accoutrements of different personifications, namely *vrou Minne* (Lady Love) and *vrou Werlt* (Lady World). These poems thus seem to give us a summary of a late medieval discourse on Fortuna, which is not the forefront of intellectual development, but rather its sediment in the vernacular. By studying it, we perceive that "older ways of thinking about Fortune persisted alongside the new".[5] But which notions of Fortuna can be called old, and which ones new? And does it matter if the medium "of thinking about Fortune" is a text or a picture?

Methodically, we have to take into account the fact that the boundary between text and image does not conform to that of the abstract phenomenon of fortune and the figure of it. Instead, the texts and the images of Fortuna always treat fortune in a concrete or figural form *and* in a conceptual or abstract form.[6] But having acknowledged this, we must ask how the textual and the pictorial

---

[4] Frenzel, Peter, "Sangspruch", in: John M. Jeep (ed.), *Medieval Germany. An Encyclopedia*, New York 2001, 694. "Unlike the polystanzaic songs of *Minnesang*, *Sangspruch* was customarily confined to a single stanza. [...] and though the single stanza could stand by itself, thematic connections existed between some [...] stanzas" (ibid.). The recently published *Repertorium der Sangsprüche und Meisterlieder (RSM)* gives a comprehensive overview of all texts and melodies (*Ton*); I cite for each text the number of the *Repertorium*.
[5] Kiefer, "Conflation", 26.
[6] See Thürlemann, "Narrative Sequenz", 148.

media handle these two aspects of Fortuna and how they are related. If the lyric texts, as we will see, conflate different verbal images of Fortuna, we have to examine the conceptual consequences. We must also thereby pay attention to the differences between Latin and the vernacular languages: which connotations bear the vernacular semantics of fortune and how do the vernacular literary traditions transform the image of Fortuna? In the following contribution, I will thus not attempt to grasp Fortuna as a *topos*, which characterises an era, but rather to focus on the specific traits of its lyric representation in the Middle High German *Sangsprüche* through delineation of its representation in pictures or philosophical texts.

The first part of the paper will concentrate on the so-called "wheel of fortune". Scholars assume that Fortuna loses her various antique accoutrements in the Middle Ages and only the wheel remains.[7] On the conceptual level this is interpreted as part of the Christianisation of the goddess, since the wheel does not (only) represent instability, but also can stand for providence. But how is the relationship between stability and instability depicted or described in the different textual and pictorial representations? To examine these questions more closely, I will begin with a closer look at one miniature of the wheel of fortune and compare it to a poem, which presents us with an *ekphrasis* of a painted wheel of fortune (2). Some linguistic remarks on the terminology of fortune in medieval German will then be necessary, since there is not one, but indeed two terms for fortune (3). The vernacular semantics of *saelde* and *gelücke* as well as the literary means to represent an abstract power (e.g. *apostrophe*) alter the traits of Fortuna compared to the miniatures of the wheel of fortune. I would like to show this by analysing poems that describe the wheel as an autonomous power which acts on its own (4) and through a discussion as to whether and how the wheel can be brought to a standstill (5). In the last section, I would like to study poems that do not evoke the wheel of fortune any more, but instead address *vrou Saelde* or *Gelücke* from the first person perspective and with a distanced or even ironic attitude. I will ask how those personifications can be treated as personifications of Fortuna and how the ironic attitude changes the representation of the personification (6).

---

[7] Doren, "Fortuna", 76–86; Patch, *Goddess Fortuna*, 152–159; Pickering, *Augustinus oder Boethius?*, 21–25; Schilling, "Rota fortunae", 296; Radding, Charles M., "Fortune and Her Wheel. The Meaning of a Medieval Symbol", *Mediävistik* 5 (1992), 127, 130.

2 The *ekphrasis* of the Wheel of Fortune

Although the so-called "wheel of fortune" was very popular in miniatures, mosaics and rose windows from the twelfth century onwards,[8] we have an unexplained "time lag",[9] between Boethius's *Consolatio* and the earliest known miniature of the wheel of fortune from the eleventh century (Codex Casinensis 189). This is all the more astonishing considering the broad transmission of the *Consolatio* (in over 400 manuscripts) and the early translations into the vernaculars.[10] But as soon as we take a closer look at the verbal image of the wheel in the *Consolatio*, its vagueness is striking as well. Boethius[11] does not present one well-defined notion of a wheel of fortune, but instead offers a number of verbal images: sometimes the wheel (*rota*) rolls away (II 1p 59–60), sometimes it is responsible for the ascent or fall of somebody (II 2p 32–33), and sometimes it is depicted as a rotating disk (*orbis*). [12] While Boethius, on the conceptual level,

---

[8] There are several impressive overviews on this subject, see Appuhn-Radtke, "Fortuna"; Courcelle, *consolation*; Meyer-Landrut, Ehrengard, *Fortuna. Die Göttin des Glücks im Wandel der Zeiten*, München / Berlin 1997; Schilling, "Rota fortunae".
[9] Kitzinger, "World Map", 362; cf. Patch, *Goddess Fortuna*, 151; Radding, "Fortune", 129; Wirth, Jean, "L'iconographie médiévale de la roue de Fortune", in: Yasmina Foehr-Janssens (ed.), *La fortune. Thèmes, représentations, discours*, Genève 2003, 105–127; Tilliette, Yves, "Eclipse de la Fortune dans le haute moyen âge?", in: Yasmina Foehr-Janssens (ed.), *La fortune. Thèmes, représentations, discours*, Genève 2003, 93–104.
[10] See Courcelle, *consolation*, 29–90, 239–332; Gibson, Margaret T. / Smith, Lesley / Passalacqua, Marina (eds.), Codices Boethiani. A conspectus of manuscripts of the works of Boethius. London 1995–2009. Gruber, Joachim, *Kommentar zu Boethius, De Consolatione Philosophiae*. 2 erw. Aufl. Berlin / New York 2006, 46–51; Glei, Reinhold / Kaminiski, Nicola / Lebsanft, Franz, "Einleitung: Boethius Christianus?", in: iidem (eds.), *Boethius christianus? Transformationen der Consolatio Philosophiae in Mittelalter und Früher Neuzeit*, Berlin 2010, 1–17.
[11] Not only Boethius's notion of Fortuna but also the wheel of fortune is based on antique traditions: while Fortuna often stands on a rolling sphere (as an indicator of her instability), there are a number of proverbs which refer to *Tyche*, *Nemesis* or *Fortuna* with a wheel, which sometimes also has figures on it. Walther, Hans, "Rota Fortunae im lateinischen Verssprichtwort des Mittelalters", *Mittellateinisches Jahrbuch* 1 (1964), 48–58, 48–49; Courcelle, *consolation*, 129–134; Wackernagel, Wilhelm, "Das Glücksrad und die Kugel des Glücks", *Zeitschrift für deutsches Altertum* 6 (1848), 135; Patch, *Goddess Fortuna*, 150.
[12] He differentiates on the one hand between the centre and periphery of the circle or wheel (*orbis*): if man stays in the middle (by focusing on eternal values), he is not affected by the volatility of the periphery of the circle (IV 6p 61–90). On the other hand, he links the volatile personification to a mechanical, regular action: Fortuna says in a famous quote: *hunc continuum ludum ludimus: rotam volubili orbe versamus, infima summis, suma infimis mutare gaudemus; Ascende, si placet, sed ea lege, ne, uti cum ludicri mei ratio poscet, descendere iniuriam putes*. (II 2p 30–33). See also the reflection on the relationship of regularity and irregularity: *Tu vero volventis rotae impetum retinere conaris? At [...] si manere incipit, fors esse desistit*. (II 1p

reduces the power of the personification to the periphery and thereby stresses the factor that men are responsible for being victims of Fortuna,[13] he evokes a large number of verbal images of the wheel of fortune on the figurative level and transforms one verbal image into another. Several key traits of the wheel thereby remain undetermined, for example whether Fortuna embodies the wheel or whether she governs it, or whether she or the wheel stand for a mechanical or an anthropomorphic power. We can assume that this is one reason for the popularity of Boethius's Fortuna, since various discourses can use one aspect and drop another.

If we go on and examine more closely the "earliest known miniature", we realise that there is not one, but in fact there are two. On a leaf of the Codex Casinensis 189 (fol. 73^r und 73^v) we find two miniatures, possibly a draft (fol. 73^r, fig. 1) and a finished version (fol. 73^v, fig. 2).[14] Both miniatures depict a circle with four male figures on it, and the one on the top is "extraordinarily large"[15] compared to the wheel and the other figures. In both miniatures, the figure on the top has a staff in her hand, whose double end points downwards. But while the figure in the "unfinished version" (fol. 73^r) bears the iconography of God[16] (with a beard and falling hair), the figure in the "finished version" (fol. 73^v) is drawn like a king (with a crown and a richly decorated vesture). The "un-

---

59–61); which sounds like a paraphrase of Ovid, *Tristia* V,8,15–18): *Fortuna [...] manet in nullo certa [...] et tantum constans in levitate sua est.* I cite Boethius, Anicius Manlius Severinus, *De consolatione philosophiae*, Claudio Moreschini (ed.), München 2005.

13 It is well known that Boethius brings in a differentiation of perspectives: what seems arbitrary to men is, from the perspective of the divine will (*sub specie aeternitatis*), part of the providential order. In the Fourth Book (IV 6p 20–60) he differentiates between *Providentia* (eternal *ratio divina*) and *Fatum* (execution (*dispositio*) of this providential will). By doing so, he reduces the personification of *Fortuna* almost to an empty name as Philosophia claims in the Second Book (II 4p 8–9; 6p 62–70), see e.g. IV 7p 4–9. For the (non-) distinction of fate and fortune in the Middle Ages, see Patch, *Goddess Fortuna*, 79–80.

14 Cf. Orofino, Giulia (ed.), *I codici decorati dell'Archivio di Montecassino*, vol. 3: *Tra Teobaldo e Desiderio*, Roma 2006, 17, 83–86, who provides a close description of the codex and the miniature. Older scholars see a close link to Boethius's *De arithmetica* in the beginning of the codex: Courcelle, *consolation*, 141–142; Vollmer, Matthias, *Fortuna diagrammatica. Das Rad der Fortuna als bildhafte Verschlüsselung der Schrift "De consolatione philosophiae" des Boethius*, Frankfurt a.M. 2009, 151–152; Doren, "Fortuna", 89 n. 41. In contrast, Thürlemann "Narrative Sequenz", 154–156 assumes that the two drawings were produced individually and were later added to the last quire of the manuscript. For the relationship of the draft and the finished version, see Kitzinger, "World Map", 362–363; Thürlemann, "Narrative Sequenz", 155; Vollmer, *Fortuna*, 143–144.

15 Kitzinger, "World Map", 363.

16 In the miniature of the Codex Buranus, the figure of Fortune is also depicted in iconographically similar fashion to the *Majestas domini*; see Steer, "Fortuna-Bild", 189.

finished version" (fol. 73ʳ) thus presumably shows the Last Judgement with God pushing the three kings into the abyss, therefore using the wheel diagram.¹⁷ In contrast, the "finished" miniature (fol. 73ᵛ) depicts a wheel of fortune with four

Fig. 1: Wheel of fortune, pen drawing, 11th century, Archivio Storico di Montecassino, codex 189, fol. 73ʳ – © Archivio Storico di Montecassino.

---

17 For the popular use of circle and wheel diagrams in medieval miniatures, see Vollmer, *Fortuna*, 14–15, 90–100.

kings on it, but the one on the top is considerably larger. This raises the question of whether the figure on the top rules over the wheel or whether this figure has to be seen as a future victim of the wheel. This question is underlined by the draft, but also by the reference to the antique iconography of Fortuna standing on a sphere.[18]

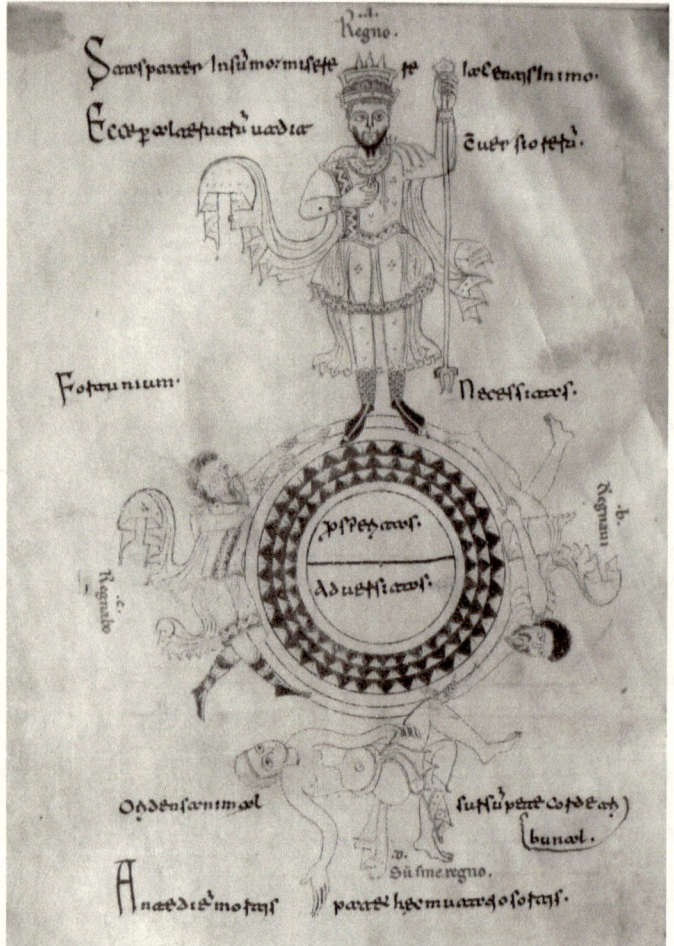

Fig. 2: Wheel of fortune, pen drawing, 11th century, Archivio Storico di Montecassino, codex 189, fol. 73[v] – © Archivio Storico di Montecassino.

---

18 Kitzinger, "World Map", 363; Courcelle, *consolation*, 142.

The inscriptions, which we only find on the "finished version" (fol. 73ᵛ) and which are written with another ink and are therefore assumed to be slightly younger,[19] stress this ambiguous meaning of the figure on the top: we find on the right and on the left of the king the words *necessitas* and *fortunium*. The circle or wheel[20] is divided into an upper and a lower half by the words *prosperitas* and *adversitas*.[21] We thus have two pairs of semantic oppositions which divide the drawing into four quarters. The two semantic pairs stress the ambivalence of the phenomenon depicted: the figures seem to be ruled by a positive *fortunium*, when they ascend and by a negative *necessitas* when they descend.[22] They suffer *adversitas* or are supported by *prosperitas*, according to the turning of the wheel. In addition, we find above and below the drawing a short poem, which speaks in the first two verses not of Fortuna, but of the *pater*, who stands *in summo*, and who is asked for mercy for the figure at the bottom. In the second half, it addresses the recipients and reminds them of the *mutatio sortis* and the coming *tribunal*.[23] The textual layer of the miniature therefore provides more than one interpretation of the wheel and the figure standing on the top. On the one hand, the wheel embodies an inevitable volatility, while on the other hand, it is seen as a punitive instrument of a Christian God.[24]

Finally we have a second layer of inscriptions, which derive from a much younger hand and emphasise again the four axes of the drawing. Beside each of the kings, we read: *regno, regnavi, regnabo, sum sine regno*.[25] The so-called "for-

---

[19] Thürlemann, "Narrative Sequenz", 155; Vollmer, *Fortuna*, 144.

[20] The so-called wheel bears six rings on the periphery, three of them are filled with spikes. The circle thus refers not only to a wheel, but also to world maps, see Kitzinger, "World Map", 365.

[21] This is usually interpreted as a reference to the *Consolatio* (II 4p 2–5), although this reference seems to me to be quite vague; cf. Courcelle, *consolation*, 142 n. 1.

[22] Courcelle, *consolation*, 142.

[23] Two verses are above, two underneath (they are written by the same hand as the inscriptions mentioned above). *Stat pater in summo; miserere iacentis in imo / Ecce per alterutrum vadit conversio rerum. / O ridens animal sursum pete corde tribunal. / Ante diem mortis patet haec mutatio sortis*. Cited according to Orofino, *codici*, 86, with minor differences to older quotes; Thürlemann, "Narrative Sequenz", 149; Courcelle, *consolation*, 143.

[24] See the stanza of Dietmar der Setzer (Dietm/3), which gives a similar interpretation of the wheel of fortune as an executive power of the divine will: *swer übermuotes und unrehtes gwaltes pfligt, / den selben got vil gerne vallen lât* (v. 12–13 "God lets willingly fall (of the wheel) the one, who is full of *superbia* and is abusing his power"; v. 12–13). Due to his fall, man recognises that he has a 'master' (*meister*) above him (v. 11); I cite de Boor, Helmut (ed.), *Mittelalter. Texte und Zeugnisse*, München 1965, 719–720.

[25] The quoted order is indicated by four letters beside each word (abcd) and adds up to a hexameter but is opposed to the pictorial order and the supposed temporal order of the circle; see Thürlemann, "Narrative Sequenz", 155. Walther, "Rota Fortunae", 49, provides evidence for

mula of the four"[26] (*Viererformel*) not only supports the equality of the four figures, but also introduces a different point of view: the perspective of the individual (king). The four verbs stand for restricted perspectives, since the four kings are – in contrast to the recipient – not able to perceive all four positions or the full circle.

Due to the draft and the inscriptions, we thus perceive several indeterminacies of the pictorial scheme of the wheel of fortune. The miniature leaves pictorially undetermined the question of who is ruling and who is ruled, and whether it is an anthropomorphic or a mechanical power which governs the wheel. On the one hand, rise and fall are depicted as mechanically following each other, and when the poem on the bottom of the page announces the *mutatio sortis*, the wheel is used as a prediction of change. But on the other hand, this is logically opposed to the volatility of Fortuna (as well as to the mercy and omnipotence of a Christian God, to which the inscriptions refer). On a more conceptual level, we thus do not know if the revolving of the wheel has an ultimate cause or if it rather stands for chance and arbitrariness. The subsequently added "formula of the four" makes additionally visible the fact that the claims of chance, luck or necessity (*fortunium/necessitas*) are themselves interpretations, which can derive from a restricted perspective.

In the miniatures of the twelfth and thirteenth centuries, the relation between the personification of Fortuna and the wheel are often pictorially specified – Fortuna can stand beside the wheel and turn it (mechanical representation) or she is depicted in the middle of the wheel (in a so-called symbolic representation), while the rose windows normally depict the wheel of fortune without Fortuna.[27] But this does not mean that the indeterminacies mentioned are always clarified.[28] The pictorial scheme of the wheel rather seems so successful

---

several miscellanea, in which the hexameter is preserved independently of a drawing. In the famous miniature of the Codex Buranus, the four words are also added by a younger hand from the fourteenth century; see Vollmann, Benedikt K. (ed.), *Carmina Burana. Texte und Übersetzungen mit den Miniaturen aus der Handschrift*, Frankfurt a.M. 1987, 941–942; Diemer, Peter / Diemer, Dorothea, "Die Illustrationen der Handschrift", in: Benedikt K. Vollmann (ed.), *Carmina Burana. Texte und Übersetzungen mit den Miniaturen aus der Handschrift*, Frankfurt a.M. 1987, 1289–1298, 1291; Steer, "Fortuna-Bild", 184.

26 Patch, *Goddess Fortuna*, 165.

27 Cf. Hahnloser, Hans R., *Villard de Honnecourt. Kritische Gesamtausgabe des Bauhüttenbuches ms. fr 19093 der Pariser Nationalbibliothek*, Graz 1972, 128–129; Kitzinger, "World Map", 364–365; Steer, "Fortuna-Bild", 184–186; for the pictorial tradition, see also: Schilling, "Rota fortunae"; Meyer-Landrut, *Fortuna*; Appuhn-Radtke, "Fortuna"; Vollmer, *Fortuna*, 142–233.

28 E.g. the dispute concerning the relationship of Fortuna and the wheel in the miniature in the Codex Buranus, Steer, "Fortuna-Bild", 184, 188–189; Diemer, Peter / Diemer, Dorothea,

because it is not always necessary to specify the connection of contradictory notions.

The Latin and the German poems often refer to the wheel of fortune in a proverbial style,[29] i.e. they do not describe it in full length, but use it instead as evidence for the moral teaching that they propagate.[30] When we find an elaborate description, the wheel is often depicted as an artefact or a painted wheel.[31] The last entry in the *Frau-Ehren-Ton* (of Reinmar von Zweter) in the *Kolmarer Liederhandschrift*[32] are three stanzas (*Bar*), which are captioned *aber iij vom gluck* ("three other [stanzas] of fortune"). In the first stanza, the wheel of fortune is introduced by an *ekphrasis*:

Ich sach gemâlt an einer want,
die aller schœnsten vrouwen, gelückes rat stuont an ir hant:
si treip ez umbe geswinde, alsô ez si selben dûhte guot.
Viere ich an dem rade sach:
der eine der saz dar ûf, der was ein künec, als er verjach;
der zweite ûf steic behende: 'nû bin ouch ich ein künic hôch gemuot'.
Der dritte der sprach: ich mac niht vil geschallen,
ich was ein künec unt bin her abe gevallen'.
der vierde niden lac in der crumbe,
der was sô gar ein unvrô man,
dêr heil noch trôstes mê gewân. (ReiZw/1/508a, v. 1–11)

'"Qui pingit florem non pingit floris odorem". Die Illustrationen der Carmina Burana (Clm 4660)", *Jahrbuch des Zentralinstituts für Kunstgeschichte* 3 (1987), 43–75, 63.
29 Cf. Walther, "Rota Fortunae"; Wackernagel, "Glücksrad", 137–138.
30 E.g. Dietmar der Setzer (Dietm/3) v. 7: *Daz bewæret uns gelückes rat* ("the wheel of Fortune gives evidence for this"); Johann von Ringgenberg (JohR/13) v. 1,7: *Gelükes rat nit stille stât [...] Hiebî is uns bezeichenlich* ("The wheel of Fortune stands still, this signifies for us..."); for the latter I cite the edition of Schiendorfer, Max (ed.), *Die Schweizer Minnesänger Bd. 1 (nach der Ausgabe von Karl Bartsch)*, Tübingen 1990.
31 *Crône* v. 15853–15894, see above n. 42; Wirnt von Grafenberg, *Wigalois. Text nach der Ausgabe von J.M.N. Kapteyn*, Sabine Seelbach / Ulrich Seelbach (ed.), Berlin 2005, v. 1036–1053; further examples are provided by Wackernagel, "Glücksrad", 140–141.
32 The *Kolmarer Liederhandschrift* (Munich, cgm 4997, 667rv) is an important and extensive collection of *Sangsprüche*. The beginning of its production is assumed to be in the period 1459–1462, but a significant part of the collection of songs dates from before 1350, other songs are from a later period, see Wachinger, Burghart, Art. "Kolmarer Liederhandschrift", *Die deutsche Literatur des Mittelalters. Verfasserlexikon* (1985). The stanzas are arranged according to the melodies (Töne), with the authors not seeming to be of interest; for the order of the *Töne*, see Schneider, Karin, *Die deutschen Handschriften der Bayerischen Staatsbibliothek München: Die mittelalterlichen Handschriften aus Cgm 351–500*, Wiesbaden 1996, 440. I cite here the edition of Roethe, Gustav (ed.), *Die Gedichte Reinmars von Zweter*, Leipzig 1887, nr. 246–248, who qualifies the stanzas – other than the RSM – as part of the oeuvre of Reinmar von Zweter; see the discussion on the authenticity of the stanzas, ibid. 133, 155, 157.

> I saw the most beautiful maiden painted on a wall, she grabbed the wheel of fortune with her hand. She turned it as quickly as it seemed alright. I saw four people on the wheel: the first one was a king, as he said; the second one was ascending: 'finally, I am a joyful king as well'. The third said: 'I am not in the mood to lose many words, I was a king and have been falling down'. The fourth lay down in the curve, he was a miserable man, who will not gain any consolation or salvation any more.

The poem describes a mural painting, which seems very close to the miniatures mentioned above: a maiden turning a wheel with four kings on it, and even "the formula of the four" (*regno, regnavi, regnabo, sum sine regno*) seems to be paraphrased. Therefore, the stanza is often used as evidence that the miniature of the wheel and "the formula of the four" is well known or that the literary texts depend on the pictorial documents.[33] But if we take a closer look at the stanza, we can perceive some decisive differences between text and image: firstly, the text specifies how the maiden is turning the wheel. She is not turning it regularly, but rather according to her whim: the aforementioned inconsistency between regularity and irregularity is thus clarified. The up and down of the wheel is regular and therefore predictable, but its rotational speed is irregular and depends on the mood of the maiden. Regularity and irregularity are thus split into two figures: the incalculable and anthropomorphic maiden and the mechanical regularity of the wheel.

The poem begins with the expression *Ich sach* (v. 1, cf. v. 4) and thereby introduces the *ekphrasis*. But as the poem goes on, the lyric persona not only sees, but also listens, since he primarily tells us what the kings tell him. Their explanations paraphrase the *regno, regnavi, regnabo, sum sine regno*. But presented by direct speech, the vividness of the mural painting is intensified, especially because the poem also works with the difference between direct and indirect speech to characterise the four figures: only the lateral kings, the one who ascends and the one who descends, are quoted directly and in contrast to each other. While the second figure proclaims, relieved, that he has finally become a king, the third figure does not want to cheer, since he has ceased to be a king. With the expression *ich mac niht vil geschallen* (v. 7), he is indicating that the loss of power also means a loss of the possibility to speak. This is underlined by the fourth king, who is described as desperately lying at the bottom and not being able to speak any more.

But while the four figures are becoming livelier, the maiden, with whom the *ekphrasis* began, is moving out of focus. Indeed, she was the first to be de-

---

33 Doren, "Fortuna", 87; Wackernagel, "Glücksrad", 140–141; de Boor, "Fortuna", 319; Schmidt-Wiegand, "Fortuna", 200; Müller, Ulrich, *Untersuchungen zur politischen Lyrik des deutschen Mittelalters*, Göppingen 1974, 524.

scribed and she is said to have power over the wheel. But at the same time, she does not talk at all (neither directly nor indirectly). The phrases of the four figures do not refer to her and she does not bear a name, in contrast to the wheel, which is identified as *gelückes rat* (v. 2). It is not until the closing of the stanza that we find a potential reference to the maiden. In the last verse, the lyric persona draws a moral conclusion (as is typical for the genre of the *Sangsprüche*): *seht, alsô gât diu welt hie mit uns umbe!* (v. 12: Watch out, that is the way that the world is treating us here).[34] The experience of the four kings is – also typical for the *Sangsprüche* – thereby transformed into the experience of everybody (*uns*), but not of a past experience, but rather a future one. So the wheel of fortune is again used as an admonition. However, it is neither Fortuna nor *vrou Saelde* which is held responsible, but rather *diu welt*. Although this expression does not depict the world as an anthropomorphic power, it still evokes the personification of *vrou Werlt* (World), which is described as seducing her lovers (*werlt diener*) with her beautiful front in the German literature of the time. Her ugly back, draped with spiders, ulcers and worms, displays the false pretence of worldly affairs.[35] The poem conflates the traits of the two personifications without representing either of the two as fully vested personifications. Instead, it plays with the lyric ability to relate the traits of a nameless figure to different traditional personifications.

The poem thus indeed describes a painted wheel of fortune (*ekphrasis*). It thereby underlines the predominance of the visual arts by its representation and marks it as a commonplace. But at the same time, the stanza uses literary modes of representation such as the combination of seeing and listening, the alteration of direct and indirect speech, and the namelessness of the maiden. It uses the difference between text and image to intensify the impact of the commonplace. When the last verse begins with the request *seht*, the lyric persona does not refer to a painting, but to its own verbal artefact.

---

34 We find a similar verse in the closely related poem of Johann von Ringgenberg (JohR/13) v. 7–8: *Hiebî ist uns bezeichenlich / der welte manicvaltiu grôz unstæte* ("this signifies for us the huge volatility of the world").

35 See Skowronek, Marianne, *Fortuna und Frau Welt. Zwei allegorische Doppelgängerinnen des Mittelalters*, Berlin 1964, 45–68; Kern, Manfred, *Poesie und Poetik der Vergänglichkeit in der weltlichen Dichtung des 12. bis 15. Jahrhunderts*, Berlin 2009, 43–68, 99–151. In the poems of Walther von der Vogelweide in particular, the personification of *vrou Werlt* bears different traits from stanza to stanza and looks sometimes like Fortuna, sometimes like *vrou Minne* (Love); cf. L 59,37; 100,24.

3 The Lexis of Fortune in Medieval German

In the stanza discussed above (ReiZw/1/508a), the wheel of fortune was called *gelückes rat* (v. 2), and the maiden who turns it remained nameless. To understand the significance of this naming, a closer look at the Middle High German semantics of fortune is necessary. In the literature of the time, we find three terms to name the personification of Fortuna. Sometimes *fortuna* is not translated into Middle High German, but named using the Latin term.[36] One of the first and most prominent examples is found in the so-called *Straßburger Alexander: Fortuna di ist sô getân / ir schîbe lâzet si umbegân / si hilfit den armen, sô si wile, / den rîchen hât si ze spile; / umbeloufet ir rat, / dicke vellet, der dâ vaste saz.* (v. 3416–3421/2964–2969) "Fortuna has such a condition, she lets her wheel turn, she helps the poor if she is in the mood to, and she plays her game with the rich. If her wheel revolves, frequently the one who was sitting solid (on the top) falls".[37] This Latin name for the personification is typical for the *Antikenromane* (epics of antique *materia*), which are retold in close dependency on their Latin or French pretexts.[38]

In other genres such as the *Sangsprüche*, the Latin name of the personification is translated into the vernacular. The poems speak of the *gelückes rat* or of *vrou Saelde*. Since the semantics of those terms are unique and differ from each other as well as from the Latin noun, this translation has consequences for the personification and the wheel of fortune, even if the commonplace elements

---

[36] Notker, who glosses and translates Boethius's *Consolatio* into Old German, uses *fortuna* for the personification, while for the phenomenon, he uses different terms, such as: *sâlda, unsâlda, uuîlsâlda, sâligheit, uuerltsâlda*; see Schröbler, Ingeborg, *Notker III von St. Gallen als Übersetzer und Kommentator von Boethius' "De consolatione philosophiae"*, Tübingen 1953, 134–150; Hehle, Christine, *Boethius in St. Gallen. Die Bearbeitung der 'Consolatio philosophiae' durch Notker Teutonicus zwischen Tradition und Innovation*, Tübingen 2002, 207–210; Sanders, Willy, *Glück. Zur Herkunft und Bedeutungsentwicklung eines mittelalterlichen Schicksalsbegriffs*, Köln et. al. 1965, 17.

[37] *Alexanderroman. Mhd./Nhd.*, Elisabeth Lienert (ed.), Stuttgart 2007. For further semantic sources, see: Sanders, *Glück*, 23–29; de Boor, "Fortuna", 314–320; Wackernagel, "Glücksrad", 141–143.

[38] Haug, Walter, "O Fortuna. Eine historisch-semantische Skizze zur Einführung", in: Walter Haug / Burghart Wachinger (eds.), *Fortuna*, Tübingen 1995, 1–22, 12–14 and Haug, Walter, "Eros und Fortuna. Der höfische Roman als Spiel von Liebe und Zufall", in: Walter Haug / Burghart Wachinger (eds.), *Fortuna*, Tübingen 1995, 52–75, 64 assumes *vrou Âventiure* (Adventure) to be an equivalent to *Fortuna*, since *Âventiure* stands for a coincidence which the hero has to master, and which normally serves a higher purpose. Here, we must not discuss this – from my point of view quite problematic – equalisation, since *Âventiure* is not a subject of the *Sangsprüche*.

seem the same. The word *saelde*[39] has, on the one hand, a highly positive Christian meaning, and besides fortune it can also mean grace, blessing or salvation. The denominated *felicitas* is in this case of a constant and not of a transitory nature, and is finally owed to God, although it is often linked with *virtus*.[40] But on the other hand, *saelde* also has a more profane meaning and stands for a fortune which is volatile and fragile or even an illusion, and is awarded in an arbitrary manner.[41] The personification of *vrou Saelde* is often represented with

---

39 Lexer Bd. 2, col. 579–580; BMZ II/2, col. 35a–38a. There are countless studies on the term *saelde*. See the older quantitative and all too general studies of Strümpell, Regine, *Über Gebrauch und Bedeutung von saelde, saelic und Verwandtem bei mittelhochdeutschen Dichtern*, Leipzig 1917, and Scharmann, Theodor, *Studien über die Saelde in der ritterlichen Dichtung des 12. und 13. Jahrhunderts*, Würzburg 1935; and the younger and more focused comments of Sanders, *Glück*, 82–85; Schouwink, *Fortuna*, 79–91, 179–193; de Boor, "Fortuna", 314–316.
40 In the courtly epics, this Christian meaning is conflated with a courtly one and *saelde* stands for success in a courtly world. It is a lifelong aristocratic quality of the hero, which is often said to have been given to him at his birth, see *Erec* v. 3460, 9899–9902; *Gregorius*, v. 1235–1242; *Wigalois* v. 1036–1052; *Crône*, v. 412. In historiographic texts, we find a similar *fortuna*, which stands for a personal, inherited *felicitas* or an *Amtscharisma*, see Schouwink, *Fortuna*, 26–28; Steer, "Fortuna-Bild", 187–190.
41 Sanders, *Glück*, 26–27. This double meaning of *saelde* and the personification of *Saelde* is semantically reflected in the late courtly epics (*späthöfische Dichtung*) in particular: Rudolf von Ems differentiates in his *Alexanderroman* between the *glesîn saelde* and the *staete saelde* (v. 20553–20558), and the latter is able to raise Alexander on the wheel without letting him fall down afterwards; see Schouwink, *Fortuna*, 92–100; Janota, Johannes, "Fortuna vitrea", in: Burghart Wachinger / Walter Haug (eds.), *Fortuna*, Tübingen 1995, 344–362, 347–350; Weber, Regine, *Die Inszenierung der Divina Providentia im Oeuvre Rudolfs von Ems*, Hofkirchen 2012, 160–165. The ambivalence of the personification is also figuratively shown in Heinrichs von dem Türlin *Crône*. The personification of *Frow Salde* is elaborately described as a two-sided figure, whose one side is beautiful and whose other side is old, blind and pale (v. 15853–15867). When the hero enters, the wheel of *Frow Salde* stands still, *Frow Salde* converts into a wholly beautiful and richly dressed figure and all the people whose destinies were determined by the wheel are made happy (v. 15870–15894). But after *Frow Salde* has blessed the hero, promised him worldly fortune (v. 15898–15900) and given him a ring as a present, he has to leave again (v. 15923). Of semantic interest is that the child of *Frow Salde* is called *Heil* (salvation) and is likewise two-sided. This description of *Frow Salde* takes up motifs of the *Anticlaudianus* of Alanus ab Insulis. See *inter alia* de Boor, "Fortuna", 320–328; Ebenbauer, Alfred, "Fortuna und Artushof. Bemerkungen zum 'Sinn' der *Krone* Heinrichs von dem Türlin", in: id. / Fritz Peter Knapp / Ingrid Strasser (eds.), *Österreichische Literatur zur Zeit der Babenberger*, Wien 1977, 25–49; Knapp, Fritz P., "Virtus und Fortuna in der *Krone*. Zur Herkunft der ethischen Grundthese Heinrichs von dem Türlin", *Zeitschrift für deutsches Altertum* (1977), 253–265; for the *fortuna bifrons* or *anceps*, see: Appuhn-Radtke, Sibylle, "Fortuna bifrons. Zu einem mittelalterlichen Bildtyp und dessen Nachleben in der Ikonographie Albrecht Dürers", *Das Mittelalter. Perspektiven mediävistischer Forschung* 1 (1996), 129–149.

a wheel, but this wheel is usually called *gelückes rat*.⁴² The word *gelücke* was presumably incorporated into German in the middle of the twelfth century from Dutch (Limburgish).⁴³ In the thirteenth century, the term is closely associated with the wheel and denotes a transitory state of fortune which is promising and desirable, but which is also associated with instability, fragility⁴⁴ and bad luck. Since the grammatical gender of *gelücke* is neuter, we never find a Lady or Mister *gelücke*.⁴⁵ Nevertheless, the poems address *gelücke* quite often, praising or criticising it. Using the rhetorical device of the *apostrophe*, they evoke the impression of an anthropomorphic counterpart, although the personification has a more transient nature than, for example, the Philosophia in the *Consolatio*.

These linguistic peculiarities have consequences: firstly we have two terms: *gelücke* and *saelde*, with a similar meaning. The meaning of both is ambivalent: they can denote a wholly positive notion of a desirable condition. *Saelde* in particular has a Christian connotation and can refer to a state of grace and salvation. But *gelücke* and *saelde* can also mean a transient moment of luck or happiness or a false pretence of fortune. The poets play with the possibilities of the

---

42 There is rarely the expression of the *saelden schîbe*; see *Pfaffe Amis*, v. 1829–1831, 2053; *Studentenabenteuer*, v. 471. In both texts, the *saelden schîbe* is not a wheel with four figures on it, but a sphere or ball, which is turned by the protagonist, and who wants to turn it even faster to be more fortunate; See Wackernagel, "Glücksrad", 146–147; Reichlin, Susanne, "Zeitperspektiven. Das Beobachten von Providenz und Kontingenz in der *Buhlschaft auf dem Baume*", in: Cornelia Herberichs / Susanne Reichlin (eds.), *Kein Zufall. Konzeptionen von Kontingenz in der mittelalterlichen Literatur*, Göttingen 2010, 245–270, 145–148. The term *schîbe* can mean a sphere, ball, bowl as well as a flat disk or wheel; see BMZ II/2 col. 95b; Lexer II col. 715–716. Wackernagel, "Glücksrad", 147. See here as well for all sources with *schîbe*; quite often, the poets speak in the context of Fortuna of the *schîbe*, without specifying whether it is the *gelückes schîbe* or the *saelden schîbe*. See, for example, Gottfried's *Tristan*, in v. 7161–7162. (I would suggest that in this verse, the *schîbe*, which is struck by Morold, means not the wheel of fortune – as the critics and translations usually assume – but rather a sphere or a ball, as in the citations mentioned above).
43 According to Sanders, *Glück*, 12, 229–232, the word *gelücke* bears first the meaning of destiny or fate, but is then semantically affected by the Latin and French Fortuna traditions, and is thus associated with chance and instability. Around 1200, the meanings of the *gelücke* and *saelde* converge. Cf. Strümpell, *Gebrauch*, 17–26. The ambivalence of the word *gelücke* is reflected by Frauenlob V,52, when he claims that there are two forms of *gelücke:* one is *gut* (v. 2) and is due to God, the other is the fortune of the sinners and is *böse* (v. 7); cf. Ganz, Peter, "Fortuna bei Frauenlob", in: Burghart Wachinger / Walter Haug (eds.), *Fortuna*, Tübingen 1995, 76–87, 79–81. For the ambivalence of the word *gelücke*, see also *Passional* I, v. 2784–3195 (the word bears here the meaning of chance and contingency as well as that of providence).
44 Gottfried von Straßburg is popularising the *fortuna vitrea (daz glesîn glücke)*; cf. section 4, n. 59.
45 Sanders, *Glück*, 25–27; Ganz, "Fortuna", 78.

two terms and their double meaning. Therefore, the semantics of *saelde* and *gelücke* have to be analysed from case to case.⁴⁶ Secondly, the wheel and the personification of fortune are semantically divergent; the wheel is related to *gelücke*, and the personification to *saelde*. This might be one reason why several poems describe the wheel without a personification or the personification without a wheel. The wheel thereby loses the status of an accoutrement and becomes an independent verbal image. Thirdly, the studies on the semantics of *saelde* and *gelücke* show how difficult it is to differentiate precisely between the several meanings of the concept of fortune. The studies work with a large number of oppositions: for example fate and destiny on the one hand, chance and contingency on the other;⁴⁷ or: pagan fate versus Christian providence; or the stable and well-deserved happiness (*felicitas*) and the instability of a transitory luck or a false pretence of fortune.⁴⁸ However, a closer analysis of the vernacular sources shows that these oppositions do not conform to the semantic distinction of *saelde* and *gelücke*, or that of an early – or medieval Fortuna – and a late or humanistic or Renaissance Fortuna. The personifications of *saelde* and *gelücke* are indeed so fascinating because at least semantically, they have the ability to stand for fate *and* contingency, stability *and* instability and they conflate Christian notions of providence with the experience of a seemingly brute contingency.

4 The Wheel of Fortune Acting on Its Own and the Different Perspectives on It

Literary texts have, other than images of the wheel of fortune,⁴⁹ the possibility to describe accurately the turning of the wheel, its speed, its acceleration or de-

---

46 Also Weber, *Inszenierung*, 159.
47 E.g. Sanders, *Glück*, 28–29.
48 Scharmann, *Studien*, 37, for example, attempts to separate *saelde* (as the personification of a highly positive and invariable value) from Fortuna (and her arbitrariness and inconstancy). See the critic of Sanders, *Glück*, 26–27.
49 The miniaturists also find possibilities to represent the revolving of the wheel. In the two miniatures of the Codex Casinensis 189, for example, the garments of the kings flutter in the wind and are indicating the movement; cf. Vollmer, *Fortuna*, 144. It is striking that in the so-called draft, the garment of the figure on the top is not fluttering, while on 74r, the garment of the fourth king is fluttering; Additionally Thürlemann, "Narrative Sequenz", 143–150, has pointed out that the miniatures of the wheel of fortune represent the passing of time by a *kontinuierender Stil mit verteilten Rollen* (Panofsky): one image depicts several *stadia* of a process, although the figures in the sections are not thought to be the same, but are marked by

celeration. In the second stanza of the above-quoted poem (*Bar*) in the *Frau-Eh-ren-Ton* (ReiZw/1/508a),[50] the lyric voice describes a wheel which revolves so fast that the lyric persona is not able to ascend smoothly.

> *So wol ym den fraw [Saelde]*
> *begryffet unde rüret der kumpt wo[l] vff gelückes rat*
> *daz ist mir leyder ture. doch kam ich dar daz ich es han gesehen*
> *Das selbe rad daz ist so snell*
> *es lauffet vmb vnd vmbe recht alz ein schyybe sinnewell*
> *Im tuot doch nieman sture also hör ich die wysen mei[n]ster jehen*
> *Y doch kam ich im einest also nahen*
> *Ich want ich woltz mit armen vmbefahen*
> *velg vnde nab darzu die sinen speichen*
> *Ich tet zu ym ein snellen swa[n]g*
> *Es stiess mich gar on minen dang*
> *so ferre von ym Ich kunt sin nit her reichen.* (ReiZw/1/508a II)

Blessings to him who is seized and moved by Lady [*Saelde*], he gets on to the wheel of fortune well. Unfortunately, this never happened to me; but once I got so far to have seen it. This wheel is so fast, it turns round and round as a round sphere, though nobody governs it, as I hear the philosophers say. But once I got so close to it, I thought I was able to grasp it, rim and hub and in addition its spokes. I made a quick move to get close to it, I was thrown down so far against my will that I never had the possibility to reach it (again).

The motion of this wheel is a double one: it not only revolves fast, but also moves onwards and backwards without guidance (v. 6). In contrast to the first stanza of the poem, in which the maiden was held responsible for the irregularity of the revolving of the wheel, mechanical regularity and human irregularity are combined here in one figure, that of a volatile wheel.[51] The position of the

---

similarities as part of a group that represents the process on an abstract level. For example, the figures of the four kings are different individuals, but as a group, they represent the process of the rise and fall of one.

50 I cite the text of the *Kolmarer Liederhandschrift* (667r and 667v) with slight normalizations, see http://daten.digitale-sammlungen.de/~db/0010/bsb00105055/images/index.html?id=00105055&groesser=&fip=qrsenxdsydwsdasxsqrseayafsdrewq&no=77&seite=1341 (19.3.2016). Roethe's edition of the stanza (no. 247) follows the *Heidelberger Liederhandschrift cpg 350*, 44v-45r, which preserves the stanza in a quite different version (= ReiZw/1/246a).

51 The personification, which is indicated in the first verse, is not held responsible for the wheel and its movements. The version of this stanza in the *Heidelberger Liederhandschrift cpg 350* (= ReiZw/1/246a) omits the personification of *vrou Saelde* completely. It preserves the first verses (v. 1–2) as follows: *Wol ieme der den bestin phat begrifit. der ien fuorit ebin uf des gluckis rat* ("Blessings to him, who seizes the optimal way, which is leading him even on to the wheel of fortune."), see http://digi.ub.uni-heidelberg.de/diglit/cpg350/0096?sid=0932f6f-ba7d39ce333a7bea2c758cc4a (3.12.2016).

victim of Fortuna has also changed: he is not on the wheel, determined by its ups and downs, but he first has to seize and get on it before he may profit from it. This volatility seems even more ungovernable because there is no personification which is responsible for the motions of the wheel. It is indeed acting on its own.

The poet conflates different literary *topoi* of fortune: firstly the personification of fortune, which helps her favourites (v. 1–2); secondly the wheel of fortune, with figures on the rim (v. 1–2), thirdly the rolling sphere (*schîbe*), on which Fortuna is standing (v. 4–6)[52] and fourthly *gelücke* or *saelde* as something which is unattainable (v. 7–12)[53]. By conflating these images,[54] the poet merges on the one hand the regular turning of the wheel (with four kings on it) with the quick and multi-directional movements of a rolling sphere, and is thus able to represent the irregularity *and* the regularity of the wheel of fortune. On the other hand, he also merges the notion of an anthropomorphic and that of a mechanical power and thereby heightens the impression of incalculability and volatility.

Compared to the stanzas discussed above, the volatility is also intensified by a change of perspective: the lyric persona is not contemplatively looking at a wheel and thereby being warned or instructed morally, but attempts to ascend the wheel. So the experience of pursuing fortune and the suffering of the victim of Fortuna or of the wheel of fortune is emphasised. This raises the question of who is responsible for the misfortune, but the stanza does not provide any hint of an answer. Correspondingly, the passing of time is (other than in the miniatures) not represented by four different *stadia*, but rather by the memories and hopes of one person. But the course is thereby a different one: it is not an ascent followed by a descent, but the protagonist instead describes several attempts to get on the wheel, all of which fail. Only one stands out because the short moment of fortune proves – retrospectively – to have been an illusion. Therefore, not only the motion of the wheel is shown as irregular, but also its effect on man is incalculable because he is deceived.

---

[52] See above n. 43.
[53] This is often expressed by verbal images which are not connected to a wheel. In the third stanza of ReiZw/1/508a, the lyric persona describes how Fortuna never offered him her hands and when she did offer them, she struck him (v. 4–6). In stanza Mei/16/9, the lyric persona claims that fortune is slipping through his hands like an eel (v. 4–5). In a stanza attributed to Rubin (26A, 31C), the lyric persona compares *vrou Saelde* to a wild and shy deer, which always escapes although the lyric persona tracks her (KLD 47 XII, v. 5–9).
[54] Kiefer, "Conflation" describes some of the famous Renaissance paintings of Fortuna as a conflation of Fortuna and Occasio. For a medieval example of the conflation of Fortuna and Occasio, cf. the poem in the *Codex Buranus* CB 16,1,3–4.

I will come back to the effects of a first person perspective in section 6, but prior to that, I would like to have a closer look at another poem in the *Frau-Ehren-Ton* (ReiZw/1/91).[55] This stanza addresses almost the same phenomena as the stanza just quoted, namely the deception and the wheel as an unattainable object, but from the perspective of the third person.

> *Gelückes rat ist sinewel,*
> *im loufet maneger nâch, doch ist ez vor im gar ze snel*
> *unt lât sich doch erloufen williclîch, den ez beswîchen wil.* (ReiZw/1/91, 1–3)
>
> The wheel of fortune is round, many are chasing it, but it is too fast, though it can be reached willingly by whomever it wishes to deceive.

From the third person perspective the wheel looks like an anthropomorphic figure which deceives on purpose.[56] But it is not the experience of being deceived, but rather the question of how to remain in the fortunate position on the wheel that is discussed (to remain on it, one has to be witty or wise; *der darf wol guoter sinne;* v. 5). It is not the argument here, but rather the handling of perspectives that is remarkable: in the first two verses and in v. 4–6, fortune is presented as something which is desirable, but not attainable. But in the third verse, the perspective is a different one. The lyric voice reveals that whoever reaches fortune is just deceived by it. So the poem is playing a similar game with its recipient that it attributes to fortune. It presents something as attractive (v. 1–2) and then reveals it to be unattractive, since the one who seemingly seizes fortune is just deceived (v. 3). But in the next verse, sitting on the wheel of fortune is again presented as desirable (v. 4–6). So the stanza does not stick to a didactic perspective on fortune, but rather contrasts two perspectives on fortune with each other, knowing that the latter is only plausible because the former is inevitable.[57]

---

[55] This stanza is preserved in the *Heidelberger Liederhandschrift cpg 350* (15v), but in part D from the late thirteenth century, which contains almost only stanzas in the *Frau-Ehren-Ton;* it is also found in the *Codex Manesse* (Heidelberg, cpg 848, 331v) and is attributed to the author Reinmar von Zweter. Part of the stanza (v. 1–6) is also found in the fragment UB Basel, Cod. N I 1, 73c, 1v; see Meyer, Karl, "Bruchstücke mhd. Dichtungen aus der mittelatlerlichen Sammlung zu Basel", *Germania. Vierteljahrsschrift für deutsche Alterthumskunde* 18 (1873), 80–96, 82. I cite Roethe, *Gedichte*.

[56] The deception is nominally credited to the wheel, but this is not to be taken literally. As we will see, the stanza suggests in accordance with Boethius (cf. section I) that he who is conned is responsible, because he was pursuing the "wrong" values. See section 6 for the peculiar and transient status of the personification.

[57] Stackmann, Karl, "*Gîte und Gelücke*. Über die Spruchstrophen Gotfrids", in: Hugo Moser (ed.), *Mittelhochdeutsche Spruchdichtung*, Darmstadt 1972, 288–305, 291–292 compares Rein-

In the conclusion at the end of the stanza, the poet quotes a phrase from a stanza of Gottfried von Straßburg (Gotf/1/2), who speaks about the *glesîn glücke* (the vitreous fortune, v. 9).[58]

ez [gelücke] gît vil manegem ê der zît
unt nimt hin wider swaz ez gît
ez tœret den, swem ez ze vil geborget. (ReiZw/1/91, 10–12)

Fortune gives too early and reclaims what it has given. It deceives those whom it has lent too much.

Reinmar's stanza comes back to the question of deception and links it with the topic of Fortuna's gifts. As Boethius's Fortuna already asserts (II 2p), her gifts are not to be taken for granted, but rather as a loan, since she reclaims them. But this well-known argument is doubled with a temporal argument. In Gottfried's stanza (Gotf/1/2, 4), the vitreous fortune not only gives too much, but also gives too early (*ê der zît*). The stanza of Reinmar von Zweter (ReiZw/1/91) links the time of giving and taking with the wheel of fortune. The wheel, the lyric persona suggests, raises the people too early, for example from a didactic and normative perspective "too easily", and lets them fall too early, according to their own perspective. So the arbitrariness of the wheel of fortune is also a temporal one, since it does not wait with the ascent until someone has earned it fairly.[59]

---

mar's stanza with that of Gottfried (see below n. 59). He claims that Reinmar von Zweter presented fortune as a "false idol", while Gottfried does not dissuade his recipients from pursuing fortune. It seems to me that Stackmann downgrades Reinmar all too much. Gottfried also warns his recipients of the false shininess of fortune (v. 11–12), and Reinmar's stanza presents the two perspectives as being tied to one another.

58 *es [gelücke] wenket, dâ man ez niht wol besorget. / swen ez beswaeren wil, dem gît es ê der zît; / und nimt ouch ê der zît wider, swaz ez gegît.* (Gotf/1/2, 3–5) "it [fortune] totters, when you are not looking for it. Whoever it wants to burden, it gives to him too early, and also reclaims what it has given too early". Gottfried refers in this stanza to the *Pubilii Syri sententiae*. In the part which is not quoted by Reinmar, namely in v. 10–12, he refers to the *fortuna vitrea* (F 24), but in the part quoted by Reinmar von Zweter, he refers to L4: *Levis est fortuna, cito reposit quod dedit;* For the quotes and the transmission of Publilius Syrus see Janota, "Fortuna vitrea", 351–352. The stanza of Gottfried (Gotf/1/2) is found in the Codex Manesse (cpg 848) at the end of the songs of Ulrich von Liechtenstein. But since Rudolf von Ems quotes them in reference to Gottfried, they are credited to the latter. I cite Moser, Hugo / Tervooren, Helmut (eds.), *Des Minnesangs Frühling = MF. 38. rev. Aufl. Unter Benutzung der Ausgaben von Karl Lachmann u.a.*, Stuttgart 1988, 431–432.

59 We also find this notion of a normative time in other poems. For example, the lyric voice in a stanza of Meissner (Mei 16/9) says to the addressed fortune: *nu kum zuo mir, des ist zît.* (v. 8) "now come and visit me, because it is time for it".

Additionally, Gottfried stresses that the vitreous *glücke* not only gives but also reclaims its gifts "too early" (*und nimt ouch ê der zît wider*; v. 5).[60] This second *ê der zît* cannot (as the first one) refer to the time of a fair relation of service and reward, since in this respect, *glücke* reclaims its gifts right on time. Instead, the "too early" refers to the subjective perspective of those who have received something from *glücke* and do not want to give it back. So the two phrases *ê der zît* refer each time to different notions of what is "on time". It thereby becomes visible that volatility and irregularity always refer to a norm (the "on time"), and as soon as a representation of fortune or Fortuna refers to different inconsistent norms, the volatility is intensified, since the clear distinction of regularity and irregularity is questioned.

5 The Pausing of the Wheel

The irregularity of the wheel of fortune can be represented by unexpected movements of the wheel, but also by its deceleration or pausing. The idea of the pausing of the wheel refers *ex negativo* to the proverbial saying that the wheel never stands still and thus the fall of those who ascend is inevitable (see Boethius II 1p 59–61). This saying is repeated in a long series of sources[61], quite often it is also marked as proverbial: in the above-quoted poem by Reinmar von Zweter, the poet refers to the authority of the wise man: *ez [rat] stât joch nimmer stille, als ich die wîsen meister hœre jehen.* (ReiZw/1/246a, v. 6) "It [the wheel] never pauses, as the wise men say."

But despite the proverbial truth, there are several poems and literary texts which describe the pausing of the wheel.[62] We have seen that Reinmar von Zweter (ReiZw/1/91)[63] already raised the question *wie er behalte Gelückes stat*

---

[60] This is also an addition compared to the *sententia* of Publilius Syrus: *Levis est fortuna, cito reposit quod dedit* (L4).

[61] Patch, *Goddess Fortuna*, 157 n. 4. Johann von Ringgenberg (JohR/13) v. 1–3 also emphasises that the wheel never stands still: *Gelükes rat niht stille stât: / vro Sælde, diu ez trîbet, daz erzeiget hât / an vieren, die da wonent bî, dáz ez umbe loufet zaller stunt.* ("the wheel of fortune never stands still, it turns always; Lady *Saelde* gave evidence for this with four figures, which inhabit the wheel.")

[62] Patch, *Goddess Fortuna*, 157; de Boor, "Fortuna", 318–319; see above n. 42 for the pausing wheel in the *Crône*.

[63] The stanza is only transmitted in a neatly written supplement in the precious manuscript of the *Jenaer Liederhandschrift* (Jena El. 101–102, 10r) from the beginning of the fourteenth century; see Wachinger, Burghart, Art. "Jenaer Liederhandschrift", *Die deutsche Literatur des Mittelalters. Verfasserlexikon* (1983), col. 512–518; see http://archive.thulb.uni-jena.de/hisbest/rsc/

(v. 5: "how he [who is at the top] keeps his fortunate position"). The question is also discussed in a panegyric song of "Bruder Wernher" (Wern/1/26). The lyric voice praises a young king (*edele[] küneg[] [...] in sîner jugent;* v. 1, 7), whom the critics assume is Heinrich VII (the son of Friedrich II).[64] The lyric voice enumerates different requirements one by one, all of which the young king fulfils: he has *künecliche vuore* ("a royal behaviour"; v. 3) and carries his crown rightfully (v. 6). Despite his youth, he has earned such a reputation that those who have power respect and fear him (v.7–8).[65] But by lauding the king in this manner, the stanza sounds like a denial of reproaches concerning his lack of authority or virtue. And this would indeed support the reference to Heinrich (VII), who was elected in 1220 at the age of nine.[66] Towards the end of his praise, the lyric persona refers to the wheel of fortune and describes the ascent of the king: *daz enirret niht sîn miltekeit, sîn reinez herze, sîn edel tugent, / daz er in rehter küneges vuore ûf stîget* ("it does not vex his generosity, his pure heart and his virtue when he ascends in a rightful royal manner"; v. 9–10). Again, the panegyric seems to deny a reproach of that manner that the king ascends without the necessary virtues such as generosity and clemency.

Scholars have pointed out that the wheel of fortune is commonly used in historiographic texts to explain the rise and fall of sovereigns or dynasties.[67] In the Bavarian continuation of the *Kaiserchronik*, the rebellion of Heinrich (VII) against his father and his dethronement in 1235 is announced as follows: *Der chünec saz ûf gelückes rat: / daz rat saic umbe und tet im mat, / daz ich iu her nâch wol sage* ("the king sat on (the top of) the wheel of fortune, it turned down,

---

viewer/HisBest_derivate_00001155/Ms-El-f-101_010r.tif (19.2.2016). In the two columns of the same page, the stanzas Wern/1/1b and Wern/1/10b are written, which scholars both interpret in reference to Friedrich II and his son Heinrich (VII), although the reference in 1/1b is vague (Schönbach, Anton E, *Beiträge zur Erklärung altdeutscher Dichtwerke. Die Sprüche des Bruder Wernher I*, Wien 1904, 4–8, 32–36; Schmidt-Wiegand, "Fortuna", 201–202; Müller, *Untersuchungen*, 90–92); see concerning stanza Wern/1/10b below n. 72.

64 Schönbach, *Beiträge*, 59–61 (cited); Gerdes, Udo, *Bruder Wernher. Beiträge zur Deutung seiner Sprüche*, Göppingen 1973, 75; Schmidt-Wiegand, "Fortuna", 199–200. All underline the close relations of this stanza to the *Erste Philippston* of Walther von der Vogelweide, especially L 18, 29. According to Gerdes, Bruder Wernher – other than Walther – bases the fortune of the sovereign not only on birth, but also on virtue (*Geburts- und Tugendadel*) ibid. 75–77.
65 The lyric voice exclaims additionally that had the king not been born as a king, he should have been crowned as a king (v. 4).
66 Koch, Walter, Art. "Heinrich VII, dt. Kg. von Sizilien", in: *Lexikon des Mittelalters* (1989), col. 2047.; Schmidt-Wiegand, "Fortuna", 197–198.
67 Pickering, *Augustinus oder Boethius?*, 21–25; for a closer and less problematic view see: Schouwink, *Fortuna*, 21–50; Schmidt-Wiegand, "Fortuna", 202–203.

and he was placed in checkmate, as I will tell you as follows" v. 653–655).[68] In contrast, in the quoted stanza of Bruder Wernher, the wheel of fortune is not used to interpret the fall of the king, but instead to praise a disputable, adolescent king (v. 7). Therefore, the poem does not mention the fall of that which is at the top, but ends with the question of how the king is able to stop the wheel:

> *nû sitzet er ûf gelückes rade; wil er, daz ez im wenke niht,*
> *sô rihte er, swaz die armen klagen, sô gît im got ze sælden phliht.* (Wern/1/26, 10–11)
>
> Now, he is sitting at the top of the wheel of fortune. If he wishes to cease the tottering of the wheel, he has to judge in favour of the accusations of the poor, then God will let him have a share of *saelde*.

In these last verses of the poem, the tone of the lyric persona has altered. He does not praise the king any more, but instead warns and advises him. He is telling him under which conditions he is able to maintain his fortunate position. To attain it, he should judge in favour of the poor. So unlike in the Bavarian chronic, the wheel of fortune is not used as a means to interpret history, but rather as a threat which legitimises the lyric voice to give advice to a king (the literary tradition evoked is the mirror-for-magistrates, i.e. *Fürstenspiegel*).[69]

The pausing of the wheel is thereby linked to moral values. The wheel can be brought to a pause, but virtue is necessary for this.[70] When the wheel pauses, it is not *gelücke* which the king obtains but *saelde*, and it is not Fortuna who dispenses *saelde* but God who "lets him have a share". So we can observe here the aforementioned distinction between the terms *gelücke* and *saelde* which differ from case to case. *Gelücke* stands in this case for the volatile state, caused by the revolving wheel, and *saelde* stands for a stable happiness, which is attained through virtue, but awarded by God. But this *saelde* is not – as the

---

68 The Bavarian continuation (Schröder, Edward (ed.), *Die Kaiserchronik eines Regensburger Geistlichen*, Hannover 1892, 393–408) was written around 100 years later than the *Kaiserchronik*, and it ends with the death of Friedrich II. Schönbach, *Beiträge*, 61–62 reads both texts as part of the mystification of the reign of Heinrich (VII) as a time of peace. Schmidt-Wiegand, "Fortuna" presents the different contemporary German sources about Heinrich (VII) and shows how ambivalent the reign of Heinrich (VII) was seen in in the eyes of his contemporaries.

69 See the stanza of Sigeher (Sigeh4/2) in which the wheel of fortune is used in a similar way (mirror-for-magistrates). But the lyric voice refers not to the standstill of the wheel, but rather to the ascent of the King; see Brodt, Heinrich P., *Meister Sigeher*, Hildesheim 1977, 92–93, 14–15.

70 See, similarly, the stanza of Johann von Ringgenberg (JohR/13), who promises that after the descent with the wheel, a new ascent is possible if one is able to gain the favour of God and one's fellow man. For the combination of *fortuna* and *virtus* as a model to describe a perfect sovereign, see *inter alia*: Schouwink, *Fortuna*, 21–35; Schmidt-Wiegand, "Fortuna", 202–203.

Christian use of the term would suggest – an eternal or heavenly salvation, with the term rather describing a political and worldly state which is just – for the sake of the panegyric – associated with heaven.

The sudden standstill of the wheel is linked to the question of how man can influence fortune or Fortuna and whether he can influence it by virtue. But this emphasising of the responsibility of man is ambivalent, since the *saelde* of the pause is credited to God and not to Fortuna. This leads to the puzzling impression that the ups and downs of the wheel of fortune are considered regular and credited to Fortuna, whereas the irregular pausing of the wheel is caused by God – a prerequisite but not a guarantee for the pausing is virtue. This raises difficult questions about the relationship between God, Fortuna and virtue. They are indeed not solved, but rather dissolved by giving the pausing of the wheel a utopian notion.[71] The lyric voice suggests that we all know that the wheel never stands still, but as a wish and as praise of the young king, and to persuade him to be charitable, we assume it can. So while the regular ups and downs are related to reality, the standstill is presented in a mode of imaginary hopes and wishes.

6 The Personification of *Gelücke* and *Saelde*

I began this examination of the *Sangsprüche* on Fortuna with a stanza that presented an *ekphrasis* of the wheel of fortune and a maiden who turned it (I). We then went on to look at stanzas in which the wheel acted on its own and the lyric persona attempted to grab it (II). The wheel was thereby presented as an autonomous power which was responsible for the well-being of the lyric persona. Another way of evoking an autonomous power is the rhetorical device of the *apostrophe*. By addressing an abstract quality in a personal way and by referring to its power over the speaker, the abstract quality receives anthropomorphic traits. The *Sangsprüche* address in this form *gelücke* and *saelde*: *Gelucke, wa bistu so lange* ("fortune, where have you been for such a long time" Mei 16/

---

[71] In several epic texts, the cessation of the wheel of fortune is also described as a short moment of a utopian condition, see above n. 42, especially Heinrich von dem Türlin, *Crône*. Stanza Wern/1/10b also refers to the standstill of the *gelückes rat*. But in contrast to our stanza, the standstill refers to or announces the misfortune of the imperator (presumably Friedrich II): The lyric voice claims that if the imperator does not dispense justice, then *sô vürhte ich, daz gelückes rat noch vor dem rîch stille stê* (v. 9: "I fear, that the wheel of fortune will stand still before the empire"). The *gelückes rat* has the form here of a rolling sphere, which brings fortune to the person or – precisely – to the area into which it rolls.

9, v. 1) or *Gelücke, wol man dîn bedarf / bî fiure [...], ûf erde / swaz kunst ein man gelernet hât, / diu frumt in ân dich niht* ("Oh fortune, we need you with fire, on earth [...]; whatever skill a man has learned, without you, it is useless" Kanzel 5/7, v. 1–4[72])

The *apostrophe* to Fortuna is frequent in antique and medieval Latin poetry.[73] The *Sangsprüche* combine it with the literary tradition of the *Minnesang*, in which a beloved but distant lady is addressed, and with the tradition of the political *Sangsprüche*, in which sovereigns are addressed, criticised or flattered and asked for *milte*. The personification is not precisely described (as in the *Consolatio* or in epic texts such as the *Crône*[74]), but its personal character originates from the accusations and flatteries, the insults or praises of the lyric voice. But the *Sangsprüche* address not *fortuna*, but *gelücke* or *sælde*, the vernacular translations of "fortune" or "Fortuna". Whether those personifications are identical or similar to the Latin personification of Fortuna, has to be considered from case to case.

So let us have a closer look: *Vil rîche Sælde, mich nimt immer wunder / daz dû die êren gernden êres niht besunder* ("O though almighty Sælde, I ask myself on and on, why you are not honouring those who strive for honour" Kel/2/1a, v. 1–2).[75] The stanza of Kelin begins with the well-known reproach to *Saelde*, that she spreads her gifts in an arbitrary and unfair way and does not distinguish between the honourable and the unworthy.[76] The lyric voice uses strong expressions such as "shame on you" (*Nu scham dich, Sælde*; v. 4) to accuse her of not helping the pious, honourable and generous. The *apostrophe* goes along with the first person perspective, which emphasises the emotions of the lyric personae, their anger and surprise, their complaints and accusations. Despite the expressive language, the *Sangsprüche* do not express individual feelings, but rather exemplary ones, with which the audience is invited to identify. The stanzas thus quite often end with a didactic conclusion. However, we hardly find the Boethian argument that the wise man should concentrate on the tran-

---

72 I cite KLD 28, XVI,7 (64C).
73 Appuhn-Radtke, "Fortuna", 273–281; Walther, "Rota Fortunae", 56; Courcelle, *consolation*, 127–134.
74 Cf. n. 42.
75 The stanza Kel/2/1 is preserved in the *Jenaer Liederhandschrift* 17v (see no. 64) and in the corresponding fragment Ba (UB Basel N.1.3, 145), 1v–2r; the texts of both manuscripts are closely related (see von Wangenheim, Wolfgang, *Das Basler Fragment einer mitteldeutsch-niederdeutschen Liederhandschrift und sein Spruchdichter-Repertoire (Kelin, Fegfeuer)*, Bern 1972, 18–29); for our stanza, there are no semantically important variations, see the cited edition of Wangenheim, *Fragment*, 84–85.
76 Cf. Kanzel 5/7, v. 13–14.; Walther von der Vogelweide L 43,1.

scendent values and not expose himself to Fortuna.⁷⁷ Instead, the lyric personae adopt an angry and sometimes ironic attitude, which also gives a characteristic trait to the stanza of Kelin: towards the end of the stanza, the lyric voice presents an explanation for the incomprehensible and seemingly unfair behaviour of *Saelde*.

> ôwê, daz dû dîne helfe zun milten nicht enswers! / Ich weiz wol, dû wilt sie hin heim in dînen hob behalten. / du quæme alrêst dâ her von himelrîche, / dâ wiltu die getriuwen milten sicherlîche. / lâ die gar verschamten argen hie mit schanden alten! (Kel/2/1 v. 7–10)

> O, that you are not assuring your help for the generous. I know you want to keep them with you at your court. You recently came from heaven, there, you want to conciliate the faithful for sure, and you let the shameless bad people here [on earth] grow old in disgrace.

The lyric persona assumes that Lady *Saelde* normally stays in heaven and has just come to earth for a short visit. He depicts her as a selfish lady who wants to be surrounded by the good and generous. That is why she gives her gifts to the unworthy, in order that they stay on earth and grow old there. So Lady *Saelde* prevents the world from being appealing to the honourable and generous. This explanation is, at first glance, structured like a standard providential argument. A negative experience caused by chance or fortune is unveiled as part of a hidden providential plan, in which the negative event serves a higher purpose. But in the explanation of this stanza, the higher purpose is a selfish action on the part of Lady *Saelde*. The stanza only evokes the pattern of the providential explanation, but misuses and ridicules it, since it is not a divine and good-natured will that organises the world, but rather an ambivalent and selfish one. The stanza thereby also intermingles what we would separate logically: *Saelde* as an autonomous power, which acts arbitrarily and without foundation, and *Saelde* as a mistress of God who lives in the *himelrîche* and executes a divine will. This intermingling is eased by the term *saelde*. As we have seen, the noun *saelde* bears either a strong Christian connotation and denotes a steady fortune or even salvation, or it means luck or misfortune by chance (section 3). Since the two meanings are logically incompatible with each other, *saelde* normally bears either the first or the second meaning.⁷⁸ Only in our stanza has the poet found an ironic way to combine the two meanings. We can thus also read the stanza as a reflection on the ambiguity of the term *saelde*.

---

77 See for one of those cases above n. 24.
78 Wangenheim, *Fragment*, 87 claims that in the first part of the stanza (v. 1–6), *Saelde* stands for Fortuna, and in the last part (v. 7–19) for *Salus*.

Additionally, the good are specified as being generous towards the end of the stanza (v. 6, 9). The motif of generosity (*milte*) is a frequent one in the *Sangsprüche*, since the poets are directly affected by it. In many stanzas, the generosity of the patrons is discussed: either praised in a flattering manner or criticised as too avaricious.[79] When the lyric voice suggests that Lady *Saelde* supports the unworthy or avaricious[80] to let them grow old on earth, this bears implications for the audience. The recipients might belong to the group of the avaricious, which have been maliciously favoured by Lady *Saelde*, in order to stay on earth. This implication might help the singer, since his audience now has to be generous in order to prove that they are not part of the avaricious who are left behind by Lady *Saelde*.

Whereas the stanza of Kelin (Kel/2/1a) reflects on the personification as a means to persuade, other stanzas use the first person perspective to revolt rhetorically against fortune. Meissner (Mei 16/9)[81] addresses fortune (*gelucke*) and asks why it takes so long to come to him: *Gelucke, wa bistu so lange, / daz du nu nicht ne kumst zů einem male* ("fortune, where have you been for such a long time, that you do not come to me (just) for one time" ; v. 1–2). He is expressing his dependency on it and is appealing for support.[82] He is begging and lamenting for quite a while, until he ends with a sudden change of perspective: *Wiltu dir lenc von mir unthalten / so tustu mich in grozen sorgen alten. / ich entétes niht, muchte ich so wol din sam du min gewalten* ("Do you want to withdraw even longer, then you will make me grow old in sorrows. I would not do that if I were master over you, as you are over me" v. 9–11).

The lyric persona hypothetically takes over the perspective of the addressed *gelücke* (fortune). If he were in her position, he would not abuse his power and would look after everyone who depends on him. So again we have a lyric persona who is trying to seduce someone, but this time it is not the audience, but *gelücke* itself. This way of addressing someone, at the same time lamenting and

---

[79] Quite often, the poets also complain about the lack of distinction between the qualified and the unqualified poets, see Strohschneider, Peter, "Fürst und Sänger. Zur Institutionalisierung höfischer Kunst, anläßlich von Walthers Thüringer Sangspruch V,9 (L. 20,4)", in: Ernst Hellgardt / Stephan Müller / Peter Strohschneider (eds.), *Literatur und Macht im mittelalterlichen Thüringen*, Köln / Weimar / Wien 2002, 85–107; cf. Walther von der Vogelweide L 20,4 where the lack of *milte* of the sovereign is described as the locked gate of *saelde* (*Mir ist verspert der sælden tor*).

[80] The adjective *arc* in v. 10 can mean both.

[81] The stanza is only preserved in the *Jenaer Liederhandschrift* 96v–97r, I cite Objartel, Georg, *Der Meissner der Jenaer Liederhandschrift. Untersuchungen, Ausgabe, Kommentar*, Berlin et al. 1977, 220.

[82] *Ich lene mich of dinen trost. wiltu, du macht mich wol vurterben* ("I am hoping for your help, it is up to you, you are able to perish me." v. 7).

trying to seduce the addressee, is very often used in the *Minnesang*.[83] The beloved lady in the *Minnesang* is addressed and accused of not rewarding the *dienst* of the singer fairly. She is also said to act arbitrarily and is reminded of her responsibility, because she has so much power over the lyric persona.[84]

We will come back to the meaning of those parallels after a short look at a stanza of Walther von der Vogelweide (L 55,35), which uses the subjunctive mode in a similar way. This stanza is preserved in the *Weingartner Liederhandschrift* (B) as a single stanza, but is part of a song of five or six stanzas in other manuscripts.[85] The transmission as well as the subjects of the stanzas mark them as being between the two genres of *Sangspruch* and *Minnesang*. For example, the ties between the stanzas are not strong and they do not express the experience of love, but reflect on love and address repeatedly the personification of love.[86] In the version with five or six stanzas, the lyric persona first addresses three times the personification of love (*Vil minneklîchiu Minne*) and asks her for help to conquer the heart of the beloved lady (L 55,8, 55,17, 55,26). Then he suddenly seems to change his subject and speaks about *vrô Sælde*. He does not address her, but reflects on her (L 55,35): *Vrô Sælde teilet umbe sich / si kêret mir den rugge zuo*. ("Lady Saelde spreads [her gifts] / she turns her back on me").[87] So the stanza evokes the well-known trait of Fortuna to distribute her gifts arbitrarily, and the lyric persona is excluded from her benefits and laments about it (v. 2–7). The further development of the stanza, however, is atypical. The lyric persona attempts to outwit the personification. First, he aims to understand the

---

83 In our stanza (Mei 16/9), the addressed *gelücke* is neuter, but there are several semantic references to the *Minnesang*, e.g. *trôst* (v. 7), *tuo mîn ungelücke sterben* (v. 8) or the speech act of threatening at the end (v. 9–10).
84 Albrecht von Johansdorf MF 89,9; Heinrich von Morungen MF 134,14; Reinmar der Alte 164,3; 166,16; 171,18; See also Kaiser Heinrich MF 5,23, where the experience of love is compared with the ascent and descent of the wheel of fortune.
85 This applies to the Minnesang manuscripts A, C and E, whereas F preserves two two-stanza songs; see Bein, Thomas (ed.), *Leich, Lieder, Sangsprüche: 15., veränderte und um Fassungseditionen erweiterte Auflage der Ausgabe Karl Lachmanns*, Berlin et al. 2013, 210–217; Schweikle, Günther (ed.), *Walther von der Vogelweide: Werke Bd. 2: Liedlyrik. Mhd./Nhd. 2. durchges. Aufl.* Stuttgart 2005, 580; see Schuchert, Carolin, *Walther in A. Studien zum Corpusprofil und zum Autorbild Walthers von der Vogelweide in der Kleinen Heidelberger Liederhandschrift*, Frankfurt a.M. 2010, 201–203 for a detailed commentary on the variations of the manuscripts.
86 Schweikle, *Walther von der Vogelweide*, 581.
87 The variations between the different manuscripts concerning our stanza are not small, Bein, *Leich, Lieder, Sangsprüche*, 210–217 edits three versions, I cite the C-Version (*Heidelberger Liederhandschrift*). In the *Weingartner Liederhandschrift* (83B) the stanza begins with *Diu sælde teilet umbe mich* (v. 1, ibid. 214). This opening stresses the reflection on the personification, in contrast to a direct address. Another major difference concerns v. 3 and the question of whether *Saelde* is not able to take pity (B/C) or if she does not want to take pity (A).

laws of *Saelde* and to use them for his own purposes: he moves around the personification so that she has to look at him, but: *gen ich hin für, ich bin doch iemer hinder ir* ("even if I go to stand in front of her, I am always standing at her back"; v. 6). So he has to acknowledge that the volatility and unpredictability of *Saelde* is greater than he expected, and he is not able to predict her movements. That is why he ends by expressing the wish that *vrou Saelde* should have additional eyes on her neck, so that she would be forced to look at him (v. 8–9) – and thus give her gifts to him. So the lyric persona strikes back with the power of imagination. He invents a hypothetical scenario in which *vrou Saelde* is forced to act according to his will.[88]

The stanza thus shapes the personification of *Saelde* at the beginning like the personification of Fortuna, in the role of the one who donates blind and therefore arbitrarily.[89] The personification is also incalculable and almost invincible, because she moves quickly and irregularly, as we know from the personification of the wheel or sphere of fortune (section 4). But unknown to the Fortuna tradition is the emphasis on her gaze. This refers undoubtedly to the *Minnesang-topos* that *Minne* conquers the lover through his eyes.[90] So there are again parallels between the beloved lady of the *Minnesang* and the personification *Saelde*. These parallels concern not only the personification, but also the way the lyric persona speaks about her, for there are many *Minnesang* poems which use the subjunctive mode and imaginary scenarios to wield power over the invincible and unattainable lady.[91]

The *vrou Saelde* of Walther and Kelin and the addressed *gelücke* of the Meissner thus refer undeniably to the Fortuna tradition, but the specific traits of the personification are shaped by the lyric genre and the literary tradition of the vernacular literature. If the parallels between the personification of fortune and the beloved lady of the *Minnesang* are stressed, the personification of fortune is

---

[88] In the context of the song with five or six stanzas (A, C, E) the reflection on *Saelde* has to be seen as part of the reflection on and the dethronement of *vrou Minne*. In the antecedent stanzas (L 55,8, 55,17, 55,26), the power of the personification of *Minne* is contrasted with the powerlessness of the lyric persona. In our stanza, the lyric persona shows how to cope with a seemingly autonomous power ironically. In the subsequent stanza (L 56,5) the power of the personification of *Minne* is placed into question and the lyric persona refers to God (v. 5); cf. Wisbey, Roy A, "Fortune and Love. Reason and the senses: Traditional Motivs in Walther's Song *Ich freudehelfelôser man* (L 54,37–38)", *Oxford German Studies* 13 (1982), 115–142.
[89] Walther delineates the personification in other stanzas with the same trait, cf. L 43,1. Concerning Fortunas blindness, see Appuhn-Radtke, "Fortuna bifrons", 130–132, 135.
[90] Bernger von Horheim, MF 112,1; Heinrich von Morungen MF 124,32; 126,8; Reinmar der Alte MF 164,12; cf. Neumeister, Sebastian, "Das Bild der Geliebten im Herzen", in: Ingrid Kasten (ed.), *Kultureller Austausch und Literaturgeschichte im Mittelalter*, Sigmaringen 1998, 315–330.
[91] Vgl. Bernger von Horheim MF 113,1; Morungen MF 140,11; Reinmar der Alte MF 153,14.

evoked as an attractive and seductive lady, whose attractiveness and gifts are not wholly despicable (as we would assume according to the common view of the "medieval Fortuna"), but at most as ambivalent. But the attitudes of the lyric personae are also atypical when compared to the common view that the "medieval Fortuna" is part of a providential will. In all three stanzas, the lyric personae acknowledge their dependency on the personification of fortune. Nevertheless, they are not overwhelmed by the invincible power, but instead show a distanced, ironic or combative attitude. Since they are powerless in reality, they help themselves through the invention of imaginary scenarios – a motif which can be traced back to *Minnesang*, but at the same time has conceptual consequences: the arbitrariness of *Saelde* is not something which one has to accept, but one has to find ways to cope with it. Even if it is not possible to figure out the laws of this volatile and arbitrary power and to revolt against her with rational means, the stanzas show other means, such as the power of imagination or irony. But these means also shift the status of the personification. The personification of *Saelde* is not so much connected to a metaphysical question (in that case, the distanced and ironic attitude would be much harder to achieve[92]), but is shown as rhetorical device which can be transformed with rhetorical means.

7 Summary

This paper has examined late medieval poems (*Sangsprüche*) that address the wheel of fortune and the personification of fortune (*Saelde*). In contrast to the general historical view, which claims that there is a concentration on the wheel of fortune in the Middle Ages, we observed that in the vernacular poems, the wheel is just one verbal image among others. It was combined or conflated with the image of Fortuna as a bestower of gifts, with the notion of Fortuna as unsteady ground or as a sphere and with fortune as a desired and pursued good that proves to be an illusion. By transforming one verbal image into another, the poems are able to contrast different perspectives and to reflect on different notions of fortune.

The wheel of fortune, which stands for a regular rise and fall, and which should at the same time explain the experience of the unpredictable, volatile and sudden (mis-)fortune, raises the question of how regularity and irregularity

---

[92] Cf. Walther von der Vogelweide L 20,16; in this stanza, the arbitrary donor is God and not *Saelde*, and of course the tone and the attitude of the lyric persona are different, although the observations about the arbitrariness of giving are the same.

of Fortuna go together: the *Sangsprüche* take up this question, but only rarely answer it as the philosophic texts do with a hierarchy of entities (God overrules Fortuna) or by making man wholly responsible for his misfortune and advising him to concentrate on eternal values. They instead focus on the first person perspective and its experience of deception about fortune, the contrast of different perspectives on fortune and the reflection on the personification as a figure of speech. They not only avoid the metaphysical questions about last causes, but also they play with literary traditions of the *Minnesang* and *Sangspruch*: some stanzas stress the similarities between the personification of fortune and the personification of *Minne* and *vrou Werlt* or that with the beloved lady of the *Minnesang* or the implicitly addressed donor of the *Sangsprüche*. They thereby alter some of the traditional traits of Fortuna or carve them out more concisely, but the reference to Fortuna always remains visible. Nevertheless, the status of the personification or even that of an anthropomorphic power remains diffuse. Therefore, scholars have sometimes considered not taking the *Sangsprüche* into account for a history of Fortuna.[93] In contrast, I would like to suggest that this transient and variable nature of the personification is a specific trait of the textual media (and especially the lyric genre) and its representation of Fortuna. The *Sangsprüche* do not present the personification of fortune as a fully vested allegory, but they are interested in the fluent transition between speaking in figurative terms of an abstract phenomenon and depicting this phenomenon as a concrete figure or even as an anthropomorphic power. And one cannot deny that this form of representation demonstrates the represented qualities of volatility and incalculability.

So if we do not assume a history of Fortuna in which the pictorial and the literary, the intellectual and political history run parallel to each other, we are able to see traits of Fortuna that are primarily emphasised in literary texts: the first person perspective, which presents us with an affected individual who is not interested in the metaphysical reasons for his misfortune; the imaginary and ironic mode of coping with fortune, the reflection on fortune and Fortuna as something which always combines different inconsistent perspectives; and last but not least, the transient mode of representation as part of the represented phenomenon.

---

93 Sanders, *Glück*, 28–29; de Boor, "Fortuna", 312.

Burkhardt Wolf
Fortuna's Sea Change
Renaissance Poetics of Contingency

1 Introduction: Fortuna and the Sea

Since time immemorial, Fortuna and the sea have made a fickle couple. They lived, so to speak, in concubinage – and with good reason. In ancient times, the sea in its threefold sense of *thalatta, pontos* and *okeanos* was already considered a space of insecurity, instability and unpredictability. Those venturing onto the high seas were considered neither dead nor alive,[1] but seemed to float in a state of mere possibility. At the same time, Fortuna represented uncertainty; she either appeared as mere chance, or she personified a fortuitousness that concealed some hidden fate. She originated as an Italianate goddess invoked during land-based cults of harvest and fertility. But sometimes she appeared as a syncretic creature and was eventually "maritimised". In Hellenistic times, she fused with the Egyptian goddess Isis, especially with Isis Euploia, the mistress of wind and sea, and she merged with the Greek deity Tyche ("the one who strikes from a large distance," as her name was translated), Thethys's daughter and therefore the sister of the Oceanids. Although Homer never names her as such in his epics, but rather deals with the Moirai and particularly with Lachesis, Tyche is mentioned as a nymph in the *Homeric hymn* (Dem. 420) and as Okeanus's daughter in Hesiod's *Theogony* (v. 360). Eventually, Pindar praised her as nothing less than the *kybernétes*, the steersman of the way of the world. Only after having been conflated with Tyche and her double agency of *eutychia* (luckiness) and *atychia* (misfortune) did Fortuna assume her Janus-faced appearance and henceforth personify *felicitas* (happiness) and *fors* (chance).[2]

---

[1] This saying was credited to the ancient Scythian Anarcharsis in Diogenes Laertius, *Lives of Eminent Philosophers*, ed. by Robert D. Hicks, Harvard 1925, Book I., Chapter 8, § 104.
[2] Cf. Doren, Alfred, "Fortuna im Mittelalter und der Renaissance", in: Ernst Cassirer / Fritz Saxl (eds.), *Vorträge der Bibliothek Warburg 1922/23*, Wiesbaden 1924, 71–144, here 135; Göttlicher, Arvid, *Nautische Attribute römischer Gottheiten*, Bremen 1981, 80–81, 131; Meyer-Landrut, Ehrengard, *Fortuna. Die Göttin des Glücks im Wandel der Zeiten*, München / Berlin 2007, 14–15, 24; Tanzer, Ulrike, *Fortuna, Idylle, Augenblick. Aspekte des Glücks in der Literatur*, Würzburg 2011, 69, 166; Vogt, Peter, *Kontingenz und Zufall. Eine Ideen- und Begriffsgeschichte*, Berlin 2011, 93–108.

In Rome, Fortuna was worshipped for countless reasons by the lower classes. Being a goddess for everyone, she appeared in *plurale tantum*.³ In the long run, however, a kind of standard image was established: she was occasionally depicted with a wheel, but most often with a sphere, symbolising instability and change, or, in later Roman times, particularly with a globe, thus transforming into Victoria. Once in a while, she displayed a horn of plenty in her left hand and a rudder in her right hand, implying her double agency (as Lady Luck and as the goddess of destiny) with respect to land and sea. Philosophically, she was related to the discussion of *automaton* and *tyche*, of unpredictability and *causae per accidens*. She belonged to a realm beyond knowledge and science, as Aristotle had already suggested. But, at the same time, philosophers proposed specific remedies against her actions.

Whereas *fatum* was deemed irrevocable, Fortuna's domain seemed confined to external assets such as wealth, power or beauty. She could not impair the ethical realm and the inner dispositions, meaning that *sapientia* and *prudentia*, as Seneca wrote, or *virtus*, *fortitudo*, *ratio* and *diligentia*, as Cicero claimed, acted as cures against her harmful actions.⁴ Fortuna therefore served as a touchstone for manifold virtues, and interlacing these ethical, philosophical and religious dimensions, Fortuna was put in the service of power. Augustus considered her a decisive factor at the sea battle of Actium,⁵ thus installing the official glorification of *Fortuna Dux*, a sort of maritime Lady Luck, being in the service of the Roman Empire's providence. On the stage of imperial politics, Fortuna was enhanced to the "Fortuna of the sea", guiding the world's destiny with her rudder, the only nautical attribute elevated to an imperial insigne.

The Church Fathers, of course, would not tolerate her entitlement to providence. Lactantius and Augustine in particular despised her as a ridiculous spawn of pagan misbelief, and although she survived as one of the few ancient deities in post-Roman folk religion, Fortuna, was henceforth subject to a further iconographic change: *fortuna maris* became a minor element within patristic allegories of *navigatio vitae*.⁶ Accordingly, in Boethius's *Consolatio philosophiae*, the *gubernatio* and the rudder were confided to God, while Fortuna was down-

---

3 Cf. Pfeiffer, Helmut, "Glück und List. Decameron II 4 und II 9", in: Walter Haug / Burghart Wachinger (eds.), *Fortuna*. Tübingen 1995, 110–142, here 116.
4 Cf. Fichte, Jörg O., "Providentia – Fatum – Fortuna", *Das Mittelalter* 1 (1996), 5–19, here 7.
5 Patch, Howard R., "The Goddess Fortuna in the Divine Comedy", *Annual Reports of the Dante Society* 33 (1914), 13–28, here 15; id., "The tradition of the goddess Fortuna in Roman Literature and in the Transitional Period", *Smith College Studies in Modern Languages* 3/3 (1922), 127–177, here 144–145.
6 For the "nautical theology" of the Church Fathers see Rahner, Hugo, *Symbole der Kirche. Die Ekklesiologie der Väter*, Salzburg 1964, 239–270.

graded to an emanation of God's will, administering His providential scheme on the level of human existence. On the sea as well as elsewhere, she appeared as pure chance and contingency, since man, confronted with interweaving causalities, was considered unable to figure out God's *praescientia* and *providentia*. For Boethius, Fortuna's mutability seemed to be her only constant trait. But it was precisely as personified instability that she uncovered the caducity of mundane goods, therefore forcing man to contemplate his proper disposition.[7]

By and large, the Fortuna of the sea disappeared from medieval imagination. Iconically, the *rota fortunae* dominated, and expressions such as *fortuna ventosa*, as mentioned in a Genoese document from 1242, were used rather in a technical manner (signifying indefinite dangers connected to the weather). Against this background, Dante's *Commedia* is a milestone on Fortuna's course into modern times. From an overall theological perspective, she is interpreted here as an angel in the service of providence, as a "general minister and guide who shifts those worthless goods, from time to time, from race to race, from one blood to another beyond the intervention of human wit." (*Inf.* VII. 78–79) In philosophical terms, everything foreseen by God, the prime cause, will happen, but not as a matter of necessity; contingency is part of His general scheme. Fortuna not only symbolises the potentiality of creation, but also acts as a second cause and assumes the paradox function of *gubernatio*: of directing man to fulfil God's providence by nothing other than his free will.[8] In the mundane perspective of *Inferno*, however, Fortuna is criticised as the idol of the greedy, the vain and the liars. Dante indeed hints firstly at the *avarizia* amongst Florence's early capitalists. Secondly, Fortuna's deceit is part and parcel of the sea adventurers' vain *curiositas* that, by ignoring the maritime hazards, flouts God's providential order, as exemplified in the 26th canto by Ulisse's fatal journey on the Grand Sea of Being (the *Gran mar de l'essere* in *Par.* I. 113). And thirdly, Fortuna is presented as the prophetess of a language that does not signify the things as such, but that boils down to rhetoric, delusion and imagination.[9] In a way, Fortuna becomes the protective goddess of fiction – of a "fittizie parole," as Dante called his own poem (*Convivio* II. 12, 8). In the waning of the Middle Ages, Fortuna's ambivalent agency bears on the worldly spheres of trade, seafaring and fiction.

---

7 Cf. Boethius, *Consolatio philosophiae*. Liber Secundus, 8.p., passim. – Cf. Müller, Jan-Dirk, "Fortuna", in: Almut Schneider / Michael Neumann (eds.), *Mythen Europas. Schlüsselfiguren der Imagination zwischen Mittelalter und Neuzeit*, Darmstadt 2005, 145–162, here 147.
8 Cf. Münchberg, Katharina, *Dante. Die Möglichkeit der Kunst*, Heidelberg 2005, 160.
9 Initial commentators distinguished between Dante's theological, philosophical and poetical interpretation, each one corresponding to the sections of *Paradiso*, *Purgatorio* and *Inferno* and to Thomas Aquinas's, Aristotle's and Augustine's conceptions of Fortuna. – Cf. *Le Chiose Ambrosiane alla Commedia*, ed. by Luca Carlo Rossi, Pisa 1990, 29.

And these were the very terms for Fortuna's rebirth at the dawn of modern times.

2 Fortuna's Maritime Renaissance

Starting from ancient ethics, as propagated by Aristotle, Seneca and Cicero, the fifteenth century's maxim became: *virtù vince fortuna* ("virtue overwhelms Fortuna"). The goddess of chance was not to be avoided any more, but rather to be conquered by brave men, even if she displayed the unfavourable side of *fortuna bifrons*: the view of *mala fortuna*. And if this overpowering should be attempted not through action, but in the mode of humanist erudition, Renaissance men opposed Fortuna with *ratio* and *diligentia*, rather than with sheer austerity. Now, in collective imagination, the daredevils would no longer perish, as Dante's curious Ulisse did, when challenging Fortuna. For the future, she was to be subdued in the concerted action of *vita activa* and *vita contemplativa*, by coordinating enterprise and science. Whilst ancient and - *a fortiori* - medieval ethics had already aimed at the true goods and spiritual values beyond Fortuna's scope, the new morals deemed wealth and power to be a necessary means for self-assertion and self-improvement. Fortuna was thus no longer in opposition to man's virtues. Incorporating happenstance, she represented the very conditions for successful action. Niccolò Machiavelli therefore related Fortuna to a wide array of possibilities that must be narrowed down: *Occasio*, here, was the link between Fortuna (as the master of possibilities) and princely virtue (that realises the best of all options). Applying her to the hazards of being flooded, Machiavelli advises his prince to "take precautions with dikes and dams", in order to ward off and control Fortuna's sneak attacks.[10] But apart from *ratio status* and dominion, mercantile virtues were also set against – or rather in accordance with – Fortuna, since she ruled, as described famously by Leon Battista Alberti (1404–1472) in his *Libri della famiglia*, not merely in political, but also in commercial affairs. "There is a tide in the affairs of men, Which, taken at the flood, leads on to fortune", as William Shakespeare put it in *Julius Caesar*, one of his political, but also commercially grounded plays, "And we must take the current when it serves, Or lose our ventures. " (IV. 3, 216–222)

---

10 Machiavelli, Niccolò, *The Prince*, translat. and ed. by Peter Bondanella, Oxford / New York 2005, 84.

Not merely the princes, but also the self-confident new merchants represented themselves more and more in maritime terms. In *Fortune's ship*, for example, an engraving celebrating the marriage of Bernardo Rucellai and Nannina Medici in 1466, the groom is transmuted into the mast that spans the sails (fig. 1). On the one hand, he replaces Fortuna, while on the other hand, he

Fig. 1: *Fortune's ship* (1466). (Source: Reichert, Klaus. *Fortuna oder Die Beständigkeit des Wechsels*. Frankfurt am Main: Suhrkamp, 1985, p. 27.)

seizes the rudder for himself and essentially *fortuna* and *virtù* are espoused.[11] In sixteenth-century allegories, as in Nicoletto da Modena's depiction from 1506 (fig. 2), the *rota* is finally superseded by a sphere that is not merely an attribute of global power, as in ancient Rome, but part of a nautical system: it is Fortuna who achieves a subtle balance between the sphere, the rudder and the sail, thus conflating the elementary forces of the wind and the sea through elaborate

Fig. 2: Nicoletto da Modena: *Fortuna* (around 1506). (Source: Berlin: Kupferstichkabinett.)

---

[11] Cf. Warburg, Aby, "Francesco Sassettis letztwillige Verfügung (1907)", in: *Werke in einem Band*, ed. by Martin Treml / Sigrid Weigel / Perdita Ladwig, Berlin 2010, 234–280, here 260.

navigation. In other images, cast dice are added that signify chance and its usefulness in gambling, as soon as its laws are understood. Notably, those depictions appeared just as Gerolamo Cardano was working on his theories of gambling, bookkeeping and the – now so-called – Cardan rotation sequence. Even in architecture and sculpture, Fortuna left her mark: the *Dogana da mar* (fig. 3),

Fig. 3: Bernardo Falconi: *Fortuna di mare* (1678), Venice, Dogana da Mar.
(© Photo: Franz Huber/ Florian Runschke)

for example, the Venetian tollhouse at the entrance to the *Canal grande*, carries Bernardo Falconi's figure group of *fortuna di mare* (from 1678) that unites rudder and sail in a weather vane, while Fortuna presides over a globe, carried by several atlantes. This Fortuna seems to await future possibilities and the advent of *prospera fortuna*: of goods arriving from the open sea. But at the same time, she signifies state power, the governmental collection of customs and taxes, and the mercantile calculation of values resulting from Venetian sea ventures.

Altogether, Renaissance Fortuna, especially *fortuna di mare*, merges myth and calculation, figure and concept. She represents the governing of chance and danger, acquired through new nautical and commercial technologies. The historical frame of Fortuna's iconological "sea change", as one might say, is twofold. During the fourteenth century, two crucial improvements were accomplished at the seaports of northern Italy: the so-called "nautical revolution" concerned innovations in ship-building, as well as the introduction of the mariner's compass and of the first sea charts. From then onwards, ships could be en route throughout most of the year and could sometimes even comply with a proper timetable. The so-called *rivoluzione commerciale*, in turn, was based on the introduction of paper and the Indian-Arabic numerals, along with the invention of double-entry bookkeeping; these innovations allowed not only for commercial partnerships between merchants, shipmasters and captains, but also for a separation *and* cooperation between the *routes* of seafaring and the *routines* of bookkeeping. Both revolutions led to a commercial boom, to growing investments in overseas trade and, in light of the increasing losses at sea, to a huge demand for nautical safety and commercial security. This is why a further revolution eventually took place: the introduction of insurance.

Since ancient times, the bottomry bond had served as a speculative trade in maritime business: merchants or shipmasters could borrow money that, in case of bad fortune, namely of shipwreck, did not have to be paid back. Only if the defaulter's business succeeded did he have to reimburse the credit *plus* an interest rate of about 30 percent. The 1230 canonical ban on usury, however, scared the moneylenders away from sea trade: why should they bear all of the risk for the mere expectation of a small profit? Under these circumstances, Italian merchants, eager to benefit from overseas trade, found a remedy in inventing the *assecurazione* (first documented in 1347): they defined their business as a credit without interest, supplemented by a contract which ascertained that they would accept the sea dangers, the *fortuna di mare*, in exchange for a certain charge. This so-called *premio* was to be payable in advance, whereas the credit should be disbursed only *ex post*, if the ship actually went down. This arrangement was approved by the church (by Pope Gregory IX's decretal *Naviganti* in 1234), allowing for new partnerships between capital and labour, inasmuch as the transfer of dangers was made explicit. For this reason, the merchants introduced the concept and term *risco*, derived from the Greek word *rhiza*, meaning "cliff ". In the long term, this invention of "risks" supported the modern spirit of enterprise, especially of maritime ventures, and by rewarding the merchants for participating on a monetary level, it worked around the ban on usury.

Risks are dangers converted into merchandise. As such, they are specifications and enumerations of what had previously been thought of as Fortuna and treated as a shapeless and nameless threat. Following the emergence of risks in the maritime business, it was utterly impossible not to take these risks: people either ran the risk of needlessly insuring themselves, or they ran the risk of not being insured. For this reason, dangers, the former *fortunae malae*, were no longer threats assigned to a mysterious goddess; now they were threats not yet taken into account by insurance, or threats exceeding its scope, tellingly referred to as *acts of God*. In any case, the invention of risks led to a pragmatic approach towards Fortuna. By converting dangers into risks and by trading those risks on the market, diffuse fears of loss could be turned into expectable, probable and thus somehow calculable profits. As on the stock market, with which maritime insurance was very quickly aligned, the risk trade established a kind of feedback link between contingent future and present action. Henceforth, one no longer dealt with Fortuna and her unfathomable temper, but rather with virtual realities, virtual values and virtual goods.

3 Fortunatus as Modern Man

Against this backdrop, Renaissance Fortuna was subject to a long-term change not only in visual arts, but also in literature: in late-medieval novellas such as Boccaccio's *Landolfo Rufolo* (around 1350), she comes to the fore not allegorically, as the figure of fickleness herself, but rather through the ups and downs in matters of sea fortune. However, those tales do not yet circumscribe commercial virtues that serve to overpower Fortuna or to cope with her. Usually, they recommend the *vita contemplativa*, the retreat from mundane affairs governed by Fortuna, and especially from the sea and its contingencies, as is still suggested in Sebastian Brandt's *Ship of fools* (1494). To put it simply, there seem to have been no proper sea adventures in literature before the sixteenth century, if one understands the term in its original Latin sense of *ad-venire*: as an orientation towards "what approaches or comes about." In the medieval genre of *aventures* or *avantiuren* that particularly dealt with errant knights, the adventure consisted of the hero's encounter with the world outside the court: Fortuna's dominion of chance, chaos and unforeseeable dangers. But as soon as merchants literally "deal" with this outer world, an "adventure" becomes a business opportunity. Since 1443, English cloth traders, travelling on the sea regardless of uncertain market demands, called themselves "merchant adventurers", and in fifteenth-century German, a long-distance trade exposed to dangers and uncertainties was called *auventura* or *risigo*, while the personification of *ventura* was increasingly equated with Fortuna. Consequently, the first German prose novel, published anonymously in 1509 and probably originating in Augsburg, is, amongst other things, an adventure of sea trade. Named after the protagonist, the book *Fortunatus* mingles diverse narrative and didactic, legendary and novelistic elements, using motifs of the *Gesta Romanorum* and of *Il Decamerone*. Fortunatus is a modern adventurer: having left his impoverished family home, he becomes lost in a forest, where a "maiden of fortune" approaches and offers him diverse goods such as wisdom, wealth, strength, health and beauty.[12] Fortunatus chooses wealth, and thereupon supplied with a wondrous money bag that generates endless amounts of coins in any currency, he is able to travel throughout the whole world. He establishes an ever-expanding network of trade relations and, in the end, dies as a made man.

On the one hand, the novel is surprisingly realistic in its numerous details, while on the other hand, the workings of money, the self-increase of capital and its power to dissolve any social boundary is shrouded in mystery. After Fortunatus has proven himself a proper "stallion " in front of ladies and maidens, he receives Fortuna's money bag as a further phallic enhancement, finally becoming a ruthless and dishonest capitalist, seizing any occasion for further profit. He is a *homo fortunatus*, a darling of fortune, as described by Giovanni Pontano in his *De Fortuna* (around 1500): endowed with Fortuna's talents, he does not need to despise mundane goods, but rather makes use of them for the exercise of his virtues. Therefore, money is the prerequisite for his entire experience, development and happiness. Fortuna's favourite is a showcase capitalist, a "self-made man" made by her favour, or, as one might say, by his initial choice of the money bag. Accordingly, the novel does not so much present an allegory of Fortuna, but rather subordinates the whole world to the one and only goal: to make a fortune, i.e. to obtain and increase sufficient capital. Therefore, the novel is written like a commercial tractate for merchant adventurers; it demonstrates the bookkeeping of every event, time frame, or experience, and it trains the estimation of any chance for future profit or investment. Venice appears as the ideal setting for Fortunatus's ventures, while the only threat to his career

---

[12] "junckfraw des glücks" – *Fortunatus*, ed. according to the *Editio Princeps* by Hans-Gert Roloff, Stuttgart 2007, 46.

emerges when the unforeseen exceeds the scope of trading, when he is attacked by noblemen who do not accept him as their counterpart, for example, or when his business partners disregard the well-established rules of trade. Fortuna herself appears only in the beginning: in the primal scene of capitalism. Later, Fortunatus begs for good weather at sea, thus referring to *fortuna di mare*. But eventually, Fortuna has been "expelled from our world," as the novel concludes.[13] The demise of Fortuna as a figure seems no less irrevocable than the choice of money as modernity's prime mover.

4 The Drama of Modern *fortuna di mare*

The *Fortunatus* novel bears witness to the general boom of financial capitalism, as dominated by the Fugger family, the resulting downfall of small moneylenders and, moreover, the rise of maritime trade, as exercised by the Iberian sea powers and sponsored by the Augsburg banking house. The text contains an episode in which Fortunatus cheats the sultan of Alexandria by purloining his magic hat, the bearer of which is miraculously transferred to any place he can think of. Therefore, the novel seems to be connected not only to the decline of Mediterranean trade, as symbolised by Fortunatus's disregard of the Sultan, but insofar as the wizardry hat (and its power to administer and control even the most remote places) is construed as a mystification of bookkeeping,[14] the novel also bears witness to the emergence of proper Renaissance housekeeping, as described by Alberti, or even to the "Venetian method" of double-entry bookkeeping, as presented in Luca Pacioli's *Summa de Arithmetica* (1494). *Fortunatus* was popular outside Germany, too. Shakespeare came across it through its English translation or through Thomas Dekker's adaptation entitled *Comedy of Old Fortunatus*. He unmistakably digested the motif of fateful choice in his *Merchant of Venice* (written around 1596 or 1597). Nevertheless, this play does not revolve around a solitary adventurer, but rather around commercial and amorous partnerships. Courtship as well as business follow the Venetian example, and pursuit of happiness, in either case, is under Fortuna's motto: "They lose it that do buy it with much care". (I. 1, 75)

Fortuna's power thus comprises internal as well as external goods, love no less than profit. Accordingly, the whole play is based on the permanent switching between two settings (the city of Venice and the countryside residence of

---

13 Ibid., 195 (my translation).
14 Cf. Vogl, Joseph, *Kalkül und Leidenschaft. Poetik des ökonomischen Menschen*, München 2002, 180.

Belmont) and on the entanglement of two plots: the so-called "bond plot" that relates to the merchant Antonio, who borrows money from the Jew Shylock and pawns a pound of his own flesh; and the so-called "casket plot" that relates to Bassanio, who borrows money from Antonio in order to court the rich and beautiful Portia, whereby he has to choose between three different caskets. After having opted for the right casket, namely the leaden one that promises nothing but high risk, and therefore having conquered his mistress, Bassanio learns about his friend's misfortune: Antonio's ships are reported to have sunk, and it seems that he is swiftly impoverished, while Shylock insists on the punctual repayment of his loan. In the subsequent court hearing, Portia appears, masked as a lawyer, and outplays the Jewish moneylender Shylock by construing the Venetian law in a somehow capricious way. To a certain extent, Portia acts as an avatar of the old goddess Fortuna, and as such, she opposes the new capitalists, before they expel her from the world.

The only way to defeat Fortuna is through limitless hazard or through *virtù excessiva*, as Machiavelli called it: by putting one's entire existence and future in the balance, as Bassanio does, when opting for the leaden casket. In contrast to the *Gesta Romanorum* (and its English edition), where the topic of option first appears, the right casket is no longer marked by providence: the *Gesta*'s wording "Who chooseth me, finds what God has prearranged for me,"[15] in Shakespeare is turned into: "Who chooseth me, must give and hazard all he hath" (II. 9, 21). Famous commentators interpreted the casket procedure as a fateful choice of partner. Sigmund Freud, for example, says that caskets may house an entire body, as mothers do. Bassanio, at last, thus chooses his mother, or perhaps more the archetypical mother: mother Earth who will finally enclose him as a grave. Fortuna thus seems to be a "deity of death".[16] In Shakespeare's text, however, the expression *casket* supersedes the term *vessel*, as it reads in the *Gesta*. The concept of casket thereby encompasses the meaning of a "receptacle" as well as that of a "vehicle". Consequently, and in contrast to Freud, one could easily claim that there is a completely different series of substitutions in Shakespeare's play: Bassanio does not simply choose mother Earth and eternal rest, but rather a sea voyage and therefore eternal unrest. He opts for the maritime sphere of risk and hazard; he is a sea adventurer, and his bride is Fortuna in her most powerful guise as *fortuna di mare*. Respectively, the term "casket" could be related to the vulgar Latin *quassicare* and its modern derivations *casco*

---

[15] Theisen, Joachim, "Fortuna als narratives Problem", in: Haug / Wachinger (eds.), *Fortuna*, 143–191, here 154.
[16] Freud, Sigmund, "Das Motiv der Kästchenwahl", in: *Gesammelte Werke*, 18 vols, Frankfurt am Main 1999, Vol. X, 24–37, here 37.

and *cascare*, denoting the marine hull, its concussion and its *kasko* (the Italian expression for the comprehensive insurance). The casket plot thus links the bond plot to maritime affairs.

Bassanio, previously nothing but an errant soldier of fortune, becomes the darling of fortune by choosing the right casket. But in contrast to the novel *Fortunatus*, Shakespeare's play also portrays plainly unfortunate capitalists. Above all, the Jewish moneylender Shylock is despised: he is treated like an enemy and, ultimately, is completely disfranchised. He is reproached for spurning labour, for leading an essentially infertile life and for dealing in God's property, namely for dealing with time. In a way, Shylock is the scapegoat for every sin that financial capitalism around 1600, with its credits and banking houses, commits as a matter of course. Shylock, and no one else, seems to be mistreated or even punished according to the – outdated – polemics against usury. The play's second anachronism concerns Antonio: why in the world did he not simply insure his ships? If he had done so, he would not be in the debt of his creditor. However, in contrast to Shylock, the royal merchant has no understanding of sea fortunes. He is not sad because he has missed the opportunity of insuring his ships, but he does not insure them because he is a sad "want-wit" (I. 1, 6), recognising no opportunity in sea ventures, but merely danger and misfortune.[17] Whereas Shylock is overpowered by Fortuna, as if she punished modern capitalism (that will finally subdue her) *in effigie*, Antonio is all the more unable to defeat her. Both are melancholics, born under the sign of Saturn, being endowed with the gift of counting and calculating, weighing and measuring, but determined in large part by the stars.[18] Untimely characters, both set their own calculations against modern contingencies in vain; both seem overpowered and finally depressed by capitalism's incessant fight against the infinite uncertainties of old Fortuna.

5 Poetics of Contingency

Against this background, an old riddle of Shakespearean scholarship might now be viewed in a different light: the lack of maritime insurance seems to be the prerequisite for Fortuna's chronologically misplaced performance. Had mar-

---

17 Cf. Wilson, Luke, "Drama and Marine Insurance in Shakespeare's London", in: Constance Jordan / Karen Cunningham (eds.), *The Law in Shakespeare*, Basingstoke 2007, 127–142, here 129.
18 Cf. Reichert, Klaus, *Fortuna oder Die Beständigkeit des Wechsels*, Frankfurt am Main 1985, 123.

itime insurance been established in Antonio's Venice, as it had been long ago in Shakespeare's London, the old goddess would have been expelled. But in this anachronistic setting, Fortuna, in the disguise of Portia (or Portia in Fortuna's disguise), may firstly act like a sadistic Lady Luck: she crushes Shylock by adjusting Venetian law to the "occasion" and by interpreting his case in terms of equity, as was customary at Elizabethan Chancery Courts in Shakespeare's time. She thereby demonstrates the law as being essentially "contingent", as being dependent on the economic and power circumstances within capitalism. Secondly, she appears as a bountiful goddess of luck, since she allows for modern partnership in its double, commercial and amatory sense, as long as it is conceived as a true venture. And thirdly, Fortuna intervenes in the communication necessary for any risk management in business and in love: it is she who brings the crucial letters and news about what occurred. Especially in the case of Antonio's ships, whose possible perdition is vital for the plot, she mysteriously reports about their rescue, but adds: "You shall not know by what strange accident / I chanced on this letter." (V. 1, 278–279) In the form of *fortuna di mare*, she controls the knowledge about things being or not being, and therefore directs the goings-on. In a way, she acts as if she were engaged in the business of a "lost-or-not-lost contract", a specific type of hazard insurance that was still custom at London's seaport around 1600.[19] Her fickleness thus infects not only talk, but the crucial events themselves: they could have happened or not. Ultimately, Shakespeare's play pivots on events outright contingent.

The concept of contingency goes back to Aristotle's effort to evade Fortuna's mystification through meditating about chance and merely possible events. In *Peri hermeneias*, he limits true propositions to statements about a completed past or about a fully tangible present. Things are different if one turns one's hand to the future. For Aristotle, a sentence like "Tomorrow there will be a sea battle," is neither true nor false.[20] It refers neither to something existent nor to something non-existent, but rather to something insisting: to something with the potential to be and, at the same time, not to be. Boethius later translated Aristotle's respective term *endechomenon* into *contingentia*, attributing this specific modality to the events themselves as well as to the language referring to them. A language without definite truth values, referring to events that have the power "not to be", is itself contingent, or, as we would call it today: it is

---

19 On the – not rarely fraudulent – insurance practices at the Royal Exchange after 1577 cf. Kepler, J. S. "The Operating Potential of London Marine Insurance in the 1570s: Some Evidence from 'A Booke of Orders of Assurances within the Royall Exchange'", *Business History* 17/1 (1975), 44–55.
20 Aristotle, *Organon II*: *Peri hermeneias*, 18b.

poetic or *fictional*. Notably, the modality of contingency was, for Aristotle, already irrevocably entangled with the sea. It is not without cause that he chose the example of a naval battle, because in ancient Greece, the sea was considered a region without firm grounds of being and without proper *nomoi* (without fundamental laws and borders) – a space where people are neither dead nor alive, a district that suspends the bivalent logic of true or false, and a realm beyond the exclusive choice between to be and not to be.

Last of all, one could ask what mode of being applies to Shakespeare's Fortuna herself. Obviously, she is not presented in a schematically allegorical manner. She is not an ideograph that could be translated back into firm concepts. Portia is instead vivid and concrete, without losing the general traits of the goddess.[21] This Shakespearean character, in a sense, incorporates Fortuna's mode of simultaneous being and not being. Portia is a figure of potentiality, of becoming and occasion. At the same time, she is a *figura etymologica*, since Fortuna has been derived from Latin *fors* and *ferre*, meaning the advent, the bearing and bringing of possible futures – just as Portia could be translated as the porter or bearer of possible futures. As such, Portia or Fortuna is never completely present in the play: she always wears the masks of the uncertain or upcoming, whereby she is the opponent of merchant adventurers. She is the figure of instability that is consequently unable to become a proper figure, but which is existent only as a figure. Not being Janus-faced, being neither merely *fortuna bona* nor merely *fortuna mala*, but being both at the same time, she "cannot but distinguish herself from herself".[22] If one wants to devise a formula, one might say: Portia = Fortuna ≠ Portia. At any rate, she is the figure of contingency in its double meaning: a figure tainted by contingency, and, at the same time, the only figure representing contingency itself. And finally, even her dwelling is a paradigmatic setting of contingency. Portia's or Fortuna's home is not the commercial city of Venice, but rather "Belmont." This putative country residence turns out to be an island with winds "blown in from every coast." (I. 1, 170) It is the utopian goal of true *homini fortunati*. And in that respect, her final retreat "Belmont" is exactly the opposite of direful Mount Purgatory, where Ulisse, Dante's unfortunate adventurer, once sank.

---

21 Cf. Reichert, *Fortuna*, 133.
22 Heller-Roazen, Daniel, *Fortune's Faces. The Roman de la Rose and the Poetics of Contingency*, Baltimore / London 2003, 89.

6 Conclusion: Modernity and Fortuna's Sea Change

To conclude, Fortuna's "demise" in early modernity, corresponding to the waning of the Renaissance, is not entirely a downfall or cessation. Quite rightly, demise could also be understood as a *translatio* of power: as a transfer on the one hand between antiquity and the Renaissance, involving the passage from mythology and religion to rationality and technology, and on the other hand between Italy and England, involving the expansion of sea trade from the Mediterranean Sea to the oceans. On the occasion of the Sea Venture's loss on a Bermudan reef, Shakespeare's very last play, *The Tempest*, introduced the term "sea-change" (I. 2, 403) for a profound transformation of being on the level of politics and poetry (involving Shakespeare's own leave as a playwright). Therefore, in the Renaissance, a double sea change is connected to Fortuna. Firstly, concerning the three revolutions described (the nautical and the commercial revolution, both resulting in the revolution of insurance), the adventurous encounters with the sea have changed as much as the sea itself, and secondly, Fortuna herself has been profoundly changed. In her incessant fickleness, she is no longer an allegory of luck, but rather the figure of contingency. Therefore, she becomes truly maritime, and her unstable presence as *fortuna di mare* seems to be not merely one of her many disguises, but her appearance as such. Although the notion of Fortuna, in the long term, was superseded by the estimations, calculations and pricings of modern risk management, it is still somehow present. Because in maritime insurance, immeasurable uncertainties are far more frequent than measurable ones, practical calculation dominates mathematical computation in this field. When directed to maritime affairs, modern insurance, which was born of the sea, offers practical stability, but not theoretical certainty – it is rather a matter of complex (or in itself contingent) market action than of simple computation. Therefore, a technical term was already coined in Renaissance times for the totality of uncontrollable and unpredictable sea dangers, for storms as well as, for example, piracy or human error in general. And taking into account the history of maritime risk management, this term seems to be most felicitous: *fortuna di mare*.

Nicolette Mout
Justus Lipsius (1547–1606): Fortune and War

1 Lipsius, Fate and Fortune

"It is a poor soldier that follows his commander grumbling."[1] This quotation from Seneca's *Letters* appears in Lipsius's book *Politica* (first published in Leiden in 1589).[2] In Seneca's as well as in Lipsius's view, the commander was like life itself, with all its vicissitudes, good or bad. According to Stoic precepts, the wise man should be aware that his fortune was wont to change: "No man has ever been so far advanced by Fortune that she did not threaten him as greatly as she had previously indulged him". [3] In the sixteenth century, however, *fortuna* – as well as *fatum* – had become slightly dangerous words, as Lipsius was to find out to his discomfort soon after he had published his book *De Constantia* (Leiden 1584). As a philosopher with a penchant for political thought Lipsius developed his line of reasoning about fate and fortune mainly in two of his publications that both became hugely popular: *De Constantia* and *Politica*. In other works as well as in his letters he refers to these concepts only occasionally. As a humanist scholar frequently caught up in the troubles of his time, particularly the revolt of the Netherlands and the concomitant religious strife, he had every reason to link the concepts fate and fortune to his personal experiences. Finally, however, he settled for a thoughtful treatment of the relation between fortune and the practice of war, albeit only as a side-line to his arguments concerning political life and moral philosophy. In line with Jacob Burckhardt's remark that

---

[1] "Malus ille miles, qui imperatorem suum gemens sequitur", quoting Seneca, Ep. 107, cf. Lipsius, Justus, *Politica. Six Books of Politics or Political Instruction*, Jan Waszink (ed.), Assen 2004, 276–277. I have followed the translation in Seneca, *Letters from a Stoic. Epistulae Morales ad Lucilium*, Robin Campbell (ed.), Harmondsworth 1969, 199.
[2] Cf. for the literary form of the *Politica* Moss, Ann, "The *Politica* of Justus Lipsius and the Commonplace-Book", *Journal of the History of Ideas* 59 (1988), 421–436; Lipsius, *Politica*, 49–79; Tucker, George H., "Justus Lipsius and the *Cento* Form", in: Erik De Bom / Marijke Janssens / Toon van Houdt / Jan Papy (eds.), *(Un)masking the Realities of Power. Justus Lipsius and the Dynamics of Political Writing in Early Modern Europe*, Leiden 2011, 163–192.
[3] Seneca, Ep. 4, *Ad Lucilium Epistulae Morales* I, Richard M. Gummere (ed.), Cambridge (Mass.) /London 1917, 17.

https://doi.org/10.1515/9783110455045-004

fortune is more often depicted as the bearer of disasters than praised as a force to the good,⁴ Lipsius's view of the concept ran the risk of ambiguity.

What meaning did the word *fortuna* have for Lipsius? He must have been familiar with the rather down-to-earth use that merchants made of the word, where it simply meant success in material aspects of life. In early modern iconography pertaining to commercial activity, the images of Fortuna and Mercurius were sometimes coupled together. Many a merchant's house in town, be it Amsterdam or Prague, had a house sign showing the goddess Fortuna. ⁵ Lipsius must have been conscious of the political use of the concept of fortune as well, as was the case, for instance, in Florence where the facade of the Palazzo del Podestà carried an inscription praising the city that obviously enjoyed fortune's favour.⁶ Perhaps Lipsius would have liked Erasmus's quotation of Cicero's words about high achievements attained while "guided by virtue, accompanied by fortune". These words lived on in many variations well into early modern times.⁷ Lipsius would probably not have wholeheartedly supported the idea of Fortuna as the last goddess surviving from antiquity into a Christian world, but if she was not that goddess, what was she – or it?⁸ Lipsius must have been aware of the caution if not outright suspicion with which some had come to consider the concept of fortune. As Lipsius's older contemporary, the Anglican bishop Thomas Cooper, wrote, perhaps echoing Saint Augustine: "That which we call fortune is nothing but the hand of God [...]. Chance or fortune are gods

---

4 Burckhardt, Jacob, *Die Kultur der Renaissance in Italien. Ein Versuch*, Walter Goetz (ed.), Stuttgart 1966, 479.
5 González García, José M., *La diosa Fortuna. Metamorfosis de una metáfora política*, Madrid 2006, 66–108, esp. 93–108; Bec, Christian, *Les marchands écrivains à Florence, 1375–1434*, Paris / The Hague 1967, 301–317; Elias, Johan E., *De vroedschap van Amsterdam 1578–1795* [The Town Council of Amsterdam], vol. I, Haarlem 1903, 57, and vol. II, Haarlem 1905, 730, 739, 832, 859, 953; Winter, Zikmund, *Z městkých živností* [From urban crafts], Prague 1911, 285; Volf, Josef, *Geschichte des Buchdrucks in Böhmen und Mähren bis 1848*, Weimar 1928, 28.
6 Rubinstein, Nicolai, "The Beginnings of Political Thought in Florence. A Study in Mediaeval Historiography", *Journal of the Warburg and Courtauld Institutes* 5 (1942), 198–227, esp. 213.
7 Erasmus, Desiderius, *Adagiorum Chilias Quarta (Pars Altera) necnon Adagiorum Pars Vltima* (= Opera Omnia Desiderii Erasmi Roterodami (henceforth ASD), vol. II, 8, Ari Wesseling (ed.), Amsterdam 1997, Adag. 3947: "Omnia summa consequutus es virtute duce, comite fortuna" ("Guided by ability and accompanied by fortune you have achieved the highest success in everything"). Cf. Volkmann, Ludwig, *Bilderschriften der Renaissance*, Leipzig 1923, 120. Cf. also Wittkower, Rudolf, "Chance, Time and Virtue", *Journal of the Warburg Institute* 1 (1938), 313–321; González García, *diosa*, 287–292.
8 Patch, Howard R., *The Goddess Fortuna in Mediaeval Literature*, Cambridge 1927, 3–6; Doren, Alfred, "Fortuna im Mittelalter und in der Renaissance", in: Fritz Saxl (ed.), *Vorträge der Bibliothek Warburg. Vorträge 1922–1923*, vol. I, Wiesbaden 1924, 71–144; González García, *diosa*, 221–274.

devised by man and made by our ignorance of the true, almighty and everlasting God". A plan for a disputation at Cambridge University about fortune and fate in the presence of Elizabeth I of England was disapproved of because the topic "might yield many reasons [arguments] impertinent for Christian ears, if it were not circumspectly used".[9]

In his popular philosophical work *De Constantia*, Lipsius was offering the reader moral consolation in troubled times. At the same time, he was attempting to revive Stoic tenets in a world of divided Christianity. He, like the Neapolitan humanist Giovanni Pontano, author of another popular philosophical treatise, *De fortuna* (1500–1501),[10] wrote about fate and, to a much lesser degree, about fortune. Lipsius took great pains to make it clear that he was just a philosopher, declining to write about religious matters: "It is said that elephants, although they are very much attracted to streams, nevertheless do not go in rashly because they do not know how to swim: that is how I feel about theology", he wrote to a friend when sending out the first complimentary copies of *De Constantia*.[11] In his eyes, contemporary religious discord, fuelled by dissenters of every hue, was becoming a stumbling block on the road to wisdom. Pontano believed in fortune being governed, to a certain degree, by the stars. Through the prudent use of his free will, man was able, as Pontano argued, to thwart the negative effects of fortune. Lipsius, on the other hand, did not discuss the influence of the heavens on human affairs. On the contrary, he criticised the belief in celestial power popular with astrologers and even, as he wrote, with several theologians. In *De Constantia*, he approved solely of the concept of the true or pious fate of the individual. According to Lipsius, this fate was exclusively subject to divine providence coupled with necessity – the latter being the universal law behind the course of creation.[12]

---

9 Quoted in Keith Thomas, *Religion and the Decline of Magic*, Harmondsworth 1973, 91–92, footnote 4.
10 Pontano, Giovanni, *La fortuna*, Francesco Tateo (ed.), Naples 2012.
11 Lipsius, Justus, *Iusti Lipsi Epistolae* (henceforth *ILE*), vol. I: 1564–1583, Aloïs Gerlo / Marcel A. Nauwelaerts / Hendrik D. L. Vervliet (eds.), Brussels 1978, 83 10 15 P², l. 14–16. Cf. also Mout, Nicolette, "'Elefanten tauchen nur mit Vorsicht in die Flüsse ein, weil sie nicht schwimmen können.' Justus Lipsius und die religiösen Auseinandersetzungen seiner Zeit", in: Heinz Schilling / Heribert Smolinsky (eds.), *Der Augsburger Religionsfrieden 1555. Wissenschaftliches Symposium aus Anlaß des 450. Jahrestages des Friedensschlusses, Augsburg 21. bis 25. September 2005*, Münster 2007, 439–454.
12 Lipsius, *De Constantia Libri Duo*. Leiden 1584, Book I, Cap. 18, f. 55–60. I used Lipsius's own copy with his marginal notes: Leiden University Library, 765 B 22. Cf. also Mout, Nicolette, "Trost im Unglück? Lipsius und Fortuna", in: Walter Haug / Burghart Wachinger (eds.), *Fortuna*, Tübingen 1995, 297–301.; for the similarity between ancient Stoic teachings about fate

The concept of fortune was only mentioned in passing. Aristotle was chided because he had mentioned luck, in the forms of fortune and chance, as a possible cause of things. Lipsius, however, credited the ancient Stoics for "drawing blind mortals away from that blind goddess, I mean Fortuna, whose name and power they strongly opposed", as Saint Augustine did as well, he added in the margin.[13] "We" – and here Lipsius means his fellow Christians – "shun the deceitful blasts of fortune and chance, so that our ship is not wrecked on the cliffs of necessity".[14] Despite Lipsius's prudently formulated arguments about the role of fate in human life, several readers of *De Constantia* took him to task on his views, relating them, contrary to Lipsius's intentions, to certain controversial theological issues of the day, such as the cause of sin and the importance of free will versus predestination. Lipsius replied to their censorious and sometimes quite abusive remarks with his usual circumspection, explaining that he had only wanted to adapt ancient Stoic philosophy to reveal Christian truth. He considered the reproach of not incorporating enough Christian doctrine into his arguments unfair, as even Saint Augustine had recommended that Christians make use of what ancient pagan philosophy had to offer. Lipsius repeatedly made a point of stressing his pure intentions, which should be obvious to the benevolent reader of those difficult and much criticised passages about fate.[15] In the foreword to the second edition of *De Constantia*, however, he went as far as to ask his readers for clemency.[16]

In his *Politica*, a mirror for princes (Leiden 1589), Lipsius attempted to be very judicious as far as the concept of fortune was concerned.[17] He focused even more than in *De Constantia* on fortune's subordinate relation to fate. Quoting again from Saint Augustine, Lipsius stressed that fate is nothing other than "the decree and the voice, so to speak, of the divine order." He prudently declined to discuss the theologically controversial role of man's free will in relation to his individual fate.[18] Nevertheless, this very passage was censured by the ecclesiastical authorities prior to the publishing of the book's second edition in 1596. By

---

and Lipsius's tenets, cf. Sellars, John, "Stoic Fate in Justus Lipsius's De Constantia and Physiologia Stoicorum", *Journal of the History of Philosophy* 52 (2014), 653–674.
13 Lipsius, *Constantia*, Book I, Cap. 18, f. 60.
14 Ibid., Book I, Cap. 20, f. 66.
15 Mout, Nicolette, "'Which Tyrant Curtails my Free Mind?' Lipsius and the Reception of De Constantia (1584)", in: Karl Enenkel / Chris Heesakkers (eds.), *Lipsius in Leiden. Studies in the Life and Works of a Great Humanist on the Occasion of his 450th Anniversary*, Voorthuizen 1997, 123-140.
16 Lipsius, *Constantia*, Antwerp, second edition, 1585, Foreword of the second edition.
17 Mout, "Trost", 301–303.
18 Lipsius, *Politica*, 270–271. Cf. also Brooke, Christopher, *Philosophic Pride. Stoicism and Political Thought from Lipsius to Rousseau*, Princeton 2012, 27–28.

then, Lipsius had returned to the Roman Catholic fold and had received a professorship at his *alma mater*, the University of Louvain in the Southern Netherlands, now firmly under Spanish rule. As soon as Lipsius was informed by friends in Rome that the papal Congregation of the Index was considering putting *Politica* on that feared list of forbidden books, he expressed his willingness to correct the text. His friends in Rome included powerful personalities such as Cesare Baronio, not yet a cardinal but superior of the Oratorians, and Roberto Bellarmino, also not yet a cardinal but rector of the Jesuit college. When Lipsius agreed to submit to the authority of the Congregation of the Index, Baronio and Bellarmino were quite prepared to assist him in turn. Lipsius also very wisely involved the ecclesiastical censor and rector of his own University of Louvain, Henricus Cuyckius (Hendrik van Cuyk), who read and approved the new version of *Politica*. The manuscript was then duly sent off to Rome, and to Lipsius's great relief, the book was not put on the Index. But the Congregation of the Index was not yet entirely content. Laelius Peregrinus, a learned priest and member of the Congregation, still found fault with a small number of passages, among them those concerning Lipsius's concept of fate. In his view, this was on the one hand based too much on the Stoa and was too similar to certain pagan concepts found in classical tragedy, and on the other hand was inimical to the Roman Catholic doctrine of free will. Lipsius thereupon made several changes to the text, adding a note that he had used the ancient word fate as an exact synonym of providence in the Christian sense. In his *Breves Notae*, short elucidations of *Politica* published together with the book's first edition in 1589, he had already argued that his concept of fate agreed with tenets found in works by the Church Fathers, especially Saint Thomas Aquinas.[19] The same defence appears in his correspondence at the end of 1589.[20]

In *Politica*, fortune is portrayed as a power to be understood with the help of reason and consequently held in check by prudence. Whoever is able to make sense of fortune's mode of operation, particularly in politics, must also accept that fortune is not well-disposed towards everybody, but only towards the happy few who know how to act prudently. For princes, for whom *Politica* was written, it was important to know that virtue and prudence together were able to conquer fortune: here, Lipsius took up a stock argument in Renaissance politi-

---

19 Lipsius, *Politica*, 180–182, 397–399, 712–720, 727–730.
20 Lipsius, *ILE*, vol. III: 1588–1590, Sylvette Sué / Hugo Peeters (eds.), Brussels 1987, 89 11 09 and 89 12 30. Cf. also Mout, Nicolette, "Zuviel Antike? Justus Lipsius als Zankapfel zwischen Katholiken und Protestanten. Ansichten über den Staat und den Krieg", in: Ulrich Heinen (ed.), *Welche Antike? Konkurrierende Rezeptionen des Altertums im Barock*, vol. I, Wiesbaden 2011, 117–140, esp. 130–131.

cal thought.²¹ In addition, he was summing up five factors important for the prince who wanted to acquire and hold on to political power, of which fortune was only the last, after adequate financial resources, a well-equipped armed force, prudent counsel, and political and military alliances.²² Lipsius discussed the question of why fortune was the last and not the first instrument for obtaining and keeping princely power, as its strength appeared to be so great. While acknowledging the fact that glory and power were more often a gift of fortune than of virtue, Lipsius argued that they were given only to those who, born under a particular star, had fortune assigned to them by the gods.²³ In politics as in warfare, fortune's influence should nonetheless not be underrated.²⁴ In neither *De Constantia* nor *Politica*, however, did Lipsius give a clear-cut description of his particular notion of fortune, its workings, or its powers. Following in the footsteps of Boethius, he limited himself to pointing out the ancillary role of fortune to providence. This perfectly fitted his attempts to reconcile Stoic teachings with the Christian faith.²⁵

2 Interlude: Lipsius and His Experience of War

It has been shown that Lipsius liked to use military metaphors in his philosophical works from *De Constantia* onwards.²⁶ It is also undeniably true that Lipsius's personal life was deeply influenced by the course of the revolt of the Netherlands against its overlord King Philip II of Spain. Lipsius repeatedly stated that in the early 1570s, he had left his homeland, the Southern Netherlands, because of troubles related to the revolt. He, and many of his contemporaries with him, considered the revolt a pernicious civil war that was fuelled by a fatal combination of religious and political issues. Besides, it was not at all clear which of the warring parties would ultimately be victorious. Lipsius's move to Leiden in 1578, accepting a chair at a university which had been

---

21 Lipsius, *Politica*, 283–285, 306–311, 366–371, 408–413. Cf. also Skinner, Quentin, *The Foundations of Modern Political Thought*, vol. I: The Renaissance, Cambridge 1978, 119–121.
22 Lipsius, *Politica*, 432–443.
23 Ibid., 440–441.
24 Ibid., 616–617, 660–661.
25 Mout, "Trost", Papy, Jan, "Lipsius' (Neo-)Stoicism: Constancy between Christian Faith and Stoic Virtue", *Grotiana* 22–23 (2001–2002), 47–72; for Boethius's afterlife cf. Glei, Reinhold F. / Kaminski, Nicola / Lebsanft, Franz (eds.), *Boethius Christianus? Transformationen der "Consolatio Philosophiae" in Mittelalter und Früher Neuzeit*, Berlin 2010.
26 Morford, Mark, *Stoics and Neostoics. Rubens and the Circle of Lipsius*, Princeton 1991, 163–164.

founded in rebel territory only three years earlier, was inspired by his wish to escape from the theatre of war in the Southern Netherlands and find a good position elsewhere, guaranteeing him a tranquil life of study and intellectual recognition. His much commented next move, in 1591, from Leiden back to his native Southern Netherlands, meant a change of political and religious allegiance. By that time, he had lost confidence in the governmental decisions made by the States General in the Northern Netherlands. In his view, the rebellious provinces were in the throes of internal political and religious strife. In the Southern Netherlands, Lipsius, the famous former Leiden professor, now posed as a pious Roman Catholic and a loyal subject of the Spanish king.[27] He confessed in a letter that living in Leiden had meant living with the enemy, thereby turning into an enemy himself. Religious considerations along with his loyalty to the king of Spain had been the reason why he had now moved back to his native country.[28] These remarks should not necessarily be taken at face value: if anything, Lipsius very much wanted to be considered a victim of the manifold troubles of his time, not an actor on the political or religious stage. Besides, personal safety was always high on his wish list. In 1595, he repeatedly stated in his letters that he would consider immigrating to a foreign country, such as Germany or Italy, if the town of Louvain were to come under threat because of the continuing war with the Dutch rebels.[29]

The gravity of the Ottoman peril, not only to Hungary and Austria, but also to the rest of Europe, dawned on Lipsius only in the early 1590s, shortly before

---

[27] Mout, Nicolette, "In het schip: Justus Lipsius en de Nederlandse Opstand tot 1591" [In the Boat. Justus Lipsius and the Revolt of the Netherlands until 1591], in: Simon Groenveld / Nicolette Mout / Ivo Schöffer (eds.), *Bestuurders en geleerden. Opstellen over onderwerpen uit de Nederlandse geschiedenis van de zestiende, zeventiende en achttiende eeuw, aangeboden aan Prof. Dr. J.J. Woltjer bij zijn afscheid als hoogleraar van de Rijksuniversiteit te Leiden*, Amsterdam 1985, 55–64; De Landtsheer, Jeanine, "Le retour de Juste Lipse de Leyden à Louvain selon sa correspondance (1591–1594)", in: Christian Mouchel (ed.), *Juste Lipse (1547–1606) en son temps*, Paris 1996, 347–368; Tracy, James D., "Princely *Auctoritas* or the Freedom of Europe: Justus Lipsius on a Netherlands Political Dilemma", *Journal of Early Modern History* 11 (2007), 303–329; Mout, Nicolette, "Faked Conversions? The Case of Justus Lipsius (1547–1606)" in: Maria-Cristina Pitassi / Daniela Solfaroli Camillocci (eds.), *Les modes de la conversion confessionnelle à l'Époque moderne. Autobiographie, altérité et construction des identités religieuses*, Florence 2010, 87–109; De Landtsheer, Jeanine, "Juste Lipse et l'évolution politique aux Pays-Bas du Nord après 1584" in: François Guillaumont / Patrick Laurence (eds.), *La présence de l'histoire dans l'épistolaire*, Tours 2012, 295–314; Machielsen, Jan, "Friendship and Religion in the Republic of Letters: The Return of Justus Lipsius to Catholicism (1591)", *Renaissance Studies* 27 (2013), 161–182.
[28] Lipsius, *ILE*, vol. VI: 1593, Jeanine De Landtsheer (ed.), Brussels 1994, 93 12 25 H.
[29] Lipsius, *ILE*, vol. VIII: 1595, Jeanine De Landtsheer (ed.), Brussels 2004, 95 06 20 RI and other letters from the first six months of 1595, for instance, 95 02 25 and 95 03 09 O.

the outbreak of the Long Turkish War (1593–1606). Hungarian correspondents had definitively opened Lipsius's eyes to the danger of further Ottoman expansion into Europe. In his letters, desire for peace and joy at victories gained by imperial forces alternated with deeply pessimistic expressions about the fate of Europe if Ottoman attacks could not be halted on the Central European battlefields. Lipsius was indeed greatly worried by Ottoman military successes, at one point even expressing his hope that God would come to the aid of "this perishing Europe". When his old friend, the Jesuit Martinus Delrio, went to Graz in order to teach at the university there, Lipsius became even more worried, as Styria was continuously under Ottoman threat.[30]

Fearfulness about having to live in times of war, a feeling that seemed to have obsessed Lipsius since early adulthood, was thus still with him while a professor at Louvain. In his personal life, this fear indeed became reality: while on his way to the town of Spa in the summer of 1595, he had a narrow escape from Dutch cavalrymen who had captured the castle of Franchimont and were now scouring the countryside. In a letter to an old friend, written in elegant Latin and embellished with a few Greek quotations, Lipsius described how he and his companion, the Jesuit scholar Leonardus Lessius, had to jump over a hedge and flee through rough terrain to safety. This adventure upset him so much that he recounted it in other letters as well.[31] Was this a case of fortune in action?

In the same year, 1595, Lipsius ventured to give his opinion on matters of war in a public letter on Spanish foreign policy and its European repercussions. At the time, a constant theme in his correspondence was the lamentable state of European politics, of which the deeper cause, as he saw it, was religious strife and its concomitant and incessant polemics. Lipsius became particularly worried about the political and military situation in the Southern Netherlands. His heightened awareness of the possibility of a crisis might have been an incentive to him to commit to paper certain thoughts on war and politics that he would normally have reserved for himself and his closest friends.[32]

---

30 Mout, Nicolette, "'Our people are dedicating themselves to Mars rather than to Pallas.' Justus Lipsius (1547–1606) and his perception of Hungary according to his correspondence", in: Réka Bozzay (ed.), *Történetek a mélyföldről. Magyarország és Némtalföld kapcsolata a kora újkorban* [Stories about Lowlands. The Relations Between Hungary and the Netherlands in the Early Modern Period], Debrecen 2014, 398–442, quotation 437.
31 Lipsius, *ILE*, vol. VIII, 95 07 04.
32 Mout, Nicolette, "Justus Lipsius between War and Peace. His Public Letter on Spanish Foreign Policy and the Respective Merits of War, Peace or Truce (1595)", in: Judith Pollmann / Andrew Spicer (eds.), *Public Opinion and Changing Identities in the Early Modern Netherlands. Essays in Honour of Alastair Duke*, Leiden 2007, 141–162.

Lipsius had spent 1594 working on *De Militia Romana*, in which he contrasted Roman military practice, the near-perfect organisation and high morale of the Roman legions with the sorry picture of the undisciplined soldiery of his own time.[33] He must have feared that King Philip II of Spain would never be able to win any war with such armies, not even a just war against the Dutch rebels.[34] And indeed, according to Lipsius, the king had been very unfortunate so far: the Dutch rebels were in possession of all the strategic fortresses, their military force was up to the mark, they had plenty of money and their government functioned well enough, although there were internal tensions. Here, however, Lipsius saw a chance for psychological warfare. Sowing discord in the Northern Netherlands, he thought, might result in the reconversion of a few hundred or perhaps even thousands of Dutchmen to Roman Catholicism and to a re-acceptance of the king's rule. But if this kind of psychological warfare were to be effective, a truce had to be concluded first. Lipsius himself preferred a proper peace with the Dutch, but considered this an unrealistic proposal for the moment. The Northern Netherlands were prospering, their ruling elite was as wealthy and powerful as kings, they were looking for allies abroad and they had lost all respect for their natural lord, the king of Spain. The Spaniards, on the other hand, were short of good soldiers and clever politicians. If the war continued, the Spanish government of the Southern Netherlands would not have adequate opportunity to reform its army, which was essential, as mutiny was rife. The government itself suffered from disorderliness and other shortcomings; according to Lipsius, a truce would provide the necessary break so that such deficiencies could be remedied. Afterwards, the war against the Dutch would have to be resumed.[35] The concept of fortune had no place in Lipsius's public letter of 1595, as it contained mere practical advice and hardly a trace of a more philosophical approach to politics. Undoubtedly, however, Lipsius would have agreed with Erasmus: who else but the humanist should show the

---

[33] De Landtsheer, Jeanine, "Justus Lipsius's *De Militia Romana*: Polybius Revived or How an Ancient Historian was Turned into a Manual of Early Modern Warfare", in: Karl Enenkel / Jan L. de Jong / Jeanine De Landtsheer (eds.), *Recreating Ancient History. Episodes from the Greek and Roman Past in the Arts and Literature of the Early Modern Period*, Leiden 2001, 114–115. Lipsius occasionally refers to mutinies in his correspondence, cf. for example Lipsius, *ILE*, vol. VIII, 95 06 01 K.
[34] For Lipsius's ideas about a just war cf. his *Politica*, 540–551; Papy, Jan, "An Unpublished Dialogue by Justus Lipsius on Military Prudence and the Causes of War: The *Monita et Exempla Politica de Re Militari* (1605)", *Bibliothèque d'Humanisme et Renaissance* 65 (2003), 135–148.
[35] Lipsius, *ILE*, vol. VIII, 95 01 02 S. Cf. the editor's introduction for printed versions of the letter.

prince the way to perfect rule, advising him about all aspects of government, including questions of war and peace?[36]

The fact that the States General together with the provincial Estates claimed sovereign power in the rebellious parts of the Netherlands had never appealed to Lipsius. He staunchly adhered to the monarchical principle of government, defending it in his learned books. After his return to his native Southern Netherlands and the acceptance, in 1592, of the chair at the University of Louvain, his anxiety about possibly having to live in a war zone did not immediately leave him. Only from 1598, when the Archdukes Albert and Isabella of Austria began their rule of the Southern Netherlands, did Lipsius's fears gradually abate. He showed himself grateful for the gradual stabilisation of political life in the Southern Netherlands under the benign rule of the archdukes, and hoped for a reduction of the danger of military action against his native country. Around 1600, the revolt of the Netherlands had become a permanent armed conflict between the Northern and Southern Netherlands, but Lipsius was now content to live in Louvain, a town not too close to the theatres of war.[37] His worries, however, never disappeared completely, as shown by his many references to the sieges by the Dutch army of towns in the northern parts of the Southern Netherlands, such as Ostend and Bois-le-Duc.[38]

3 The Fortunes of War According to Lipsius

For Lipsius, a functioning state needed moral authority and princely power supported by an armed force. For him, military power, the organisation of warfare and army reform were not only legitimate objects of study, but also represented important issues in his own time that was ravaged by wars and other troubles. As a political theorist with a practical eye, he wanted to advise rulers and army commanders as well as the educated public on how to solve pressing problems. Machiavelli's works on the subject were known to Lipsius, and he must also have been aware of other contemporary publications touching on similar themes, although he avoided naming them in his own books.[39] Lipsius ad-

---

[36] Erasmus, Desiderius, *The Education of a Christian Prince*, Neil M. Cheshire / Michael J. Heath (transl.) and Lisa Jardine (ed.), Cambridge 1997, 2.
[37] De Landtsheer, "Juste Lipse"; Mout, "Justus Lipsius".
[38] Examples in Lipsius, *ILE*, vol. XIV: 1601, Jeanine De Landtsheer (ed.), Brussels 2006, for instance 01 07 02.
[39] Oestreich, Gerhard, "Political Neostoicism", in his: *Neostoicism and the Early Modern State*, Cambridge 1982, 71–74; ibid., "The Military Renascence", 76–81.

dressed warfare as one of the most important aspects of state policy in some of his main works: *Politica* (Leiden 1589, revised edition Antwerp 1596), *De Militia Romana* (Antwerp 1596), *Poliorcetica* (Antwerp 1596) and *Monita et Exempla Politica* (Antwerp 1605). It must be stressed, however, that he focused on the prince as the embodiment of the monarchical state and therefore its main actor, rather than on the state as an abstract concept.[40] In accordance with Lipsius's interpretation of the Stoa, utility should be one of the hallmarks of a philosophical treatise, hence the emphasis, in his *Politica*, on practical advice to princes based on sound rational principles and supported by maxims and examples mainly drawn from ancient sources.[41]

In the Fifth and Sixth Books of *Politica*, Lipsius considered external and civil war respectively, examining the moral arguments concerning the difference between just and unjust wars as well. The prince was encouraged to reform the military system thoroughly on the basis of Lipsius's teachings. The starting point of the Fifth Book was not, as in some other mirrors for princes, the prince's virtue, honour, or care for the commonwealth, but the necessary *prudentia militaris*, i.e. the military skills and good judgement of the prince at war, including strategy and tactics. This was not an innate princely virtue: even great army commanders such as Caesar, Hannibal or Alexander the Great had needed to be taught the art of war. In Lipsius's opinion, a prince needed military prudence before anything else.[42] After having explained its importance, and the difference between a just and an unjust war together with their causes, Lipsius discussed the sole object of war, namely peace. He warned against starting an armed conflict for ignoble reasons, such as ambition, greed or wrath, stating that no war should be started lightly or rashly. Quoting Livy, Lipsius wrote: "Consider your forces, the power of fortune and the even chances of war. On both sides there will be swords and men. The corresponding outcome is nowhere less certain than in war." Fortune's power, Lipsius argued, was apt to show itself particularly in war, no matter how many soldiers the prince had on the battlefield and how much terrain was covered, "so however much you trust your armed forces, you must not exchange certitude for incertitude". "The successes you have achieved, or hope to achieve, fortune can crush in a single hour."[43] Thus, fortune would become an enemy of fame.

---

40 Mout, "Antike".
41 The best short introduction to *Politica* as a work of Neostoic political theory is still Oestreich, Gerhard, "The main political work of Lipsius", in his: *Neostoicism and the Early Modern State*, Cambridge 1982, 39–56.
42 Lipsius, *Politica*, 535–541.
43 Ibid., 541–551, quotations 550, 552.

After these warnings about fortune's fickleness, and painting the horrors of war in some detail, Lipsius proceeded to discuss briefly the necessary preparations before starting an armed conflict, making sure that sufficient money, supplies and arms are available. This is followed by chapters on the usefulness of a standing army and reserve troops, and on the soldiers themselves: their recruitment, discipline and the use made of them in battle. Emphasis is given, in chapter thirteen of the Fifth Book, to one of Lipsius's favourite topics: the reinstatement, following the example of ancient Rome, of military discipline and order being essential characteristics of any army, but grossly neglected in Lipsius's own time. In his discussion of order, he propagated Roman achievements concerning the order of battle, march and encampment. Discipline, according to Lipsius, comprised systematic and frequent military drill alongside military law, upheld by commanders meting out severe punishments to offenders.[44]

The concept of fortune only returns when Lipsius starts to discuss the virtues of the good commander in the fourteenth and fifteenth chapters of the Fifth Book. He favoured professional soldiers as leaders and did not consider the presence of the prince himself on the battlefield absolutely necessary: "If the existence of the realm, or the safety of the provinces is at stake, he [the prince] would have to go into battle", but in the case of minor wars, he should stay in the town that is the centre of his government.[45] Lipsius pleaded for having only one general in command of the army as a whole, while commanders lower in rank should occupy themselves with obeying orders and leading their men accordingly.[46]

The good commander should focus on no less than five qualities: knowledge, virtue, foresight, fortune and authority. Knowledge should have been attained from extensive experience in military service, virtue rested in the strength of body and mind combined with an upright heart, authority expressed itself as severity tempered with kindness, foresight should be coupled with circumspection and a distrust of one's good luck. A good commander should have experienced the ups and downs of warfare, because, as Lipsius argued in Livy's footsteps, he who has never been deceived by fortune would not know how to act in adversity.[47]

"When you act, let reason lead you, not fortune" is a quotation from Livy with which Lipsius closed his remarks on the importance of foresight.[48] Fortune

---

44 Ibid., 556–607.
45 Ibid., 607–611.
46 Ibid., 606–607.
47 Ibid., 610–611.
48 Ibid., 616–617.

itself, however, he considered an essential, though not decisive attribute of the ideal commander. In an obvious attempt to dissociate himself from the pagan concept of fortune, Lipsius at this point avoided the word *fortuna* itself, exchanging it for the more innocent expression luck or good fortune (*felicitas*). "Good fortune", he wrote, "is definitely the companion of good counsel and reason, but God bestows it more liberally on some. He is its sole originator, and nobody can procure it for himself."[49] By considering God the source of the commander's good fortune, Lipsius hoped to avoid the pitfall of offending sensitive Christian ears. For good measure, he added a quotation from Erasmus's *Adages* expressing the same thought: good fortune is a gift from God to man. Lipsius was careful to stress again the omnipotence of divine providence, although he agreed with Plato that the art of war sometimes needed strokes of luck. He had borrowed this argument from the pseudo-Platonic dialogue *Epinomis*. At the time this antique forgery was considered genuine, serving as a supplement to Plato's *Laws* and treating of education and the road to wisdom. The short passage about war evidently suited Lipsius's line of thought: "warfare, the art of generalship: most glorified in time of need, requiring most good fortune." Supporting this view with examples from antiquity, Lipsius mentioned several Roman generals, such as Scipio Africanus, who were repeatedly given military commands not only because of their ability, but also because of their proven good fortune. Only here, in the safe context of ancient history, Lipsius ventured again to use the word *fortuna* instead of *felicitas*.[50]

Emphasising the importance of a good strategy for the successful commander, Lipsius advised not to lean too much on fortune, but to trust reason and good judgement instead. Nevertheless, one should not ignore fortune altogether, but rather follow it whenever it presented itself, making it fit into one's strategy. On the other hand, Lipsius warned the commander not to rely on fortune unnecessarily.[51] Through such rather equivocal recommendations, Lipsius obviously wanted to stress the ambivalent role of fortune in military strategy. In the case of defeat, Lipsius recommended that the prince not give up hope, but rather fight against his misfortune, as only the fearful bow to despair.[52] In the last two chapters of the Fifth Book, Lipsius discussed ways to conclude a fair and lasting peace. Again, fortune was depicted as a double-edged

---

49 Ibid., 611–619.
50 Ibid., 616–617; Erasmus, Desiderius, *Adagiorum Chilias Quarta (Pars Prior)* (= ASD, vol II, 7), R. Hoven (ed.), Amsterdam 1999, Adag. 3191. I have followed the translation of Plato, *Epinomis* 975 E 3 by W. R. M. Lamb in Plato, *Charmides. Alcibiades I and II. Hipparchus. The Lovers. Theages, Minos. Epinomis*, Cambridge (Mass.) / London 1955, 435.
51 Lipsius, *Politica*, 620–623, 630–631.
52 Ibid., 650–651.

sword. The defeated prince was exhorted to accept that fortune had turned against him.[53] The victorious prince, however, should be aware of the fact that his good fortune might change for the worse. Quoting Seneca's tragedy *Hercules on Oeta*, Lipsius pointed out that when God starts to pursue the fortunate, he bears down on them, and as a result, greatness inexorably comes to an end. Besides, in the course of an armed conflict, fortune would have taught the defeated the art of war as well. Therefore, the victor should not provoke the vanquished but rather show himself merciful in concluding a mild peace.[54]

The short Sixth Book of *Politica*, comprising only seven chapters, is devoted to what was, in Lipsius's view, the greatest calamity of his time and, as he put it, a real pest: civil war. Though neither the revolt of the Netherlands nor the religious wars in France are mentioned explicitly, it is clear that Lipsius's passionate complaint about the misery of civil war in the first chapter was fuelled by these events. He defined civil war as a war of subjects against their prince, or of subjects among themselves.[55] Both definitions would readily apply to the revolt of the Netherlands as well as to the religious wars in France. As mentioned previously, the revolt of the Netherlands profoundly affected Lipsius's own life. He specifically commented on it many times in his correspondence, depicting it as a fateful civil war. Far from limiting himself to casual remarks on the latest news about the revolt, he assessed the course of events, giving his point of view accordingly. Particularly after the murder of the leader of the revolt, Prince William of Orange, in 1584, and before Lipsius left Leiden in 1591, his analysis in his letters betrayed a deeply pessimistic evaluation of the political and military situation in the Netherlands, which was reinforced by his profound abhorrence of war in general and civil war in particular. Time and again, Lipsius expressed the view that only a Stoic attitude in the face of these troubles would bring a certain form of consolation. It was all caused by "fate, the immovable power!", he once wrote in a letter to a prominent Dutch lawyer and diplomat.[56] In January 1604, Lipsius sent a final letter about politics to a Spanish nobleman in Brussels. Now that peace between Spain and France was a fact and peace with England was within reach, Lipsius's main worry was the continuing war with the Dutch rebels. In Lipsius's view, this war was much more difficult to end, because he still regarded it as a civil war, worse than any other form of armed

---

[53] Ibid., 656–657.
[54] Ibid., 658–665. For the quotation from Seneca's *Hercules on Oeta* 713–714 cf. Seneca, *Oedipus. Agamemnon. Thyestes. [Seneca] Hercules on Oeta. Octavia*, John G, Fitch (ed. and transl.), Cambridge (Mass.) / London 2004, 394–395.
[55] Ibid., 666–670.
[56] Mout, "schip"; Mout, "Trost"; Lipsius, *ILE*, vol. II: 1584–1587, M. A. Nauwelaerts / Sylvette Sué (eds.), Brussels 1983, 87 09 15 B.

conflict. But even a civil war could be ended, for instance by following the example of Augustus, who concluded a peace with his rival Pompey, after which Pompey's men defected to him en masse.[57]

In the second chapter of the Sixth Book of *Politica*, Lipsius identified fate, in the shape of divine providence, as the first of two deeper causes of civil war, explaining that history clearly demonstrated that God himself was responsible for the destruction of great empires.[58] It was implied that the outbreak of civil war must be taken as a sign that the downfall of the realm was near, or at least that great changes were to take place. Did not Sallust, in his letter to the elderly Caesar, predict civil war among the Romans when their city had come to its predestined end? Inexorable fate would reign forever, but nevertheless, Lipsius argued, the prince should do his utmost to prevent a civil war, because once it had started, it was next to impossible to suppress. Lipsius pointed to the vice *luxuria*, by which he meant material extravagance coupled with moral depravity, as the second deeper cause of civil war. A prince was not able to change fate, as it was God's decree, but he would be wise to launch a battle against *luxuria*.[59]

Calamitous political developments such as factional strife, sedition against the prince or other authorities, and also despotic rule could provoke a civil war. Such a war always meant disaster for the state and its rulers as well as for the individual subject. Here, good fortune or similar concepts did not play a role in Lipsius's arguments. The whole of the Sixth Book was set up as a flaming indictment against the evils of civil war, denouncing the usually irresponsible behaviour of those involved in it. Lipsius prudently avoided mentioning contemporary problems, such as religious differences or political theories concerning the right to resist, as causes or aspects of civil war. According to Lipsius, even tyranny should never be deemed a valid reason for the oppressed subjects to start a civil war or to take part in it. Only a sincere attempt by the prince to make peace could end such a war. For Lipsius, even a peace that was not in all respects advantageous to the prince was considered acceptable as the lesser evil compared to the scourge of civil war.[60]

In 1605, the year before his death, Lipsius published *Monita et Exempla Politica*. The book was intended as a kind of sequel to and commentary on *Politica*, providing historical examples as illustrations of the arguments brought forth in

---

57 Frías, Duque de, "Una carta inédita de Justo Lipsio", *Archivum. Revista de la Facultad de Filosofía y Letras* 16 (1966), 91–107. My thanks are due to Jeanine De Landtsheer for placing her edition of the letter at my disposal before publication in *ILE*.
58 Lipsius, *Politica*, 672–673.
59 Ibid., 672–675.
60 Ibid., 704–709.

the latter book. The examples were to be taken from ancient and medieval history, but also from recent times. He originally planned to write such a commentary on every book of *Politica*, but in the end only managed to publish historical essays pertaining to the first two books.[61] This meant that he had to grapple again with the concept of fate, because it appeared immediately in the First Book of *Politica*. Just as he did in the revised version of *Politica* (1596), which was expurgated in accordance with the wishes of ecclesiastical censorship, Lipsius declared in *Monita et Exempla Politica* fate and providence to be identical: "You who worship God and religion are also worshipping Fate, that is Providence and the divine decree", he stated in the First Book of *Monita et Exempla Politica*.[62] Nevertheless, what at first sight appears to be Lipsius's submission to Roman Catholic teachings might still be considered compatible with the Stoic tenements so dear to his heart. It might be further proof of his constant endeavours to combine Stoic philosophy with Christian teachings. His argument would run like this: if everything is directed by divine providence, which is also the origin of every human action, then everything in the universe, including nature and mankind, is subjected to necessity. Necessity can only be an orderly and reasonable power, although its rationale is not always obvious to man. With Seneca, Lipsius had come to the conclusion that providence does not let anything happen without reasonable necessity.[63] Therefore, it was useless to resist either providence or fate. As man, however, was often not capable of understanding the workings of reasonable necessity behind the acts of either providence or fate, history presented him with a number of truly amazing developments which nobody would have been able to foresee. Lipsius provided a striking example from his own days: "How would Philip II, King of Spain, ever have become King of Portugal if not through fate?" Lipsius explained: Manuel I, King of Portugal, had married three times and fathered many children. Twenty-two of his progeny held precedence over Philip II as far as the Portuguese crown was concerned, yet all died before their time, and in this way fate favoured Phi-

---

[61] Janssens, Marijke, "De Monita et exempla politica (1605) en Lipsius' humanistische programma" [Monita et Exempla Politica (1605) and Lipsius' Humanist Programme], in: Jeanine De Landtsheer / Pierre Delsaerdt (eds.), *Iam illustravit omnia. Justus Lipsius als lievelingsauteur van het Plantijnse Huis* [Justus Lipsius as Favourite Author of the Plantin Publishing House], Antwerp 2006, 201–220.
[62] Lipsius, Justus, *Monita et Exempla Politica*, Antwerp 1605, Book I, Cap. 5, f. 23.
[63] Papy, Jan, "Fate and Rule, Destiny and Dynasty: Lipsius's Final Views on Superstition, Fate and Divination in the *Monita et Exempla Politica* (1605)", in: Erik De Bom / Marijke Janssens / Toon van Houdt / Jan Papy (eds.), *(Un)masking the Realities of Power. Justus Lipsius and the Dynamics of Political Writing in Early Modern Europe*, Leiden 2011, 200–202.

lip II to become the ruler of the whole of the Iberian Peninsula.⁶⁴ The opposite could be true as well though, as history proved that many princes lost their power or even their lives through fate. Sometimes these events were predicted, by dreams, signs, apparitions or soothsayers. Lipsius told the tale of a limping and misshapen beggar-like figure at the palace gate of Buda who repeatedly and in a loud voice requested to speak to King Louis II of Hungary, who was having a meal in the palace. Interrupting the meal, he foretold the young king's imminent death (in the battle of Mohács against Sultan Süleymān the Magnificent in 1526). Then the apparition swiftly vanished.⁶⁵

4 Conclusion

With the publication of *Monita Exempla et Politica* in 1605, the end of Lipsius's life was nigh. It seems that by then, fortune as a concept in his political thought had vanished completely. In his last years, the concept of military prudence as a safeguard against unjust wars together with the question of the causes of war still interested him. This is clear from the unpublished fragments of the dialogue *De Re Militari* (written in 1605), which were obviously meant to be included in the never-finished *Monita et Exempla Politica*.⁶⁶ It is perhaps significant that in the published version of *Monita et Exempla Politica*, it is not prudence, in some of his former books a possible opponent and sometimes even the conqueror of the vicissitudes of fortune, but faith that played a major role as the most important virtue of princes.⁶⁷

Statecraft as well as war and its consequences had been among Lipsius's favourite subjects for intellectual exploration since his famous Tacitus edition (1574, last edition revised by Lipsius 1607) and his commentary on the *Annals* (1581). He considered Tacitus the master teacher of *prudentia* as an attribute of princes.⁶⁸ His equally celebrated book *De Constantia* (1584) focused on the art

---

64 Lipsius, *Monita*, Book I, Cap. 5, f. 28.
65 Lipsius, *Monita*, Book I, Cap, 5, f. 39–40.
66 Papy, "Dialogue".
67 Lipsius, *Monita*, Book I, Cap. 2, ff. 3–12; cf. also Stanciu, Diana, "Prudence in Lipsius's *Monita et exempla politica*: Stoic Virtue, Aristotelian Virtue or not a Virtue at all?", in: Erik De Bom / Marijke Janssens / Toon van Houdt / Jan Papy (eds.), *(Un)masking the Realities of Power. Justus Lipsius and the Dynamics of Political Writing in Early Modern Europe*, Leiden 2011, 233–262.
68 The best introduction to the political importance of Tacitus's works for Lipsius is Morford, *Stoics and Neostoics*, 139–180.

of living in troubled times with the Stoa as a guiding star.[69] Apart from *De Constantia* and *Politica*, Lipsius published a number of books in which warfare played a part. These books were primarily historical, not philosophical, in outlook and he wrote them after his return to the Southern Netherlands. In *De Militia Romana* (Antwerp 1596), he produced an extensive commentary on Polybius, extolling the qualities of ancient Roman armies and warfare. Soon afterwards, he published a sequel to *De Militia Romana* entitled *Poliorcetica* (Antwerp 1596), a beautifully illustrated and detailed description of Roman war machines and projectiles used in battle, paying special attention to sieges of towns and fortresses, together with a discussion of tactics and defence systems.[70] In his book on the cultural history of the Roman Empire, *Admiranda sive De Magnitudine Romana* (Antwerp 1598), Lipsius praised the military and political virtues of the Romans as the true and only foundation of a successful empire, a glowing example to the realms governed by the Habsburgs in his own time.[71] Philosophical arguments about fate or fortune found no place in these later books.

While the philosophical notion of fortune had all but disappeared from Lipsius's late works, it seems that his perception of fate had survived, albeit in a slightly tamed form. The censors at the Vatican, by demanding a revision of *Politica* prior to the publishing of the second edition of 1596, had cowed Lipsius into rewriting – although possibly not into rethinking – passages about fate that were too close, in the censors' eyes, to pagan notions: in no way should ideas culled from the ancient Stoics interfere with the true faith. By following the censors' instructions and expurgating his text, Lipsius made a point of demonstrating his Roman Catholic piety, his submission to the Church as well as his loy-

---

69 Papy, Jan, "Justus Lipsius über Frieden und Krieg: Humanismus und Neustoizismus zwischen Gelehrtheit und Engagement", in: Norbert Brieskorn / Markus Riedenauer (eds.), *Suche nach Frieden: Politische Ethik in der Frühen Neuzeit* vol. II, Stuttgart 2003, 155–173.

70 Lipsius, Justus, *De Militia Romana Libri Quinque. Commentarius ad Polybium*, Antwerp 1596; id., *Poliorcetica*. Antwerp 1596; second revised ed. 1599; De Landtsheer, "Justus Lipsius's *De Militia Romana*"; Peeters, Hugo, "Ontstaansgeschiedenis van Lipsius' *Poliorcetica*, geschreven in aangename herinnering aan zijn verblijf te Luik" [Origins of Lipsius' *Poliorcetica*, written under the influence of pleasant memories of his stay in Liège], in: Jeanine De Landtsheer / Pierre Delsaerdt (eds.), *Iam illustravit omnia. Justus Lipsius als lievelingsauteur van het Plantijnse Huis* [Justus Lipsius as Favourite Author of the Plantin Publishing House], Antwerp 2006, 127–158.

71 Enenkel, Karl, "Ein Plädoyer für den Imperialismus. Justus Lipsius' kulturhistorische Monographie 'Admiranda sive de magnitudine romana' (1598)", *Daphnis* 33 (2004), 583–621; Laureys, Marc, "'The Grandeur that was Rome': Scholarly Analysis and Pious Awe in Lipsius's *Admiranda*", in: Karl Enenkel / Jan L. de Jong / Jeanine De Landtsheer (eds.), *Recreating Ancient History. Episodes from the Greek and Roman Past in the Arts and Literature of the Early Modern Period*, Leiden 2001, 123–146.

alty to the king of Spain. Moreover, he regularly expressed his desire to serve his fatherland, the Spanish Southern Netherlands, his hope for a Spanish victory over the rebels in the Northern Netherlands, and, implicitly or explicitly, his longing for peace. After his return to the Southern Netherlands and to Roman Catholicism, however, he did not disavow his predilection for the Stoic concept of fate, even though it was safer to consider it equal to divine providence and thus recognisably in line with Roman Catholic teachings. Seneca's bust, placed behind Lipsius in Peter Paul Rubens's painting of *The Four Philosophers* (1611), was there to stay.[72]

---

[72] Palazzo Pitti, Florence: showing Rubens himself, his brother Philip Rubens, Lipsius, and Janus Woverius, and also Lipsius's dog Mopsus.

Jürgen Müller/Bettina Gruber
Fortuna Revalued

On the Goddess's Sexualisation in the Renaissance

Fortuna balancing on her globe is the transformation of an abstract concept into a vivid image. As modern spectators, we perceive the goddess as contingency incarnate – but what do we actually mean by this? Dating back to the scholastic term *contingentia*, contingency is often casually reduced to the idea of mere chance, although it has acquired a much more complex meaning in scholastic philosophy as well as in recent cultural studies and sociological debates. The term refers to "something neither necessary nor impossible, that is, something that may exist as it is, but may just as well take on a different form."[1] Contingency presents promising and daunting perspectives, possibilities and threats, chances and risks at the same time. This aspect of uncertainty bordering on menace is appropriately expressed by the *Dictionary of Military and Associated Terms*, defining contingency as "an emergency involving military forces caused by natural disasters, terrorists, subversives, or by required military operations. Due to the uncertainty of the situation, contingencies require plans, rapid response and special procedures to ensure the safety and readiness of personnel, installations, and equipment."[2]

The sociologist Michael Makropoulos has pointed out that on the one hand, contingency is "not just a 'natural fact' at the basis of sociality", while on the other hand, it is "not a 'historical' fact in the simple positivistic sense" either, instead being defined as "a category of social self-problematisation and self-reflection inextricably linked with a society's self-perception and world view."[3]

The notion of contingency as "a category of social self-problematisation" is of particular importance to the understanding of our subject. Construing Fortuna at once as an image of contingency and a motif of special relevance to the

---
[1] Makropoulos, Michael, *Modernität und Kontingenz*, Munich 1997, 14.
[2] *Dictionary of Military and Associated Terms*. US Department of Defense 2005. www.thefreedictionary.com, article "contingency", accessed 21.11.2016. The cult of fortune seems accordingly to have thrived in times of insecurity: "Tyche gained importance during the political upheavals that followed the meteoric career of Alexander III and the establishment of new Hellenistic kingdoms in Egypt and Asia Minor after Alexander's death. No temple in the Hellenistic world surpassed the splendour of Tyche's sanctuary in Alexandria." See Littlewood, R. Joy, "Fortune", in: Michael Gagarin / Elaine Fantham (eds.), *The Oxford Encyclopedia of Ancient Greece and Rome*, vol. 3, Oxford 2010, 210.
[3] Makropoulos, *Modernität und Kontingenz*, 14.

early modern age does not imply a statement on the development of historical *realia*. We do not contend that contingency objectively increases from the Middle Ages to the modern period (something that would be very difficult to define, let alone to prove), but that the plentiful representations of Fortuna on her globe have to be read as a special *figure of self-problematisation* that is quite distinctive of the age. The increased frequency of the "Fortuna on her globe" motif goes along with a decline in the "wheel of fortune" imagery, although the latter far from disappears altogether.[4] Our assumption is that this shift indicates a ground-breaking innovation in the self-perception of early modern societies. The gracious dancer on the globe in her precarious posture differs greatly from the wheel of fortune: turning, but at least turning reliably. Niklas Luhmann has added to our understanding of contingency by stressing that it also represents the "possible worlds" complementing the one, real "Lebenswelt", the world of everyday life.[5] This makes it clear that our motif refers to the immediate problems of practical life.

With the emergence of these "'possible worlds' of one real lifeworld" that Fortuna represents, the risks and chances in life have multiplied. Consequently, Fortuna appears as *fortuna bifrons*, *fortuna bona* and *fortuna mala*, in German as "beyde[r] Glücke", a translation of the expression *fortuna utraque*. In 1555, the Italian humanist Achille Bocchi (1488–1562) stressed her elusive and malicious character – "Lusca, procax, petulans, improba, tristis, atrox, / Impatiens iuris, mendax, furibunda, superba, / Saeua, maligna bonis, benigna malis", thus branding her as wayward and promiscuous. On the other hand, a common *interpretatio christiana* views her as an instrument of God and special executive of the creator, thereby investing her with considerable dignity.[6]

Can we call Fortuna a symbol and an agent of modernity? Starting from the premise that contingency is a defining feature of modern societies, this doubtlessly seems justified. Our type of Fortuna consequently supersedes the ancient images of fate as well as the medieval "Lady with the Wheel". The reason for this iconographic development is obvious: fate as an antique goddess does not represent contingency, but rather predetermination. It is only when the aspect of Fortuna as Occasio or a decisive moment becomes central that the character of the allegory changes into an image of contingency.

---

[4] Kirchner, Gottfried, *Fortuna in Dichtung und Emblematik des Barock. Tradition und Bedeutungswandel eines Motivs*, Stuttgart 1970, 19–24.

[5] Luhmann, Niklas, *Soziale Systeme. Grundriß einer allgemeinen Theorie*, Frankfurt am Main 1987, 152.

[6] Kirchner, *Fortuna*, 19–24.

In the following investigation, we will explore examples from the critical time around 1500, which deserves to be considered a *saddle period*, i.e. a period of transition, in its own right.⁷ A chief witness for this was Sebastian Brant with his *Ship of Fools*, published for the first time in 1494. This satire can of course be read as an all-embracing sermon against vice. For our subject, however, it is interesting to note that it shows a very acute awareness of the epoch's changes and innovations, among them the discovery of America, the astronomical debates about the geocentric model, individual bible-interpretation, heretical church reform as demanded by Jan Hus, misinformation circulated by letterpress, alchemy and bogus science, to mention just a few. Brant is certainly conscious of the so-called *nova reperta*, the inventions and discoveries of the day. This seemingly modernist interest co-exists with a deeply religious attitude demonstrated, among other things, by the conclusion of his book on a truly apocalyptic note. Is it legitimate to associate the appearance of new Fortuna allegories with these developments? To clarify this, we will provide a short overview of new types of Fortuna allegories with special regard to the works of the Swiss artist Urs Graf.⁸

From the Renaissance onwards, the relation of man and Fortuna gained increasingly erotic and blatant sexual aspects.⁹ It is vital to the understanding of many of these works that the implied recipient is definitely male. Shakespeare refers to fortune several times as a whore, and Machiavelli offers the following piece of advice: "Fortuna is a woman, and to subjugate her, you have to beat her and push her around."¹⁰ The unpredictability and waywardness of Lady

---

7 For the term, referring metaphorically to a mountain saddle, and famously coined by Reinhart Koselleck, see Koselleck, Reinhart, *Vergangene Zukunft. Zur Semantik geschichtlicher Zeiten*, Frankfurt am Main 1989.

8 For a basic examination of Graf's Fortuna representations see Andersson, Christiane, *Dirnen – Krieger – Narren. Ausgewählte Zeichnungen von Urs Graf*, Basel 1978, 47–52.

9 It must be kept in mind, however, that this aspect *did* exist in antiquity: "Die gesamte Überlieferung [...] führt den öffentlichen Kult der F. auf Servius Tullius zurück. Dieser aus dem niedrigsten Stande auf den Thron gelangte König war der besondere Schützling der Göttin [...], und sollte sogar des Liebesumgangs mit ihr gewürdigt worden sein." See Otto, Walter, "Fortuna", in: Georg Wissowa / Wilhelm Kroll (eds.), *Paulys Realencyclopädie der classischen Altertumswissenschaft N.B.*, vol. VII, 1, Stuttgart 1971, 12–42; furthermore, we know about a "F. virilis" (as opposed to "F. muliebris"), who was celebrated by the visit of women from the lower classes, possibly prostitutes, in the men's *thermae*, see Littlewood, "Fortune", 211; Otto, "Fortuna", 22.

10 Shakespeare, *Macbeth*, Act I, Sc. 2; id., *Lear*, Act 2, Sc. 4; id., *Anthony and Cleopatra*, Act IV, Sc. 12; id., *Timon*, Act 4, Sc. 3; "Io iudico bene questo: che sia meglio essere impetuoso che respettivo; perché la fortuna è donna, ed è necessario, volendola tenere sotto, batterla e urtarla." See Machiavelli, Niccoló, *Il Principe / Der Fürst*, trans. and ed. by Philipp von Rippel, Stuttgart 1986, 198.

Fortune prompts the idea of likening her to a promiscuous woman. The cobbler and "Meistersinger" Hans Sachs calls her "das unsthet, untrew, waltzend glück." The Brothers Grimm in their *Deutsches Wörterbuch* inform us that "the idea of the moral shortcomings of 'Glück'" is "very widespread" and refers especially to its supposed "infidelity, factitiousness and caprice."[11] Two articles by Sibylle Appuhn-Radtke on Fortuna offer a sound basis for the study of the subject. Furthermore, we rely on an essay by Joseph Leo Koerner, who investigated the reception of Dürer's *Nemesis* in Northern European art after 1500.[12]

In contrast to Koerner, however, we focus on Fortuna and Occasio in terms of modern conceptions of art around 1500. These conceptions imply a re-orientation in the field of artistic *imitatio*: now it is not the *imitatio veterum* anymore, but rather the ironic dealing with examples and paragons that for the first time is at the artist's disposal.

Since the times of Jacob Burckhardt, we habitually associate the Renaissance with the cult of the individual and with ideas of personal achievement, culminating and converging in the discourse on (particularly artistic) genius. We view it as a period enhancing personal liberty and free choice, notions glorified for example in Pico della Mirandola's *De dignitate hominis* and Erasmus's *De libero arbitrio* – in which the latter famously refuted Luther's negation of free will.

Another aspect of this is an intensified consciousness of what is perceived as the greatness, *fama* and *memoria* of human life. Fama does not necessarily mean success or auspiciousness, but can also refer to individuality in terms of failure or tragic entanglement. Individuality in an emphatic sense is characterised by the fatefulness of human existence, by life's dependence on fortune.

Condottieri, uomini illustri or *artisti famosi* are literary characters. If we think of Renaissance artists' biographies, for example that of Michelangelo, the heroic, the tragic and the individual form an inextricable amalgam. Fortune has

---

11 Grimm, Jacob / Grimm, Wilhelm, *Deutsches Wörterbuch*, vol. 8, Munich 1999, col. 226–275, here: col. 250.

12 Appuhn-Radtke, Sibylle, "Fortuna", in: Wolfgang Augustyn (ed.), *Reallexikon zur Deutschen Kunstgeschichte*, vol. 5, Munich 2005, col. 271–401; id., "Fortuna Bifrons. Zu einem mittelalterlichen Bildtyp und dessen Nachleben in der Ikonographie Albrecht Dürers", *Das Mittelalter. Perspektiven mediävistischer Forschung* 1 (1996), 129–147; Koerner, Joseph Leo, "The fortune of Dürer's 'Nemesis'", in: Walter Haug / Burghart Wachinger (eds.), *Fortuna*, Tübingen 1995, 239–294; For the ironic reception of Dürer's *Nemesis* cf. also Kaschek, Bertram, "Kühnes Kinderspiel. Zum Motivkreis der infantia im druckgraphischen Frühwerk der Gebrüder Beham", in: Thomas Schauerte / Jürgen Müller / Bertram Kaschek (eds.), *Von der Freiheit der Bilder. Spott, Kritik und Subversion in der Kunst der Dürerzeit*, Petersberg 2013, 136–156.

taken over human destiny, marking man's predestined path to an existence as an artist or a sovereign.

Deterministic models of existence tend to interpret this with a view to a person's horoscope or place of birth. It is not a mere coincidence, therefore, that astrology plays such a large part in the *episteme* of the Renaissance. Be that as it may, individuality now becomes a constitutive factor for any concept of fate. Biographical and autobiographical texts are the corresponding literary genres. In them, Fortuna, as a character or an abstract concept, is at work as a motive force that makes drama possible. It is she who renders possible the peripety and climax of the action. She brings along all kinds of unexpected turns, unexpected rescue as well as blatant injustice. And yet, Fortuna enforces finality, because life is not only transient and brief, but also irreversible. Her categorical imperative reads "Know the right moment and catch it". The Fortuna-Occasio theme thus implies an increasing appreciation of the ability to make decisions.

This ability is a basic prerequisite for success. The German Volksbuch *Fortunatus* (first edition Augsburg 1509) offers a contemporary literary example: the protagonist manages to rise socially by dealing prudently with Lady Fortune's gifts.[13] This success, achieved due to his wise decisions, is, however, squandered by his sons. The family finishes where it began, that is in misery and poverty.

The book's tendency is comparatively conservative for its time, as right decisions reliably produce success and wrong decisions misery. Fittingly enough, Fortuna is portrayed not as a dubious female balancing on a sphere, but as a worthy Lady Fortune, two feet firmly planted on the ground, handing the modest Fortunatus a purse that is never empty (fig. 1).

Fig. 1: Lady Fortune hands a never empty purse to Fortunatus, woodcut, *Fortunatus*, Augsburg 1509, fol. 23ᵛ – © Bayerische Staatsbibliothek München.

---

13 Günther, Hans (ed.), *Fortunatus. Nach dem Augsburger Druck von 1509*, Halle a. d. Saale 1967.

In contrast to this, Fortuna now mainly stands for the awareness that the ability to make a choice is a necessary, but not a sufficient condition for success. Life is uncontrollable, as it follows the principle of causality all but stringently. Exceptions do not confirm the rule any more. Intuition and discretion are needed to discern this for each individual case. A sovereign may act adequately and still fall victim to adverse circumstances. Conversely, a gambler and reckless risk-taker may succeed in taking advantage of a fortuitous moment and rise to power.

From all this, it becomes evident that a heightened feeling of contingency increases the pressure to come to decisions and favours an active, even reckless type of person, called "Tatmensch" in German.

The importance of the Fortuna topic can be gleaned from the many examples both to the north and south of the Alps, but also from the place that the topic holds in contemporary literature and philosophy.[14] Ernst Cassirer has drawn attention to its importance for Renaissance thought, emphasising that Fortuna embodies the philosophical relation of freedom and necessity. The motif thus aligns itself with the intellectual habits of the time. With regard to the pageant staged in 1501 for the wedding of Lucrezia Borgia and Alfonso d'Este and to Giordano Bruno's philosophical dialogue *Spaccio della bestia trionfante* (1584), Cassirer remarks:

> And a figure such as Giordano Bruno teaches us that the allegorical masks which dominate these performances extend their effects far into a realm which, in accordance with our habits of thought, is the exclusive domain of abstract life, void of terms and images. In a period in which life reveals itself everywhere to be dominated and infused by intellectual forms, a period in which fundamental thoughts on the position of man in relation to the world, thoughts on freedom and fate, prove to be effective extending into such festive performances – in such a period, these thoughts do not remain contained within themselves, but indeed strive for visible symbols. [...] [Bruno] penned the idea that for human insight, ideas cannot be represented and embodied in any way other than in pictorial form. [...] For such a school of thought, the allegory is not simply an external accessory, a coincidental mantle, but indeed a vehicle of the thought itself.[15]

---

14 For a classical study see Cassirer, Ernst, *Individuum und Kosmos in der Philosophie der Renaissance*, Darmstadt 1987, especially 77–129.

15 "Und eine Gestalt wie Giordano Bruno lehrt, daß die allegorischen Masken, die diese Spiele beherrschen, ihre Wirkung bis weit in ein Gebiet erstrecken, das, unseren Denkgewohnheiten gemäß, nur dem abstrakten, dem begrifflich-bildlosen Leben vorbehalten sein sollte. In einer Zeit, in der das Leben sich überall von geistigen Formen beherrscht und mit ihnen durchdrungen zeigt, in der die Grundgedanken über die Stellung des Menschen zur Welt, über Freiheit und Schicksal bis in das festliche Spiel hinein sich wirksam erweisen – in einer solchen Zeit bleibt auch der Gedanke nicht lediglich in sich selbst beschlossen, sondern strebt nach sichtbaren Symbolen. [...] [Bruno hat] den Gedanken festgehalten, daß für die menschliche Erkennt-

The distinction between "modern" and "traditional" can help to effect a rough classification. The wheel symbolism favoured in the Middle Ages is what we call traditional. Medieval representations of Fortuna show a remarkably limited range of subjects, generally just the king and his reign. Fortuna is usually depicted standing or sitting at the hub of the wheel turning the spokes, thus effecting the sovereign's rise and fall. While the king seems to sit safely enthroned on the vertex of the wheel, he already casts his eyes down anxiously, thus anticipating his abrupt fall from power. The next stage already shows him beneath the wheel, but is only a preparation for his renewed rise to power.

It is important to note the viewing direction of Lady Fortune (here depicted as a queen) who steadfastly fixes the spectator without taking the slightest notice of the havoc she causes. The sovereign's comments on her intervention - "Regno", "regnam", "sum sine regno" und "regnabo" – illustrate the consequences of her action. A similar image can be found in an astronomical manuscript from Prague now kept in Vienna. Motifs of that kind can be traced back to the eleventh century, as an Italian codex from Montecassino shows (see pages 21–22). An illustration from Herrad von Landsberg's *Hortus deliciarum* dates back to the end of the twelfth century. Here, Fortuna is sitting *beside* the wheel, turning a crank. Again, she seems totally uninvolved, staring blindly past the unhappy kings.

Before closing the discussion on this type of Fortuna, we have to mention its last great success. The 37th chapter of Sebastian Brant's *Narrenschiff* features the rise and fall of three donkeys (fig. 2).[16] The Strassburg humanist talks about "Fortune's wheel" ("Glückes Rade") and represents his characters as hybrids of ass and man, who inform the recipient of their folly. He also deftly uses the text to denounce tyranny. Fortuna appears as the just punishment for power-crazed subjects. This tradition has it that the descent of one king automatically implies the rise of another. It operates with a kind of energy conservation law balancing power and the lack of it in eternal gyration. In this tradition, the wheel is at once a symbol of fortune and of time. Time is what brings necessary changes in its wake – everything is changing and still remains the same.

---

nis sich die Ideen nicht anders als in bildhafter Form darstellen und verkörpern lassen. [...] Für eine solche Denkart ist die Allegorie kein bloßes äußeres Beiwerk, keine zufällige Hülle, sondern sie wird zum Vehikel des Gedankens selbst." Cassirer, *Individuum und Kosmos*, 78–79.

16 Interestingly, Fortuna's wheel seems to have been rather rare in the art of antiquity "[...] obwohl die rota Fortunae nach dem Vorgang hellenist. Schriftsteller auch bei Cicero [...] erscheint, ist sie auf Darstellungen selten." See Eisenhut, Werner, "Fortuna", in: *Der Kleine Pauly*, vol. 2. Munich 1979, col. 600.

Fig. 2: Rise and Fall of the Three Donkeys, woodcut in Sebastian Brant, *Das Narrenschiff*, Basel 1494, fol. 46ᵛ – © Bayerische Staatsbibliothek München.

Contrary to these examples, we exclusively refer to as "modern" those representations that fit the following description: they show us fate as an erratic and incalculable factor irreducible to a cyclical process, while at the same time emphasising the force and energy of the individual, who is seen as a hands-on "Tatmensch".

Occasio here is the tell-tale motif. Looking at Leonardo's drawing from 1483, the technical challenge of the new pictorial type immediately catches the eye (fig. 3). The Tuscan artist, who worked at the Sforza court in Milan, in his wash drawing, aims at a suggestion of velocity. Three times he attempts to depict a rapidly advancing or a flying figure. The two figures, one above the other, their hair streaming wildly forward, clearly remind the spectator of Occasio.

Fig. 3: Leonardo da Vinci, A study for a winged figure, Allegory with Fortune, pen and brown ink, with brown wash, ca. 1480–1485, British Museum, no. 1895,0915.482 – © Trustees of the British Museum.

It is to Giovanni Bellini that we owe another image of Occasio, going back to an *ekphrasis* by Ausonius. The painting shows the allegorical figure standing on two spheres, blindfolded and with wings sprouting from her shoulders and feet, carrying two small amphoras. Created around 1500, it is possibly an allegory of life's journey, the road being clearly visible in the background. It stages the spectator's unexpected meeting with Fortuna-Occasio, the outcome of which remains dubious.

A picture from Mantegna's school of painting is just as dynamic as Leonardo's drawing (fig. 4). We see Virtù, who prevents a young man from grasping Occasio. What is suggested here, however, is less an impression of velocity than one of instability: one step further and she will fall off her globe. The youngster's wish to get hold of Occasio is evident. He is eagerly reaching for the young woman, but virtue foils his plans and frustrates his desire. Only at the second glance does one become aware that the lower part of Occasio's dress is transparent and demonstrates her sexual attractiveness. So it is sexual desire that

Virtù is so dutifully fending off. The artist vividly brings it home to us how easily we are seduced by opportunity. Mantegna's narrative framing turns Occasio into a temptress whom it now takes individual virtue to overcome. He forcefully stages temptation by merely hinting at sexuality without showing us solid evidence.

Fig. 4: Mantegna (School), Occasio and Poenitentia, fresco, ca. 1500, Mantua, Museo della Città di Palazzo San Sebastiano – © Museo della Città di Palazzo San Sebastiano, Mantua.

More explicit is an engraving from around 1500 by Nicoletto da Modena (fig. 5). It presents Fortuna with her right foot resting on a globe, checking the wind direction with her index finger, while acrobatically steering the world by means of a rudder with her left foot. Her cloak blowing in the wind like a sail, she appears more like a Venus than a goddess of fortune. Despite her decisively female character, her head reminds us of representations of Cupid. The strong wind seems to have turned her left leg outwards. The engraving is staging the moment in which she lets the male spectator see her private parts, thus producing a metaphor for sexual intercourse. It becomes obvious that Fortuna-Venus undertakes her voyage with the intention of finding a lover. Here, fate's favour is imagined as a sexual act.

Fig. 5: Nicoletto da Modena, Fortune, engraving, 1500–1510, British Museum, no. 1873,0809.695 – © Trustees of the British Museum.

The motif of Fortuna's sail and the voyage of Venus in search of a male partner were both established in Northern Europe. The engraving by Dirck Vellert (a renowned Antwerp artist and Dean of the Guild of St. Luke) draws on the same metaphors, but substitutes the ship with a large seashell to facilitate the identification of the goddess (fig. 6). Another engraving by Albrecht Altdorfer from 1511 takes the same line (fig. 7). It shows Fortuna on a globe accompanied by a young boy, who can be recognised as Cupid by his blindfold and stilts. With her relaxed and effortless contrapposto, Venus is shown to reign supreme over the world under her feet, fixing the viewer with a provocative stare.

Fig. 6: Dirck Vellert, Venus sailing in a scallop shell, engraving and etching, 1524, British Museum, no. E,1.273 – © Trustees of the British Museum.

Fig. 7: Albrecht Altdorfer, Fortune, engraving, 1511, British Museum, no. 1863,1114.757 – © Trustees of the British Museum.

In this context, we would like to add an interesting observation on the engraving by da Modena (fig. 5). As stressed before, Venus's right foot is resting on a floating globe. In order to illustrate the problem of lability and stability, the artist depicts a pedestal on the shore, thus contrasting stable earth with the untrustworthy element of water, "quadratus" with "rotundus" – they are juxtaposed in opposition like Sapientia and Fortuna. The connection of fortune with water or the sea is indeed a very old one.[17]

This iconography confers a special significance on the globe, namely that its movements are wholly unpredictable. In comparison to the geometrical

---

17 "Tyche, whose name derives from the Greek verb 'to happen', makes her first appearance in Greek literature in Hesiod's *Theogony* as a daughter of Oceanus, suggesting the goddess's affinities with the ebb and flow of the sea. Imagery associating Tyche with the sea begins with Pindar's allusion to her 'double rudder', which enables the goddess to steer either way. Marine iconography dominates Fortuna's iconography on Roman coinage from the late Republic into the second century CE, favouring principally the rudder, but also a ship's prow [...]." See Littlewood, "Fortune", 210.

shape of the globe, the construction of the wheel is relatively simple. Due to its suspension, it needs a kinetic impulse, created for instance by a crank. It can move only in defined directions: what is up must go down and vice versa. The direction of the ball, however, is not only incalculable, it is also difficult to stop once set in motion. And besides: there is no top and bottom to the globe. Its surface is a labyrinthine phenomenon, despite all ostensible simplicity. One goes up and finishes below. One sails westward to reach the East. And through its ultimately limited surface, which leads circumnavigators invariably back to the spot from which they started, it becomes a kind of prison. Man can never escape from the globe.

Fig. 8: Hans Holbein, Fortune and a fool, pen and black ink drawing in *Erasmi Roterdami encomium moriae [...]*, Basel 1515, Kupferstichkabinett, no. 1662.166, fol. S2^V – © Kupferstichkabinett, Basel.

A drawing by Hans Holbein shows Fortuna in the act of showering a fool with gold coins; he holds up his gown like an apron to collect the treasure (fig. 8).[18] The drawing is from a 1515 edition of *laus stultitiae* and comments on Erasmus's ideas on the power of Fortuna. He makes folly refer to her kinship with Fortuna, whom she calls "rerum fortunatrix", an enemy to the wise and a friend to fools. To prove this, Erasmus illustrates his assertion with a string of proverbs all concerning the feebleness of wisdom and the power of incalculable chance. The climax of his deliberations is reached with the following quotation: "Fortuna loves

---

[18] See Müller, Christian, *Hans Holbein d. J. Zeichnungen aus dem Kupferstichkabinett der Öffentlichen Kunstsammlung Basel*, Basel 1988, 20–23.

the imprudent, she loves the reckless and those who like the motto 'the die is cast'."[19]

Fig. 9: Frontispiece of Carolus Bovillus, Liber de Sapiente, woodcut in Carolus Bovillus, *Que hoc volumina continentur [...]*, Paris 1510, fol. 116ᵛ – © Bayerische Staatsbibliothek München.

The confrontation of Sapientia and Fortuna is very common, as an illustration of 1510 from the *Liber de sapiente* by Carolus Bovillus (fig. 9) can show. Holbein

---

19 "Amat fortuna parum cordatos. Amat audaciores et quibus illud placet πᾶς ἐρρίφθω κύβος" Erasmus von Rotterdam, *Moriae encomium, id est stultitiae laus*, Straßburg 1515, fol. gVIII r/v.

had a rich pictorial tradition at his disposal, which he skilfully made use of staging Fortuna once more as Occasio, who is identifiable by her tuft. To make plain the precariousness of Fortuna, the artist not only places her on a globe, but also transfers the ball into the sea. This highlights the opposition of the stable mainland and the deceptive, labile wet element.

Erasmus's text confers a vast range of meanings on Fortuna. He turns her into the essence of *mundus*, representing its whole innate and unredeemable injustice. From this perspective, the world is exactly the opposite of what it is supposed to be morally. The *laus stultitiae* does not convey a precise meaning to Fortuna. She stands for the world's status quo in general, and thus incorporates everything bad and malignant. She reigns as card or dice games, as libido or in the guise of vices such as *gula* or superstition. Her real power lies in making the world go on just as it is, thereby making injustice prevail. The globe and its surface become a prison that man can never leave.

The Swiss printmaker Urs Graf, although intermittently engaged as a mercenary, can hardly be regarded as a simple thug. His works for the Basel publisher Johannes Frobenius show that he was actually well acquainted with the pictorial and literary Fortuna-Occasio tradition. Especially important in this context is a front page that Graf created first for the 1513 edition of Erasmus's *Adagia* and later for the volume *Index in Tomos omnes operum divi Hieronymi* edited in 1515 by Johannes Oekolampad, printed by Frobenius in Basel. For this front page, the artist created an erudite architecture of knowledge (fig. 10). To the left we recognise the boy Kairos as described in ancient sources with hair hanging over his face, a razor in his hand and wings at his feet – and to the right we discover Nemesis carrying a square and a bridle.[20] On the portal itself, putti to the left and right display the escutcheons of the Holy Roman Empire and the city of Basel. The central figure is Humanitas sitting enthroned on a chariot and surrounded by four poets and orators known for their eloquence: Virgil, Homer, Cicero and Demosthenes. By contrast, the radical realignment of the artist's style in several drawings, in which Graf characterised Fortuna as a prostitute (undated pen and ink drawing by Urs Graf, fig. 11), is truly amazing. The pictorial tradition depicting the goddess in this way had first attracted the interest of Christiane Andersson.[21] But what we hope to demonstrate in this context is an ironic approach in the work of Urs Graf. But first we want to give a general description of the work of the Swiss artist. We propose the drawing originated

---

[20] For the identification of Fortuna with Nemesis ("deae Nemesis sive Fortuna") see Otto, "Fortuna", col. 41.
[21] Andersson 1978, 47–48; Andersson, Christiane, "Jungfrau, Dirne, Fortuna. Das Bild der Frau in den Zeichnungen von Urs Graf", in: *Kritische Berichte*, 16/1. 1988, 26–42.

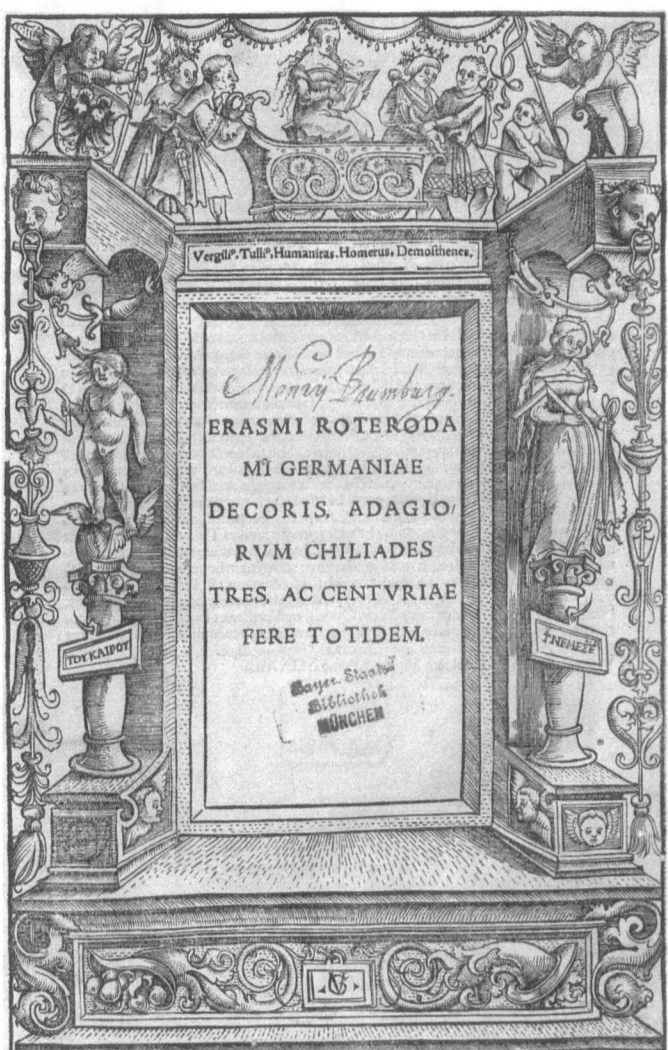

Fig. 10: Urs Graf, Title-Border with the Triumph of Humanitas, woodcut in Erasmus, *Germaniae decoris, Adagiorum Chiliades tres ac centuriae fere totidem*, Basel 1513 – © Bayerische Staatsbibliothek München.

between 1515 and 1520, as a comparison with the artist's other works suggests. It shows the goddess standing on the globe, holding the hem of her gown, which is blown upwards by the wind exposing her legs and private parts. Her face is gracefully turned to the right, and she is wearing a large hat with pompons similar to a beret. The sleeves and shoulders of her dress are decorated by vents. The Swiss dagger on her left side is a further salient feature. This type of weapon was worn by Swiss mercenaries at that time, and in his drawings Graf repeatedly vested women with this detail to mark them as so-called sutlers, or camp followers. In her right hand she carries a goblet, from which dark smoke or a stench is rising. Close beside it we spot a devilkin or little imp in profile.[22] Consequently, possible associations run in the direction of Pandora's box. The goblet with emanating smoke, which in fact represents the escaping evils of the world, resembles the box as being opened by Pandora.

Fig. 11: Urs Graf, Fortune as a prostitute, pen and black ink drawing, ca. 1520, Germanisches Nationalmuseum, Graphische Sammlung, no. Hz 160 – © Germanisches Nationalmuseum, Nuremberg.

In the whole scene, Graf stresses Fortuna's promiscuity, suggesting that she willingly denudes her genitalia. Again the representation of luck, fate and

---

22 Andersson 1988, 33.

chance is definitely genderised. The "Fortuna as a prostitute" motif with its detrimental connotations takes aim at Fortuna as a female sexual being, whereas the youth-like Kairos is spared this negative valuation.

Fig. 12: Albrecht Dürer, Nemesis (Large Fortune), engraving, 1502, British Museum, no. 1895,0915.346 – © Trustees of the British Museum.

This is especially interesting if one keeps in mind against whom the allegory is directed: the Swiss artist is alluding to the so-called *Große Glück* or *Nemesis* by Albrecht Dürer (fig. 12). Here as well, the goddess is balancing on a globe, but we watch her majestically floating by, in her right hand a cornucopia, in her left the bridle. The triangle shape that Graf gives to his clouds is also an immediate allusion to the famous engraving. Dürer takes us into heavenly regions not made for mortals – Graf, by contrast, makes Fortuna fly so fast towards us that a collision seems unavoidable.

To understand Graf adequately, a comparison to an engraving by Heinrich Aldegrever also paying tribute to Dürer's example might be helpful (fig. 13). Graf seems to refuse both Aldegrever's ambitious iconographic programme and the equally ambitious design, based on a poem by Politian and a Renaissance medal. His drawing contains a whole series of inversions and shows a very different stance on his subject.

Fig. 13: Heinrich Aldegrever, Fortune, 1555, engraving, British Museum, no. 1850,0810.279 – © Trustees of the British Museum.

A defiant attitude towards great masters is displayed by the second great model which Graf cites ironically: Raphael's *Galathea* (fig. 14). With this reference as well, the Swiss artist contradicts the Italian model that shows a particularly chaste nymph, whom he brazenly turns into a prostitute.

Fig. 14: Marcantonio Raimondi (after Raphael), Galatea, engraving, 1515–1520, British Museum, no. 1980,U.1606 – © Trustees of the British Museum.

This can be seen in an etching dated to 1513 although it was presumably created ten years later.²³ The print shows a prostitute with a leg bared in order to wash

Fig. 15: Urs Graf, Prostitute washing her leg, etching, 1513, Kupferstichkabinett, no. X.2293 – © Kupferstichkabinett, Basel.

---

23 See Müller, Christian, *Urs Graf. Die Zeichnungen im Kupferstichkabinett Basel*, Basel 2001, 289–290.

her feet in a bowl. Through this action she showcases her female charms (fig. 15). This is highly irritating, especially as the bowl does not contain any water. The attitude of the head in both works is similar, as well as one arm that is only slightly varied. Definitely changed, however, is the bust: with Graf, the viewer is invited to a clear view of the figure's breasts. A pen and ink drawing from 1513 also toys with elements from Raphael's *Galathea*, which are simply rearranged (fig. 16).

Fig. 16: Urs Graf, Foolish Virgin, pen and black ink drawing, 1513, Kupferstichkabinett, no. U.X.46 – © Kupferstichkabinett, Basel.

As far as we can see, Graf is one of the few artists to have represented Fortuna repeatedly as a prostitute, for instance by showing a mercenary at a tryst with a

Fig. 17: Urs Graf, Swiss mercenary and prostitute, pen and black ink drawing, ca. 1516, Städel, no. 15673 – © Städel Museum, Frankfurt am Main.

whore (fig. 17). Just like in Dürer's *Nemesis,* she is carrying a goblet. Sitting on the edge of a bed she is drawing the man towards her casually. He has already put cash for her on the table, where fruit, alluding to the sweetness of love, is piled up. The elegant bed and the inscriptions on it leap to the eye – they both address the topic of man's luck. "GOTT GEB U[N]S GLUK" (fig. 17) and then:

"GLUK UF MINER SITEN". We hold that Graf here simply inserts an allusion to the omnipresent threat of syphilis.[24] Graf has created a topos from the established association of Fortuna with prostitution. The starting point for this is the promiscuity of fortune, who becomes involved with everyone and just as easily walks out on them again. Her favour is therefore understood as sexual intercourse.

In a further drawing a harlot, again dressed splendidly and provokingly, is pouring out coins (fig. 18). The modern representations of Fortuna (such as Graf's) tend to present her as part of everyday life. Dressed as a prostitute, she makes blunt overtures to her male customers. As she has become venal, her services are nothing extraordinary any more. Graf thus energetically counteracts the literary appreciation of Fortuna. Remarkably, Occasio is immaterial to this scene, although the Swiss artist brings back the identification of fortune with Venus when he represents the encounter of man and fate as a sexual act.

Fig. 18: Urs Graf, Prostitute distributing money, pen drawing, 1517, Kupferstichkabinett, no. U.X.80 – © Kupferstichkabinett, Basel.

---

24 Cf. Sammern, Romana, "Die süße Milch der Venus. Zur Ikonographie der Syphilis im 16. und 17. Jahrhundert", in: Thomas Habersatter (ed.), *Sünde, Süße Laster: lässliche Moral in der bildenden Kunst*, Salzburg 2008, 133–138; McGough, Laura, *Gender, sexuality and syphilis in early modern Venice. The disease that came to stay*, Basingstoke 2011; Münch, Birgit, "Das Männerbad, der Jabacher Altar und die große Angst vor den 'frantzosen'. Albrecht Dürers vielschichtige Klagen über die Syphilis.", in: Birgit Münch / Andreas Tacke / Markwart Herzog (eds.), *Die Klage des Künstlers. Krise und Umbruch von der Reformation bis um 1800*, Petersberg 2015, 24–44.

At the outset, we inquired as to the connection between Fortuna and the category of contingency. There are, we think, several reasons for affirming this relation. Contingency, structurally seen, is not so much blind chance, but rather the relativity as an absence of necessity with which we have been confronted in Graf's work. It stands for the inaccessibility of the absolute. Most of all, the human inability to discern good and evil, the brute fact of death and the unpredictability of life are felt to be contingent. Man has a sorely limited scope for creation and free choice. The encounter with Fortuna, therefore, is the encounter with the world incarnate. Graf's Fortuna allegories are allegories of the world, she is *mundus* in disguise. The presence of sin is an implicit part in this kind of art. Fortuna lacks each and every positive aspect. She stands for man's inevitable corruptibility and points to the fact that he cannot escape a profligate world. The correspondence to the *mundus* allegory type is evident. Beauty here is just a carnal enticement and not a category of aesthetic theory.

With regard to art theory, this allows an interesting observation. As a rule, Renaissance artworks are legitimated by a theory of beauty. Raphael's *Galathea*, for instance, represents ideal beauty realising itself in the artist's work. Raphael champions a Neoplatonist theory of art. By symmetry, harmony and recourse to classical models, the individual work partakes in the idea of ideal beauty.

This platonic idealism is exactly what Graf contradicts. The Swiss artist refuses to refer affirmatively to great examples in order to inflate the value of his own work. He even disputes their claim to exemplarity. This attitude stems from the insight that the validity and prestigiousness of art and aesthetic value systems are historically relative, that Raphael and Dürer are not immortal models, but simply protagonists of a historical canon. Art does not relate to the metaphysical absolute any more, but rather to the present – a shift that wholly redefines its function. It is now supposed to make statements not on the eternal realm of beauty, but on the often dismal *present* state of human affairs.

But there is another side to the coin: the techniques of delegitimation in Graf's works are unmistakable symptoms of an enormous pressure of competition. By resorting to great examples and inserting them into inappropriate contexts, Graf decouples form and content and creates his own niche of artistic originality. He demonstrates ironically that beauty is not an expression of truth, but mere appearance, and as such a delusion ("Schein"). Beauty does not render the essence of an object, it merely unfolds the material world's seductive powers. This is the reason why Graf depicts Fortuna as a whore, whose beauty does not promise truth, but rather debauchery and decay. Fortune, despite her divine power, remains fickle and volatile.

To a certain degree, therefore, a re-arrangement in the system of allegories has taken place. The female, but erotically neutral Fortuna has turned into an attractive woman, a Renaissance *femme fatale*, bent on seducing and corrupting man. The Fortuna allegory inherits this potential of seduction from the medieval *Frau Welt* and her allurements – but she also inherits the veneer, which turns to putrefaction and decay, once her back side comes into view. It is not just fate that becomes promiscuous, but art as well. Art's promiscuity, however, is what we call venality.

José M. González García
Fortuna in Seventeenth Century Spain

Literature, Politics and the Visual Arts

As in other European countries, the goddess Fortuna had been present in Spanish literature since the Middle Ages, gained strength during the political and social crisis of the fifteenth century, broadly developed over the course of the Renaissance and reached her culmination in the baroque period. References to the goddess appear in the works of literati and moral and social essayists, and there are fundamental examples of Fortuna's presence in Spanish literature.

For example, Juan de Mena finished his epic poem *Laberinto de Fortuna* in 1444, which was published in 1481 in Salamanca. Jorge Manrique tied Fortuna's power to the force of death both in his poem *A la Fortuna* and in the *Coplas por la muerte de su padre* (1477). Fernando de Rojas's *La Celestina* (published in 1499) must be considered a transitional work between the ordered medieval world and the chaos of the modern world, in which Fortuna makes everything change constantly. And in Pleberio's final lament for the death of his daughter, we find one of the greatest expressions of complaint against unjust Fortuna. Miguel de Cervantes expresses throughout his body of work, but especially in *Don Quijote* (First part 1605, Second part 1615), the need for human effort to confront Fortuna. The Count of Villamediana (1582–1622) introduces many issues related to Fortuna in both his love poems and his political poems. Fortuna is an irrational force in life, and human reason must oppose it. Luis Vélez de Guevara in *El diablo Cojuelo* (1641) connects, like other authors, the metaphor of life as a great theatre of the world (*Theatrum Mundi*) with the idea of the goddess Fortuna. In the dramatic works of Calderón de la Barca, the subject of fortune is constantly present, for example in the titles of his comedy *Lances de amor y fortuna* (around 1625) or his Eucharistic play *No hay más fortuna que Dios* (1653). And near the end of his *La vida es sueño* (1635), Segismundo speaks the following words in his discourse to the court of Poland:

> Fate [La fortuna] should not be forced by means
> So unjust and so vindictive,
> For they but excite it more;
> And thus he who would be victor

O'er his fortune, must succeed
By wise prudence and self-strictness.[1]

In Lope de Vegas's *La noche toledana* (1612), a tree of fortune appears. From its branches hang the good and the bad that blind fortune causes to fall upon men's heads with a wand. Francisco de Quevedo offers a complex moral and political allegory in his work *La hora de todos y la Fortuna con seso*, written mostly between 1633 and 1634, but published posthumously in Zaragoza in 1650. And Baltasar Gracián presents all the allegories of fortune in *El Criticón* (first part 1651, second part 1653 and third part 1657).

Progressing from literature to the visual arts, I will deal with images of Fortuna from the Renaissance to the baroque period that are related to the virtues and challenges of political leadership.

Fig. 1: Bernhard Strigel, *Portrait of Emperor Maximilian and his Family*, after 1515, oil on lime. Kunsthistorisches Museum, Vienna. Inventory number GG_832 © 2016. Photo Austrian Archives/Scala Florence.

Detail of Fig. 1

---

[1] Calderón de la Barca, Pedro, *Life Is A Dream*, translated by Denis Florence MacCarthy, London 1873, 113.

I would like to highlight the role played by Fortuna in the creation of the image of the Renaissance prince. From an early moment, the figure of Charles V is shown to us surrounded by images of Fortuna, even before his taking possession of the crown as king of Spain and as emperor of the Holy Roman Empire. Fernando Checa Cremades's excellent monograph devoted to the study of *Carlos V y la imagen del héroe en el Renacimiento* indicates that in the collective portrait of the Maximilian family made by Bernhard Strigel, the official painter of the imperial court, the figure of Charles appears adorned by a medallion bearing the figure of Fortuna (fig. 1).[2] This transmits to us the idea of the prince's virtue as dominator of this goddess, an idea that will be repeated time and again in the iconography associated with the emperor. In the painting, we can see two levels of portraits. Above on the left is Maximilian I; on the right his first wife, Maria de Burgundy, and between them their son, Philip the Fair. Below are two grandchildren of Maximilian, Ferdinand I on the left and Prince Charles (wearing a hat with Fortuna's medallion) in the centre; and on the right is Ludwig, Maximilian's adopted son who became Ludwig II of Hungary.

The Roman Fortuna as the patron divinity of the ship of the State, whose rudder she steers, is transformed in the Renaissance into a dangerous goddess, producer of political storms that could put an end to a principality. A goddess, therefore, who we must protect ourselves from, or better said, from whom the prince must know how to protect his subjects. Therefore, dominion over fortune multiplies as a symbol of the power of the Renaissance prince, and it is no surprise that this manifests itself in the most diverse fashions. For example, the hagiographic literature that connects the Renaissance prince with the figure of the Roman caesars also insists on the link between Julius Caesar and fortune. In this way, Juan Cristóbal Calvete de Estrella, in his panegyric of Charles V, refers directly to Caesar's power over the seas, the winds and fortune:

> There are none who ignore the importance that Julius Caesar gave to Fortuna, for sailing in a small ship in the middle of high waves, he calmed a frightened sailor, telling him: 'Fear not, I guide Fortuna with this hand.' And the other Caesars endowed her with no less importance, placing her emblem not only on their camps, but also in their chambers, in the conviction that she would help them to raise the Empire and govern it with greater wisdom.[3]

---

[2] Checa Cremades, Fernando, *Carlos V y la imagen del héroe en el Renacimiento*, Madrid 1987, 34.

[3] López de Toro, José, "El panegírico de Carlos V por J. C. Calvete de Estrella", *Boletín de la Real Academia de la Historia*, CXLIII/II (1958), 114–115. See also Checa Cremades, *Carlos V*, and the detailed Chapter II dedicated to "The iconographic program" from the book by Perla, Antonio, *Historia de una estufa. Las placas cerámicas del XVI en la casa aguiberreña de Bergara*, Bergara 1998, 87–174.

It is important to underline Prince Charles's famous entrance into the city of Bruges in 1515, when he was 15 years old, and, as the count of Flanders, had

Fig. 2: On the right, Prince Charles spins the wheel of fortune in his entrance into the city of Bruges, 1515, engraving.[4] © Austrian National Library. Digitized by Google.

received the governance of his Flemish possessions from his grandfather Maximilian. Basing himself on Gilles de Gourmont's xylographs on this entrance in-

---

4 *Recueil de chroniques, chartes et autres documents concernant l'histoire et les antiquités de la Flandre-Occidentale, publié par la société d'émulation de Bruges. 3,6. La triumphante et solemnelle entree [...] de [...] Monsieur Charles prince des Espaignes, archiduc d'Austrice [...] en la ville de Bruges l'an 1515.* Bruges 1850, 54–55, http://data.onb.ac.at/ABO/%2BZ105582207, 28.01.2016.

to Bruges and, above all, on the "manuscript, with full colour miniatures, and a text by Remy du Puys, in the archives of the Austrian National Library"[5], Checa Cremades makes an interesting iconographic analysis in which he highlights the double role of Fortuna.

In the first image, Prince Charles spins the wheel of fortune producing well-being and harmony among the citizenry (fig. 2).

In this miniature, a large wheel of fortune is shown in addition to four characters: above, at the apex of power, a woman with a whip, "to indicate her cruel and tyrannical reign"; below the city of Bruges, "today poor and sad"; to the right a figure which allegorises Mars, the god of war; and to the left an allegory of Negotiation, both important figures for the opening of new markets. From outside the wheel and with one hand upon it, Prince Charles and the allegory of Commerce (a female figure with a ship) are ready to make the wheel turn to raise Bruges from its state of prostration to the highest reaches of power. Checa Cremades interprets the allegory as a medievalising vision of the prince that does not embody the Renaissance virtues, but who would instead be a figure who was "protector of commerce, material prosperity, and peace"[6]. But in my opinion, the allegory could also be interpreted with a greater emphasis given to the prince's active role in spinning the wheel of fortune in a way that was favourable to Bruges and its commerce. In this way, we would find ourselves with a typically Renaissance version of the virtue (in this case more economic than political) of the prince that defeats fortune.

On the other hand, in miniature number 21, the young Prince Charles is shown with the virtues, Fortuna, and the emperors Trajan and Theodosius (fig. 3). In the words of Checa Cremades:

---

[5] Checa Cremades, *Carlos V*, 201.
[6] Checa Cremades, *Carlos V*, 205.

Fig. 3: Prince Charles, *The Virtues* (Prudence, Justice, Fortitude and Temperance) and Fortune.[7]
© Austrian National Library. Digitized by Google.

---

7 Ibid., 33–34.

Beneath the representation of the monarch the wheel of Fortune is located, surrounded by six shields of different kingdoms of Charles V, while to the right and left of the wheel, Temperance and Fortitude halt its impetuous motion. Further below, the figure of Fortune, chained by Prudence and Justice, explains herself through the following inscription:

Je qui tous vaincz, par vertu suis vaincue. (I, who conquer everything, am defeated by virtue.)

The subject shown before the majesty of the Prince, which is none other than the triumph of Virtue over Fortuna, is a cliché of moralising literature of the period.[8]

We find a fourth example of the connections between the Emperor Charles and the image of Fortuna in the series of nine tapestries made by Pieter Coecke van Aelst in his workshop in Brussels, which are known today as the Honours tapestries, although for a long time they bore the name the *Tapestries of Fortuna*, due to the first of them being devoted to this goddess. These tapestries, finished in 1523, were presented and sold to Charles V during his residence in Seville for his marriage in 1526 to Isabel of Portugal. The following year, the tapestries adorned the church of San Pablo de Valladolid during the baptism of the emperor's first son, the future Philip II, so that the entire court could contemplate the iconographic programme full of hundreds of mythological, historical and allegorical figures. Such an educated audience certainly knew how to interpret the iconographic programme of the tapestries, which very much related to Renaissance tastes and already contained mannerist forms of expression.[9]

Guy Delmarcel rightly considers that the tapestries' iconographic programme is best assigned to the mirror for princes genre, to treatises (in this case only in the form of woven images) that attempted to teach the sovereign the virtues he must hold, the vices to be avoided and the retributions that he could legitimately expect if he behaved inappropriately. The prince's moral and political education occupies over 400 square metres of wall and is transmitted through more than 300 figures. Delmarcel summarises the iconographic programme of the nine tapestries that comprise the *Honours* tapestries as follows:

---

8 Checa Cremades, *Carlos V*, 203–204. See also Strong, Roy, *Splendour at Court. Renaissance Spectacle and Illusion*, London 1973, 19–25, and by the same author *Art and Power. Renaissance Festivals 1450–1650*, Berkeley / Los Angeles 1973, 7–11. One might add that it was also a topic of the political philosophy of the moment, because in 1513 Machiavelli wrote *The Prince*, one of the central elements of which is the struggle of Virtue against the goddess Fortuna.

9 Today, the tapestries are exhibited at the Museo de Tapices of the Royal Palace of La Granja de San Ildefonso, Segovia.

The first four tapestries illustrate the private ethics of the sovereign. This private ethics must follow the capricious course of the wheel of Fortuna, symbol of dynastic mutability, practice, above all the four cardinal virtues and also the three theological ones. This leads to the supreme recompense of royal honour, represented in *Honour*, the fifth and central piece of the series. The following four tapestries illustrate the king's public ethics. His military behaviour is worth *Fame* (number 6) which leads to *Honour* (number 5). The royal virtue par excellence is *Justice* (number 7). His entire public career is informed by *Nobility* (number 8) conferred on him by his consecration. Finally, the prince must avoid the antithesis of Honour and Fame, *Infamy* (number 9) which leads him far from happiness.[10]

The first four Honours tapestries are named: *Fortuna* (no. 1), *Prudence* (no. 2), *Divine Wisdom* (no. 3) and *The Seven Virtues* (no. 4). I shall only concern myself with the tapestry of Fortuna, the central section of which is reproduced here (fig. 4).[11] Fortuna appears triumphantly in a double version in the first of the Honours tapestries which is devoted to her, on horseback in the upper part of the tapestry and with her wheel directly below. In the middle is a sign with an inscription of a saying by Sallust: "Fortuna rules above all things". Guy Delmarcel's analysis of this tapestry is:

> The goddess Fortuna, with her eyes blindfolded, crosses the skies on horseback, in the middle and above, and throws roses with her right hand and stones with her left upon the favoured (*bona fortuna*) and her victims (*mala fortuna*) respectively. These try to cross the sea to reach the island on which the wheel is found. The fortunate remain on the left side, beneath the protection of the god Apollo; the unfortunate perish among the waves, on the right, wounded by Vulcan's forged bolts.
>
> The image of Fortuna's wheel floating above a shifting island between two contrary seas was invented by the twelfth-century theologian Alain de Lille, in his allegorical poem *Anticlaudianus*. [...] The great wheel, seen from the front, is called *Praesens*, the present. On the wheel's upper section, beneath the inscription 'Honour', one finds the imperial attributes: the crown, sceptre and sword. This tapestry, in which the date 1520 appears, signifies that Charles V's Imperial dignity reached its apogee at this moment, the Supreme Honour of the central subject of the series. This wheel is flanked by two others named *Futurum*, which seem to move the entire island. This is like a vow of happiness for the young Emperor.[12]

---

10 Delmarcel, Guy, "Colecciones del Patrimonio Nacional. Tapices I. Los Honores", *Reales Sitios. Revista del Patrimonio Nacional* 62 (1979), 42. See also the description by Junquera de Vera, Paulina / Herrero Carretero, Concha, *Catálogo de Tapices del Patrimonio Nacional. Vol. I: Siglo XVI*, Madrid 1986, 35–44, and Checa, Fernando, *Tesoros de la Corona de España. Tapices flamencos en el Siglo de Oro*, Brussels 2010, 110–118.
11 I refer also briefly to the tapestry *Divine Wisdom*, where Fortuna appears again.
12 Delmarcel, "Colecciones", 43.

Fig. 4: Pieter Coecke van Aelst, central section of the tapestry *Fortuna*, 1520. Museo de Tapices del Palacio Real de La Granja de San Ildefonso, Segovia. Inventory number 10026276. © Patrimonio Nacional.

The third tapestry, devoted to *Divine Wisdom*, acquires importance in this context because it depicts a radical departure from the triumphs of Fortuna that we have seen thus far, instead showing her utter defeat. The centre of the composition shows Virtue flagellating Vice, and just below we find Fortuna chained by two cardinal virtues: on the left Fortitude, and on the right Temperance. With both these virtues, the wise can defeat Fortuna, being strong and constant against adversity and not losing one's equilibrium when Fortuna smiles on them.

Of course, the use of images of Fortuna was not exclusive to Charles as Renaissance prince or as emperor. Other European monarchs also made similar use of the goddess. Artistic representations of Fortuna in engravings, book illustrations, paintings or sculptures were a constant in the lives of European princes. It is also worth noting that the Emperor Charles's special relationship with fortune was transferred to some of his subjects, in particular to Hernán Cortés, such that we could say that the conquest of Mexico was carried out not only in the name of the cross and the sword, but also in the name of Fortuna. John H. Elliott has analysed "the mental world of Hernán Cortés" and states that he "carried with him a strong conviction of the influence of *Fortuna* on the affairs of men"[13] when he left Cuba to head to Mexico and begin his adventure. Elliott cites a dream that Cortés had, transcribed by Cervantes de Salazar in his *Crónica de la Nueva España*. On awakening, Cortés explains his dreaming by drawing a "water-wheel" or "noria", placing one letter on the full buckets, a different letter on those that are pouring out and a third letter on those that are already empty, and driving a nail through the high buckets, signifying that he must stop the wheel of fortune. Elliott notes:

> The image of Fortune's wheel was well known to late fifteenth and early sixteenth-century Spaniards, and 'adverse fortune suddenly turns her wheel' several times in the course of Bernal Díaz's history of the conquest of Mexico. Cortés' wheel, however, has become the *noria* – the traditional water-wheel with hanging buckets to be found in Extremadura and other parts of Spain. Whether at that time this was a common conception of Fortune's wheel is not clear, although Celestina herself, in Rojas' novel, envisaged it in this form: 'We are like pots in a water-wheel [...] one up, and another down; one full and another empty; it is fortune's law that nothing can continue any long time in one and the selfsame state of being'. But the most important feature of the wheel for Cortés was that it could be stopped – a point he further emphasized when, tilting at the ring in Coyoacán after Mexico had fallen, he chose as his device a wheel of fortune and a silver figure of a man with

---

[13] Elliott, John H., *Spain and his World 1500–1700*, New Haven / London 1989, 33. See the whole chapter II entitled "The Mental World of Hernán Cortés".

a hammer in one hand and a nail in the other. The motto read: 'I shall hammer in the nail when I see that there is nothing more to possess'[14].

This constitutes an entire life plan that coincides with Machiavelli's proposed *virtù* in his struggle against Fortuna and the attempt to stop her with a nail at the most favourable position. Cortés thought that fortune could be controlled by man, even if only with divine help and the help "of the royal good fortune (*real ventura*) of Your Majesty"[15], as he writes to King Charles on various occasions. Elliott adds that in addition to counting on divine and royal favour, Cortés was aware that he must act with cunning and wit and know to recognise opportune moments and take advantage of them, for which the knowledge acquired by experience, that is to say, all the elements that Machiavelli included under the concept of *virtù*, were also necessary. We must remember that one of these ways to attain dominion over the goddess Fortuna lay precisely in stopping the eternal spinning of her wheel with a nail when the moment was favourable. Nonetheless, this endeavour is very difficult and does not usually end successfully. Machiavelli used this image in the third book of the *History of Florence* in the context of explaining a conspiracy in which Piero degli Albizzi was condemned to death, despite his noble lineage and his obvious prestige, since he had long been the most venerated and feared of the citizens of Florence:

> Some one, either as a friend to render him wise in his prosperity, or an enemy to threaten him with the fickleness of fortune, had upon the occasion of his making a feast for many citizens, sent him a silver bowl full of sweet-meats, among which a large nail was found, and being seen by many present, was taken for a hint to him to fix the wheel of Fortune, which, having conveyed him to the top, must if the rotation continued, also bring him to the bottom. This interpretation was verified, first by his ruin, and afterward by his death.[16]

Machiavelli is heir to a long tradition that harkens back to Ovid's *Metamorphosis*, where this metaphor was probably first used. In the Renaissance, its use was fairly widespread, as we have already seen in the case of Hernán Cortés and the drawing of him seeing the wheel of Fortuna in Coyoacán: "I shall hammer in the nail when I see that there is nothing more to possess"[17]. At the beginning of the seventeenth century, specifically in 1610, the image also appears in one of Sebastián de Covarrubias's *Moral Emblems*, beneath the motto *Maior*

---

[14] Ibid., 34.
[15] Ibid., 35.
[16] Machiavelli, Nicolo, *History of Florence from the Earliest Times to the Death of Lorenzo the Magnificent*, New York 1901, 155.
[17] Elliott, John H, *Spain and his World 1500–1700*, New Haven / London 1989, 34.

quam cui possit fortuna nocere, "Too large for Fortuna to hurt him" (fig. 5). In the commentary of the emblem, the author says that Fortuna is very powerful, but the virtuous, prudent and wise man does not fear her, and is always ready to be above her, being the same in a state of prosperity as in adversity.

Fig. 5: *Maior quam cui possit Fortuna nocere*, number 65 of Sebastián de Covarrubias's *Moral Emblems*, 1610, engraving.[18] © Fundación Universitaria Española.

Many noble homes also included Fortuna as a decorative motif. In the Casa Zaporta in Zaragoza, for example, one finds a bas relief of *The Occasion/Opportunity*, made in the middle of the sixteenth century. And in the Renaissance palace, ordered to be built in a small town in the heart of La Mancha, El Viso del Marqués, by D. Álvaro de Bazán, first Marqués de Santa Cruz and general captain of Philip II's Armada, a painting of a marine Fortuna can also be seen, in keeping with the owner's nautical profession, even though the palace was located in the middle of the dry Manchego plains. Built almost as an imitation of Andrea Doria's palace in Genoa, it employs a vast and complex Renaissance-style iconographic programme which includes representations of the battles and conquests of enemy ports made by Álvaro de Bazán, in the style of the narration of the battle triumphs of the great heroes. Other frescos incorporate mythological stories and a sort of treatise on the virtues of the hero, allegories of the four seasons, of the four elements, allegories of war, harmony and discord, victory, fame, sailing, or peace. It also includes portraits, like those of Alonso de Bazán and Alonso de Leyva, and allegorical frescoes of Spanish or Italian cities. Along the main stairway, the twelve labours of Hercules are depicted one after the other, as well as a version of Hercules at the crossroads, choosing between vice and virtue. And from the landing of the left staircase, in the middle of the arched ceiling, the following fresco of a marine Fortuna can

---

[18] Covarrubias, Sebastián de, *Emblemas morales*, Edición e introducción de Carmen Bravo-Villasante, Madrid 1978, emblema 65.

be seen, in reality a double Fortuna, each with a veil, but one standing atop the wheel in the shape of a ship's helm and the other fallen (fig. 6). The scene is completed by the figure of Neptune, above the waves, who emerges to greet Good Fortune on a conch pulled by fantastic sea creatures (the hippocampi) and, in the sky between the clouds, by the goddess of Victory bearing the palm and the crown of laurels. The entire allegory is indeed devoted to the Marques's good fortune, triumphant in all his seafaring endeavours.[19]

Fig. 6: Fortuna in the iconographic programme of the Palacio del Marqués de Santa Cruz, en Viso del Marqués, Ciudad Real, fresco painted between 1576 and 1586. Photo by the author.

I believe that Rubens's *Fortuna* (1636–37), which can be admired in the Prado Museum, deftly summarizes many of the attributes of the goddess in the sixteenth and seventeenth centuries (fig. 7). It was commissioned by King Philip IV for the decoration of the Torre de la Parada, a hunting lodge located near the Royal Palace of El Pardo, close to Madrid. Fortuna is represented by Rubens as

---

[19] The decoration of the palace was made between 1576 and 1586. See López Torrijos, Rosa, "Hércules, Virtud y Fortuna. Un programa iconográfico humanístico excepcional en la España de Felipe II", in: Pérez Flores, José Luis / González Varela, Sergio / Hernando Soubervielle, J. Armando (eds.), *Hércules en el mito, la historia y el arte iberoamericano: relatos de una figura de poder y dominación*, San Luis Potosí / México D.F. 2015, 53–80.

Venus in the seduction of her nudity, the beauty of her face, and the deep and attractive glance she directs at the viewer, who she seems to encourage to

Fig. 7: Peter Paul Rubens, *Fortuna*, 1636–37, oil on canvas. Museo del Prado. Inventory number P01674. © Museo Nacional del Prado.

advance alongside her without paying heed to the danger. She is a beautiful woman leaning forward with the sails held firmly in place with her hands receiving the force of the wind and facing a rough sea stirred up by the rain and the wind. Fortuna in movement, in a titanic effort to confront the storm, seduces and encourages the men to be brave, as if it were a version of the motto often repeated in that period: *Audaces Fortuna iuvat*, "Fortuna favours the brave". With one foot upon the globe that symbolises her fragility, but also her power over the world, she is not frightened off by the storm which she herself causes to blow and can end at any moment. She seems to promise a certain reward, for after the storm comes the calm, as can be seen in the calm waters and the twilight clouds on the left of the painting. Her figure splits the storm from the calm and invites the spectator to join her on her journey, with the message that no one must be frightened off by the difficulties of life, conceived as a passage through a stormy sea.

Finally, in 1640, Saavedra Fajardo devotes number 36 of his *Empresas políticas*, entitled "In contraria ducet", to the systematic comparison of the State with the ship that must sail the stormy seas, guided by the prince as an expert pilot responsible for the lives of all, who must avail himself of even the ill winds to reach a good port, overcoming adverse fortune (fig. 8). Saavedra even contemplates a definition of politics in maritime terminology in terms of understanding the storms and knowing how to make use of them to lead the ship of the State to a good port against the inclemency of the weather and the storms caused by Fortuna:

> The expert and prudent Seaman is not always carried at the Pleasure of the Wind, but rather by the Benefit of it, so disposes the Sails of his Ship, that he arrives at the desired Port, and with the same Wind lands at which he pleases of two opposite Shores, without endangering his Voyage. But when the Heaven's calm; by the help of Sails and Oars he out strips even the Wind itself. With no less Care and Diligence the Prince ought to Steer the Vessel of his State in the tempestuous Sea of his Reign, so attentively observing all Storms that he may with Prudence and Valour make use of the same in their time and place. He is a Pilot, to whose Conduct the Life and Safety of all is committed; nor is any Ship more hazardous than a Crown exposed to so many Winds of Ambition, so many Rocks of Enemies, and Storms of People. [...] Almost the whole Science of Politicks consists in knowing how to discern Times, and make use of them: A Storm sometimes bringing a Ship sooner into Harbour than a Calm. He, who can break the force of ill Fortune, renders it favourable; and one that knowing a Danger yields to it, and gives it time, at length surmounts it. When the Sailor finds there is no contending with the Billows, he strikes Sail and abandons himself to them; and because his Resistance would rather add force to the Wind, uses some narrow Creek to rest his Ship in, and shelter it from the Waves. Something must be granted Dangers, if one would escape them.[20]

Saavedra's text continues by advising the prince so that he knows how to combine strength with sagacity, so that what cannot be achieved through power might be facilitated by the art of political navigation, leading to the ship of the

---

[20] Saavedra Fajardo, Diego, *The Royal Politician Represented in One Hundred Emblems*, English translation by Sir James Astry, London 1700, vol. I, 259–260.

State arriving at a safe harbour. The governor (and never has it been more appropriate to remind ourselves that this word stems from the *gubernare* "to steer, to drive, to guide, to act as a pilot") must confront and face up to Fortuna, without despairing in his adversity, but knowing how to transform adverse fortune into a prosperous one. The allegory is completed by the metaphor of the ministers as sails of the prince's ship, and with the recommendation that they be appropriate to the size of the vessel, for otherwise they could cause it to sink:

> Ministers are as it were the Prince's Sails. Now, if they are large, and the Prince a shallow Vessel, if they are always loosed without Consideration of the Burthen of the Boat, they will certainly overset it.[21]

Fig. 8: Saavedra Fajardo, number 36 of his *Empresas políticas*, titled *"In contraria ducet"*.[22] Engraving. © Editorial Planeta.

I would like to end with a quote by Cervantes. Almost at the end of part two of the novel *Don Quijote*, Don Quixote complains bitterly to Sancho when, on leaving Barcelona, they pass through the place where he had been defeated by Sansón Carrasco, disguised under the emblem of the Knight of the White Moon (see

---

21 Ibid., 265.
22 Saavedra Fajardo, Diego de, *Empresas políticas*, Edición, introducción y notas de Francisco Javier Díez de Revenga, Barcelona 1988, 231.

O Fortuna, velut Luna). Don Quixote updates the allegory of fortune, making her responsible (instead of his own cowardice) for the end of his attained glories:

> As he left Barcelona, Don Quixote turned gaze upon the spot where he had fallen. 'Here Troy was', said he; 'here my ill-luck, not my cowardice, robbed me of all the glory I had won; here Fortune made me the victim of her caprices; here the lustre of my achievements was dimmed; here, in a word, fell my happiness never to rise again'.
>
> 'Señor', said Sancho on hearing this, 'it is the part of brave hearts to be patient in adversity just as much as to be glad in prosperity; I judge by myself, for, if when I was a governor I was glad, now that I am a squire and on foot I am not sad; and I have heard say that she whom commonly they call Fortune is a drunken whimsical jade, and, what is more, blind, and therefore neither sees what she does, nor knows whom she casts down or whom she sets up'.
>
> 'Thou art a great philosopher, Sancho', said Don Quixote; 'thou speakest very sensibly; I know not who taught thee. But I can tell thee there is no such thing as Fortune in the world, nor does anything which takes place there, be it good or bad, come about by chance, but by the special preordination of heaven; and hence the common saying that 'each of us is the maker of his own Fortune'. I have been that of mine; but not with the proper amount of prudence, and my self-confidence has therefore made me pay dearly; for I ought to have reflected that Rocinante's feeble strength could not resist the mighty bulk of the Knight of the White Moon's horse. In a word, I ventured it, I did my best, I was overthrown, but though I lost my honour I did not lose nor can I lose the virtue of keeping my word'.[23]

It is possible that in a secularised society like our own, we find this equivalence between fortune and providence to be very strange. But what I wish to stress is not this equivalence, but rather two other elements. Firstly, Don Quixote's lucidity in his reflection against deception: we should not attribute to bad fortune that which is actually the result of our wrong decisions. And secondly, the modernity of Cervantes's words: "Each of us is the maker of his own Fortune".

---

[23] Cervantes, Miguel de, *The Ingenious Gentleman Don Quixote of La Mancha, Vol. IV*, translated by John Ormsby, London 1885, 292–293.

Peter Vogt
The Death of Fortuna and the Rise of Modernity

Prolegomena to any Future Theory of Modernity

This article is divided into three parts. In the first part, I will develop my diagnosis of a so-called death of Fortuna. This section attempts to determine, to use quite a sterile and yet here rather useful term, the *explanandum* of this article (1). In the second part, I will argue on a much more abstract level. This section will present the *explanans* for the phenomenon described in the first part by connecting what I call the death of Fortuna with various historical trends and tendencies which will be taken as constitutive for early modernity (2). In my conclusion, I will use the question from the first part and the answers to this question provided in the second part as a key for distinguishing between two different versions of modernity (3).

1 Late Blossoming and Subsequent Decline: The History of Visual Representations of Fortuna in the "Waning of the Renaissance" and Beyond

What do I mean by the death of Fortuna? This article understands the time roughly between 1580 and 1650 as the period of a late – but also final – blossoming of Fortuna. In striking contrast to the late flourishing of Fortuna during this period,[1] a period William Bouwsma once called the "waning of the Renaissance",[2] the period beginning roughly with the second half of the seventeenth century saw an continuous decline of Fortuna as a visual or textual representation of chance and as the subject of an intellectual discourse on the relevance of chance for human life. While visual representations of Fortuna can only very rarely and, as we will see, only in a very limited sense be found after 1640, liter-

---

[1] I discuss the various early modern interpretations of Fortuna as they can be found in art, literature, philosophy, theology and political theory from Greek antiquity to early modernity in a separate chapter of my book: Vogt, Peter, *Kontingenz und Zufall. Eine Begriffs- und Ideengeschichte*, Berlin 2011, 503–655.
[2] Bouwsma, William, *The Waning of the Renaissance. 1550–1640*, New Haven / London 2000.

ary representations of Fortuna continue to find expression in German and Spanish literature of the Baroque period, i.e. as late as the 1660s or even 1670s. After the 1670s, however, this decline did finally result in Fortuna's death. The "classical" meaning of *tyche* and Fortuna, which represented chance as an intrinsic and inevitable element of the most fundamental dimensions of human life for almost two thousand years, finally perished. A concept which once provoked the most painful existential questions of life and death, a concept which had once haunted Boethius in his prison cell and plagued Machiavelli in his political exile, finally disappeared, or at least became a banality or a cliché.

Both to justify this diagnosis and to offer a plausible explanation of these two strikingly contrasting phenomena, namely the late blossoming of Fortuna between 1580 and 1650 on the one hand and the subsequent decline of Fortuna after 1650 and its death around 1670 on the other, one must distinguish between two manifestations thereof, namely between the references to Fortuna in various genres of texts and the use of Fortuna in visual representations. However, before going into more detail about these two aspects, I wish to highlight the contrast between the presuppositions of the entire approach of this article and one of the most commonly accepted premises in the secondary literature on the history of Fortuna.

Regarding the question of whether it is at all legitimate to speak of the death of Fortuna in early modern history as well as the question of when and why this supposedly took place, Quentin Skinner and Felix Gilbert either implicitly presuppose or explicitly formulate what might be deemed the standard answer. In their works, both Skinner and Gilbert discuss the indubitably prominent role of Fortuna in the political thought of the Italian Renaissance.[3] But they also place the decline in this prominence after the time of Machiavelli and Guicciardini, two of the thinkers in which they were especially interested. When, to quote Skinner, "the great tradition of Italian Republicanism finally came to an end", this coincided with a "loss of faith in the power of virtù",[4] thus also diminishing Fortuna's relevance as virtue's traditional and previously quite respected – though also feared – antagonist.

Both Skinner and Gilbert presuppose an inextricable link between the political world of the early modern city-republics and an intellectual discourse on the conflict between human virtue and the opposing entity of Fortuna. Both au-

---

[3] For Gilbert's discussion of Fortuna see: Gilbert, Felix, *Machiavelli and Guicciardini. Politics and History in Sixteenth-Century Florence*, Princeton 1965, 269–270. For Skinner's discussion of Fortuna see: Skinner, Quentin, *The Foundations of Modern Political Thought. Vol. 1: The Renaissance*, Cambridge 1978, 95–98, 119–122, 186–189; id., *The Foundations of Modern Political Thought. Vol. 2: The Age of Reformation*, Cambridge 1978, 277–279.

[4] Skinner, *Foundations. Vol. 1*, 187.

thors thus conclude that it is the fall of the Italian city-republics which must be regarded as the decisive event leading to the decline or death of Fortuna in early modernity.

This assumption, however, is somewhat dubious. As José Antonio Maravall made very clear in his book *La cultura del barroco*, Fortuna survived the era of early modern city-republics very well, even though this "post-republican" Fortuna, as one might put it, flourished in the very different social, political and cultural setting of the court, with its perpetual intrigues and political ups and downs.[5] While the merchant of Venice, lamenting the evils of Fortuna, was still standing on a public square desperately waiting for the return of his ships, and thus acting in a civic setting, the stage for a "post-republican" Fortuna was the princely court.

However, even if we accept this revision of a previously more or less established account of the end of Fortuna and merely postpone Fortuna's death for a hundred years or so, we still have to find a convincing answer to the much more haunting question of why Fortuna finally met its end 100 or 150 years later. Why exactly then? Why not earlier, why not later? Why was a discourse on Fortuna still so enticing to Baltasar Gracián or Andreas Gryphius? Why was Fortuna still so vividly represented by Rembrandt, Reni and Rubens? And why had Fortuna lost all intellectual credibility a few decades later?

If we survey the textual representations of Fortuna in the "waning of the Renaissance", the abundant references to Fortuna from the end of the sixteenth to the mid-seventeenth centuries in literature, philosophy, political theory or any other genre of text can be mainly understood as expressions of four intellectual, cultural and literary traditions: French and Dutch Neostoicism in the late sixteenth century, English literature and theatre at the turn of the seventeenth century, Spanish literature from Cervantes in the early seventeenth century until Quevedo's and Gracián's writings published around the middle of the seventeenth century, and, finally, German baroque poetry in the mid-seventeenth century, including works by Gryphius, Fleming, Opitz or Hofmannswaldau.[6]

---

5 Maravall, José A., *La cultura del barroco. Análisis de una estructura histórica*, Madrid 1975.
6 I have attempted to subsume the manifold textual representations of Fortuna in the decades between 1580 and 1650 under these four intellectual, cultural or literary trends: Vogt, Peter, *Kontingenz und Zufall*, 607–655; id., "'Virtù vince fortuna'. Ascesa, cambiamento e tarda fioritura di un topos dell'età moderna", *Annali dell'Istituto storico italo-germanico in Trento / Jahrbuch des italienisch-deutschen historischen Instituts in Trient* 39 (2013), 63–103; id., "Virtù vince fortuna. Aufstieg, Wandel und späte Blüte eines frühneuzeitlichen Topos", in: Hartmut Böhme / Werner Röcke / Ulrike C. A. Stephan (eds.), *Contingentia. Transformationen des Zufalls*, Berlin / Boston 2016, 75–114.

But a one-sided consideration of textual sources ignores the many visual representations of Fortuna and might thus lead to an over-simplified interpretation of the late history of Fortuna. Does a late blossoming of Fortuna between 1580 and 1650 and a succeeding decline of Fortuna after this period also characterise the history of visual representations of Fortuna?

Even though the tradition of emblematic books originated with Andrea Alciati's *Emblematum liber* in the 1530s, and thus at least five decades before the period we are investigating, the most prominent and provocative examples of emblematic representations of Fortuna can clearly be found in the years between 1580 and 1630.[7] Moreover, if we look not only at the history of emblematic representations of Fortuna, but also at the history of art in general, my suggestion of two strikingly different trends regarding the late history of Fortuna becomes even more plausible. While quite a number of paintings of Fortuna by artists of the first order can still be found at the end of the first third of the seventeenth century, nothing of comparable quantity and quality was produced after the 1640s. Therefore, the decline of visual representations of Fortuna started even one or two decades before the decline of textual representations.

This can be demonstrated by considering the representations of Fortuna which Aby Warburg collected for his *Bilderatlas Mnemosyne*. Twenty-five of the 31 pictures and images which Warburg assembled for his so-called tableau "Nr. 48", entitled "Fortuna. Auseinandersetzungssymbol des sich befreienden Menschen (Kaufmann)",[8] come from the fifteenth and sixteenth centuries. Only one painting that Warburg included here originates from a later date. This was Guido Reni's painting of Fortuna of 1623 that, as we will see later, exists in two different versions.[9]

---

7 Compare Cesare Ripa's *Iconologia* of 1593, Otto van Veen's *Emblemata Horatiana* of 1607 or Gabriel Rollenhagen's *Nucleus Emblematum* of 1611.

8 Warburg, Aby, *Gesammelte Schriften. Abteilung 2, Band 1: Der Bilderatlas Mnemosyne*, Horst Bredekamp et al. (eds.), Berlin 2000, 89.

9 The complex story of Reni's Fortuna, its two different originals and its numerous copies, is not to be retold here. Whatever the details of this story may be, Warburg chose for his tableau a version in which Fortuna holds a crown in her hand, dated it correctly as being from 1623 and described this version of the *Pinacoteca Vaticana* as Reni's original. This last piece of information can no longer be considered true. Contemporary research has found the Fortuna in the *Pinacoteca Vaticana* to be not an original, but rather a copy. However, that does not need to concern us here. Petrangolini, Rosanna / Panici, Benedetti, "La 'Fortuna' di Guido Reni", *Notizie da Palazzo Albani* 5 (1976), 53–57; Pepper, Stephen / Mahon, Denis, "Guido Reni's 'Fortuna with a purse' rediscovered", *The Burlington Magazine* 141 (1999), 156–163; Bellini, Paolo "Diffusione dello stile di Guido Reni e di taluni suoi soggetti attraverso le incisioni della sua scuola, con particolare riferimento a soggetto della 'Fortuna'", in: Henri Zerner (ed.), *Le stampe e la diffusione delle immagini e degli stili*, Bologna 1983, 55–60.

When we peruse the entire *Bilderatlas*, and not only the tableau explicitly dedicated to Fortuna, we find three further visual representations of Fortuna in Warburg's collection, all of which were produced in the 1630s.¹⁰ What is important for our argumentation here is the fact that Warburg's choice of material in the context of his project of the *Bilderatlas* confirms our view of the years around 1640 as the beginning of the decline of visual representations of Fortuna. Warburg, so it seems, found no visual representations of Fortuna of any aesthetic value or theoretical importance after the late 1630s which he considered worthy for inclusion in his *Bilderatlas*.

Before I attempt to provide a historical explanation for Fortuna's continuous loss of cultural and intellectual prominence in visual representations after 1640 and in textual representations after the 1670s at the very latest, I would like to emphasise that the manifold visual representations of Fortuna during the period of her final blossoming were characterised by specific traits or genuine iconological characteristics. Indeed, *two* such characteristics can be discovered in a closer inspection of the various visual representations of Fortuna in the late sixteenth and early seventeenth centuries.

The *first* innovative trait is an increasingly concrete association of Fortuna with commerce or, to be more precise, with the volatility of commerce. By depicting Fortuna as reigning over the entire sphere of commerce, economic success was seen as a direct result of Fortuna's favour, or economic stability – in the face of Fortuna's inimical whims – as the successful consequence of a taming of a *mala fortuna*. This tendency is illustrated in a most exemplary way by a wooden carving by the Nuremberg artist Jost Amman from 1585. Amman's work bears the title: *Eigentliche Abbildung deß ganzen Gewerbs der löblichen Kaufmannschaft samt etlich der nahmhafft und fürnehmsten Handelstädt* (fig. 1).¹¹

---

10 One is the famous etching that Rembrandt contributed in 1633 to Elias Herckmans' book *Der Zee-Vaert lof* (In Praise of Navigation). A second example is Ruben's smaller sketch from 1636 produced as a preparatory study for the famous painting of Fortuna from 1638, today hanging in the Museo del Prado. The third example is an etching from 1636 by the Dutch artist Cornelis Schut, which Warburg reproduced in tableau "Nr. 60". See for these three illustrations: Warburg, *Schriften*, 111 and 115.
11 For a more detailed interpretation of this work see the interesting remarks by Joseph L. Koerner: Koerner, Joseph L., "The Fortune of Dürer's Nemesis", in: Walter Haug / Burghart Wachinger (eds.), *Fortuna*, Berlin 1995, 239–293, here esp. 275.

Fig. 1: Jost Amman, Eigentliche Abbildung deß ganzen Gewerbs der löblichen Kaufmannschaft samt etlich der nahmhafft und fürnehmsten Handelstädt, woodcut, 1585, Germanisches Nationalmuseum, no. GM–26471–1292 – © Germanisches Nationalmuseum, Nuremberg.

Detail of Fig. 1

Fortuna is depicted by Amman as standing above the landscape of economy, which in this case is the city of Antwerp, and just underneath the scales of economy. As long as the scales of economy are well balanced, the artist seems to suggest, commerce flourishes. But due to her privileged position, Fortuna seems to be able to interrupt and destroy the balance of commerce quite abruptly. In fact, this is exactly what happened, during the years in which Amman's carving was made, to one of the richest and most flourishing European cities, due to the siege of Antwerp by Spanish troops beginning in 1584 and leading to Antwerp's surrender a year later. It is this historical context which must be kept in mind when we read the longer passage entitled OCCASIO ET FORTUNA, directly to the left- and right-hand sides of Fortuna. This text summerises the main message of the entire carving: commercial success is dependent on the benevolence of a gracious Fortuna or the domestication of a malicious Fortuna.

On a more concrete level, these allusions to Fortuna as the adjudicator of commerce resulted in numerous images in the late sixteenth and the early seventeenth centuries of Fortuna as, quite literally, the giver and lender of money or coins, pouring out either from a purse or from the classical cornucopia that Fortuna traditionally held in her hand. But while the gifts of the classical cornucopia of Fortuna originally symbolised the satisfaction of the most basic human desire for nutrition by depicting fruits and crops as the result of Fortuna's benevolence, it was now becoming increasingly common to see money as the main gift of Fortuna.

According to Erwin Panofsky's well-known interpretation, the image and the narrative of Hercules standing at the crossroads became immensely popular in fifteenth-century literature and art because it succinctly encapsulated the *quattrocento* understanding of human life as a permanent conflict between human virtue and numerous vices. But Hercules, it is worth recalling, had to choose between human virtue and vices, not between economic success and failure, and the goal of all his choices and ambitions was human glory, not financial affluence.[12]

In this context, it is quite significant that Guido Reni's above-mentioned painting of Fortuna from 1623 exists in two different versions. Reni painted Fortuna not only as holding a crown – this version was, as we have seen, part of Warburg's tableau – but also as holding a purse in her hand, thus defining the classical gifts of Fortuna in a rather mundane way.[13] This motif of a Fortuna with a purse in her hand was very popular in the 1630s. It was imitated time and again in the years immediately following Reni's work, as can be seen by the works of Girolamo Scarsello, Simone Cantarini and Bartolomeo Coriolano.[14]

A much more drastic way to illustrate the mundane gifts of Fortuna and the almost hysterical competition that these gifts could unleash – a competition

Fig. 2: Jan Harmenszoon Muller, Fortuna verdeelt haar geschenken, engraving, 1590, Amsterdam, Rijksmuseum, no. RP-P-OB-32.213A, RP-P-OB-32.213B – © Rijksmuseum, Amsterdam.

---

12 Panofsky, Erwin, *Hercules am Scheidewege*, Leipzig 1930.
13 See the articles mentioned in footnote 9 for further details about the various reproductions of Reni's "Fortuna with a purse".
14 See the illustrated catalogue of an exhibition in Carpi's *Palazzo dei Pio* in 2011. Rossi, Manuela (ed.), *Dea Fortuna. Iconografia di un mito*, Carpi 2011, 68.

neither for happiness nor for glory, but for coins, a crown, goblets and a winged trumpet – can be seen in an engraving from 1590 by the Dutch artist Jan Harmenszoon Muller entitled *Fortuna verdeelt haar geschenken* (fig. 2).[15]

What we see here appears to be something like a battlefield, dividing the receivers of the gifts of Fortuna into the two clearly distinct groups of winners and losers. The reign of Fortuna, as the Dutch artist explicitly formulated at the bottom of his engraving, follows no rules or principles, but only the capricious whims to "nunc hos extollere dextra, nunc illos variis exagitare malis."

Fig. 3: Utriusque Crepundia Merces, engraving in Francis Quarles, *Emblemes*, 1635, p. 40 – © Penn State University Libraries, Philadelphia.

---

15 For a reproduction of this engraving and a stimulating discussion of its content see: Starobinski, Jean, *Largesse*, Paris 2007, 48–49. According to Starobinski, we see "comment la Fortune prodigue d'innombrables richesses d'un côté, et oppose une main vide de l'autre. Là, une pluie des trésors; ici, le refus sans appel." (48).

A final illustration for my attempt to describe the *first* iconological innovation of visual representations of Fortuna in the period of her final blossoming can be found in Francis Quarles's emblematic book *Emblemes* of 1635. The relevant page bears the title "Utriusque Crepundia Merces" (fig. 3). Cupid and Mammon, two representatives of worldly goods, compete for the gifts of Fortuna by playing with bowls. Success in economic matters or even in love affairs is, the artist suggests by his illustration, closely related to the results of a game of chance. But the prize that Fortuna is holding aloft in the background of the page is, in this case, not wealth or luxury, but a fool's cap.[16] Therefore, one can also find in Quarles's *Emblemes* a dose of scepticism regarding the importance of worldly success and of a mundane *bona fortuna* for a good life.

It was precisely in the years in which Quarles was still criticising Fortuna as illegitimate from a normative point of view, thus still interpreting Fortuna as an opponent of human virtue, that Fortuna was increasingly being seen as an inevitable part and parcel of the economic sphere. As Simon Schama once clarified in his book *The Embarrassment of Riches. An Interpretation of Dutch Culture in the Golden Age* in the context of a discussion of the Dutch tulip mania of 1637, it became increasingly common in these years to see the "realm of queen money" as being under the control of Fortuna: "The banker and the bankrupt were separated only by Fortuna's whim."[17]

An understanding of Fortuna's reign of the genuine realm of irrational exuberance, responsible for any kind of economic crisis, a realm in which neither rationality nor honesty could prevail, was revived not only by the Dutch tulip mania, but by subsequent economic turmoil as well. Its last remnants can be found in the context of the so-called South Sea Bubble Crisis of 1721. Once again, Fortuna was used to represent economic hysteria and the irrationality of commerce. This interpretation of Fortuna was masterfully visualised by satirical engravings, such as William Hogarth's engraving *The South Sea Bubble – an allegory* or Bernard Picart's *Monument Consecrated to Posterity*, both produced in 1721.

As the date of the illustrations of Hogarth and Picart shows, a "commercialised" Fortuna survived the end of visual representations in a more "classical" sense which we had previously dated around 1640. Fortuna as an entity visualising the irrationality of commerce could easily be revived in the context of various economic crises until as late as the early eighteenth century. But this "com-

---

16 This emblem is discussed in: Thomson, Leslie (ed.), *Fortune: 'All is but Fortune'*, Washington D. C. 2000, 64.
17 Schama, Simon, *The Embarrassment of Riches. An Interpretation of Dutch Culture in the Golden Age*, New York 1987, 371.

mercialised" Fortuna as an inevitable characteristic of the economic sphere was a highly transformed Fortuna. Fortuna in its "classical" meaning had once signified chance as an inevitable element of human life. It was discussed or represented with the aim of finding answers to the most fundamental riddles of human life, such as birth or death, undeserved luck or painful suffering. In the economic sphere, however, visual representations of Fortuna succeeded in surviving the death of this "classical" meaning and happened to have a remarkable lifespan even after 1640. But the price of this survival was Fortuna's "commercialisation", and thus its vulgarisation.

A *second* innovative trait specifically characteristic for the visual representations of Fortuna in the period of her late blossoming until 1640 is the increasingly popular use of Fortuna as a rhetorical weapon in the religious conflicts of this age.

Three examples can be provided here: a good illustration of how Fortuna was used in the conflict between different religions is Martino Rota's picture of the wheel of fortune, produced immediately after the battle of Lepanto in 1572 and originally bearing the title *Il tempo che volge la ruota della Fortuna*. Chronos, standing on the grave of Constantine, is turning the wheel of Fortuna counter-clockwise, thus suggesting the rise of Christianity and the desperate attempt of the Turkish Empire to keep its position at the top of the wheel.[18]

How Fortuna could be used not only in the conflict between different religions, but also in the conflict between Catholics and Protestants, is exemplified by a pamphlet published in 1631–1632 which identified specific virtues and vices with different denominations.[19] Under the title "Tugend und Laster Kampff", the leader of the left army is followed by the personifications of ancient and Christian virtues, while the leader of the right army is riding on a wolf in a sheep's clothing, his shield showing a tiara and thus suggesting that he is the leader of the papist party. Fortuna, sailing in the background, can, due to the direction of her sail, be identified as moving steadily into the camp of the Protestants (fig. 4).[20]

---

18 See Brink, Claudia, Art. "Fortuna", in: Uwe Fleckner et al. (eds.), *Handbuch der politischen Ikonographie. Band 1*, München 2011, 353–359. For Rota's illustration see 358.
19 See Harms, Wolfgang / Kemp, Cornelia (eds.), *Die Sammlungen der Hessischen Landes- und Hochschulbibliothek in Darmstadt*, Tübingen 1987, 265.
20 An excellent description and much more detailed interpretation than the one given here is presented by Kristiina Savin: Savin, Kristiina, *Fortunas Klädnader. Lycka, olycka och risk i det tidigmoderna Sverige*, Lund 2011, 44.

Fig. 4: Tugendt und Laster Kampff, etching, 1631, Bayerische Staatsbibliothek München, no. Einbl. XI,50 – © Bayerische Staatsbibliothek München.

However, the political exploitation of Fortuna by diverse religious parties, still so vivid at the end of the first third of the seventeenth century, could quite paradoxically, also lead to a disappearance of a personified Fortuna altogether. This can best be shown by an engraving from 1630 called *Deß Römischen Reichs Grosse Welt Uhr*. The Empire is represented by a tower and the seven electors of the Empire each sitting behind a window and asking a specific question about the essence of time. A personified Fortuna does not appear here anymore. However, the engraving quite obviously plays with the medieval "wheel of fortune", but this wheel has been transformed into a cycle of power apparently directed and steered by a weight named *fatum* in the lower right-hand corner and by a person complaining "Ich bin lang genug gelegen", identified by Frederick Pickering as the Swedish king Gustav Adolf.[21] Inside the right half of this wheel, we find the members of the Catholic party. On the left-hand side we find the Protestants. The right half of the cycle is declining, the left half is moving up (fig. 5).

Fig. 5: Deß Römischen Reichs Grosse Welt Uhr, engraving, ca. 1630, SLUB Dresden, no. Hist.Germ.C.16,misc.23 – © SLUB Dresden.

---

21 See the interpretation by Frederick P. Pickering in: Pickering, Frederick P., *Literatur und darstellende Kunst im Mittelalter*, Berlin 1966, 136–137.

These *two* iconological characteristics of the visual representations of Fortuna in the decades between 1580 and 1640 – the "commercialisation" of Fortuna's benevolence in quite a literal way and the adoption of Fortuna as a rhetorical weapon in the religious conflicts of early modern Europe – offer some insights regarding the necessary explanation of the decline and death of Fortuna, and thus lead us to the second part of this article.

But before I start with this second section, I wish to summarise briefly the diagnosis of the first part. After a late blossoming of Fortuna, as it can be abundantly seen at work in visual representations from the years between 1580 and 1640, Fortuna began to suffer from a continuous decline of cultural and intellectual relevance from the mid-seventeenth century onwards. Although textual representations of Fortuna can still be found as late as the 1670s, the final agony of Fortuna irrevocably begins shortly after this date. As we have seen, however, visual representations of Fortuna could be revived easily in the context of various economic crises until as late as the early eighteenth century. But this late survival of a "commercialised" Fortuna into the early eighteenth century does not cast general doubt on our diagnosis. Fortuna as a representation and an embodiment of chance as an intrinsic dimension of human life, having provoked painful existential questions for Pindar and Pontano, for Menander and Machiavelli, for Aristotle and Ariosto, had disappeared. Fortuna, if it was indeed visualised after 1640 at all, ceased to provoke these "classical" questions and became the servant of commercial ambition and a precondition of economic success.

2 The Death of Fortuna and Five Historical Trends of Early Modernity

Why, as we asked above, was a discourse on Fortuna still so enticing to Gracián and Gryphius in the mid-seventeenth century? Why, we can likewise ask, were visual representations of Fortuna still so enticing to Reni, Rembrandt and Rubens around 1640? And why had both textual and visual representations lost all intellectual or artistic credibility from the 1670s at the latest? The main motif or ambition of this article is the idea that the answers to these seemingly very detailed questions, requiring painstaking research by the relevant experts, can finally provide us with some conclusions regarding the more general debate about the rise of modernity.

The decline and the death of Fortuna, it seems to me, must be understood in the context of *five* historical trends, covering philosophical and scientific, religious and political, cultural and social dimensions. I am far from assuming that these *five* trends constitute the entire substance of the story, but I do believe that these *five* trends, taken together, allow us not only to explain the continuous decline of Fortuna after the mid-seventeenth century and its death throes from the 1670s onwards, but also to connect in a theoretically most fruitful way this decline and death with the theoretically much more ambitious question of the rise of modernity.

The *first* – scientific and philosophical – trend that I wish to mention was once labelled by the American philosopher John Dewey as "the quest for certainty". Stephen Toulmin attempted to contextualise this "quest for certainty" in his book *Cosmopolis. The Hidden Agenda of Modernity*. According to Toulmin, the early seventeenth century was a crisis-ridden and war-torn historical period for which "the quest for certainty" in both theoretical and practical affairs seemed the only hopeful way to overcome a situation in which religious conflicts engulfed an entire continent. Any form of accepting uncertainty or even confessing the inevitable role of Fortuna in practical human affairs seemed to open the door to intellectual and practical disaster. As Toulmin writes: "In the 1580s and '90s, sceptical acceptance of ambiguity and a readiness to live with uncertainty were still viable intellectual policies: by 1640, this was no longer the case."[22]

For Toulmin, the assassination of Henri IV in 1610 had a decisive influence on this fundamental change in the cultural and intellectual climate of opinion. This murder, Toulmin conceded, might not have caused the change from the sceptical humanism of an earlier form of Renaissance thought to the philosophical and scientific quest for certainty of the seventeenth century, but it could be seen as representative of these changes. Finally, in the 1630s, the quest for certainty in science and philosophy reached, according to Toulmin, its climax. Thanks to Galilei's *Dialogo* (1632), its innovations in astronomy and mechanics, and Descartes's new method in logic and epistemology in his *Discourse de la méthode* (1637), indubitable foundations of truth seemed finally to be established.

However, the attack against uncertainty in the name of an indubitable intellectual foundation was not only a philosophical or scientific matter, but also a lively religious issue. This brings me to a *second* trend. Whereas Descartes's philosophy sought to establish logical or epistemological certainty against a philosophical scepticism in the first third of the seventeenth century, Blaise Pascal

---

22 Toulmin, Stephen, *Cosmopolis. The Hidden Agenda of Modernity*, Chicago 1990, 44.

was in search of a religious certainty against any form of fideism, against any attempt to combine religious faith with philosophical scepticism in the latter half of the century. Both Descartes and Pascal were "lecteurs de Montaigne" (Léon Brunschvicg).[23]

But while Montaigne's *Apologie de Raimond Sebond* of 1580, with its exhortation to live with ambiguity and uncertainty, was clearly one of the most significant texts for the sixteenth-century attempt to combine the revival of ancient scepticism with a fideistic form of Christianity,[24] and while his numerous references to Fortuna in the three books of his *Essais* formulated a very cautious judgement concerning the human ability to influence Fortuna, in other words connected the sceptical affirmation of human ignorance with a practical acceptance of the power of Fortuna in human affairs,[25] Descartes and Pascal discredited in the course of the seventeenth century all versions of theoretical and practical uncertainty as responsible for the religious, intellectual and political malaise that was in need of a remedy.

Early modern religious history, however, provoked a foundationalism not only in the theological genius of Pascal, but also in a broader cultural sense, which could neither accept the fragmentary character of human knowledge nor the accidental character of practical life. In this sense, Keith Thomas once emphasised in his book *Religion and the Decline of Magic* how vehemently the English Reformation reasserted the distinction between magic and religion. The protagonists of the English Reformation relentlessly criticised the rituals of the Roman Church and disqualified them as mere superstitions and as relics of paganism. But though ruthlessly inimical to any form of ritual or practice that re-

---

23 Brunschvicg, Léon, *Descartes et Pascal, lecteurs de Montaigne*, Neuchâtel 1945.
24 See Popkin, Richard, *The History of Scepticism. From Savonarola to Bayle. Revised and Expanded Edition*, Oxford 2003.
25 As Yvonne Bellenger writes: "[...] reconnaître le pouvoir de la fortune, c'est probablement, pour l'auteur des *Essais*, se montrer fidèle à soi-même et éviter de tomber dans ce défaut majeur qu'est la présomption. [...] Reconnaître le rôle de la fortune sur cette terre, c'est donc admettre qu'on est ignorant: non point ignorant accidentellement, mais condamné à l'ignorance. [...] Le mot 'fortune', les allusions au hazard, à la chance, à l'heure et au sort accompagnent dans les *Essais* [...] une vision essentiellement sceptique du monde qui, à mon sens, est celle de Montaigne. Parler de 'fortune', c'est proclamer son non-savoir, c'est refuser d'interpréter l'incompréhensible"; Bellenger, Yvonne, "La Fortune dans les *Essais* de Montaigne", in: Enea Balmas (ed.), *Il tema della fortuna. Nella letteratura francese e italiana del Rinascimento*, Firenze 1990, 490–505, here 503. According to Hugo Friedrich, Montaigne understands Fortuna as "die absolute, gleichgültige, gleichsam subjektive Willkür, das Urbild der Ferne zwischen menschlichem Willen und Weltlauf. Gelingen ist daher dem Menschen nicht als Verdienst, Mißlingen nicht als Unfähigkeit anzurechnen." Friedrich, Hugo, *Montaigne*, München / Bern 1967 (1949), 300.

minded them of superstition, Protestants also had to cope, as Thomas insists, with the recurring situations of chance. They also had to cope with "the fluctuations of nature, the hazards of fire, the threat of plague and disease, the fear of evil spirits, and all the uncertainties of life."[26] In this theoretical impasse, the Protestants, according to Thomas, did not try to deal with the undeniable facts of chance in a religious way, thus implicitly accepting their existence, but neglected these facts outright by presupposing a gapless providential necessity. "All post-Reformation theologians taught", Thomas writes, "that nothing could happen in this world without God's permission. If there was a common theme which ran through their writings it was the denial of the very possibility of chance or accident."[27] Calvin himself, it is worth remembering, had already insisted passionately in his *Institutio* that there was no role for chance in human affairs:

> It is a very bad temptation for the faithful, when things in the world are confused and it seems that God no longer engages with them but that fortune governs and rules. This has been the cause of those diabolical proverbs that everything is ruled by chance, that things happen blindly, and that God plays with men like tennis balls, that there is no reason or measure, or indeed that everything is governed by some secret necessity and that God does not bother to think of us. These are blasphemies that have always ruled. And why? Because the human mind is bewildered when we try to grasp confused things that surpass our judgement and reason.[28]

In this sense, the Synod of Dort (1619), with its most radical affirmation of a theory of predestination, can be seen as the climax of the Protestant neglect of chance in theological discourse.

In this context, it is helpful to recall that William Bouwsma once suggested understanding Renaissance humanism more as a sequel to the intellectual debates and conflicts of the Hellenistic age and its various forms of "therapeutic"[29] (Martha Nussbaum) philosophies and less as an attempt to revive Classical Greek culture. Bouwsma once classified Stoicism and Augustinianism as the "two faces of humanism".[30] This eye-opening approach allows us to understand

---

[26] Thomas, Keith, *Religion and the Decline of Magic. Studies in Popular Beliefs in Sixteenth and Seventeenth Century England*, London 1971, 77.
[27] Ibid., 79.
[28] Calvin, Jean, *Institutes*, I, xvii, 1. Here quoted from Bouwsma, William, *Jean Calvin. A Biography*, Oxford 1988, 167.
[29] See Nussbaum, Martha, *The Therapy of Desire. Theory and Practice in Hellenistic Ethics*, Princeton 1994.
[30] Bouwsma, William, "The Two Faces of Humanism: Stoicism and Augustinianism in Renaissance Thought" (1975), in: id., *A Usable Past. Essays in European Cultural History*, Berkeley / Los Angeles 1990, 19–73.

how in seventeenth-century Protestantism, Augustine finally triumphed over Seneca, providential necessity thus triumphing over a form of religious belief compatible with the experience of chance.

It is helpful to contrast the growing religious confessionalisation and its religious protest against any form of combining sceptic tolerance of ambiguity and religious belief, in other words, to contrast the religious foundationalism of the early seventeenth century and its anti-pagan consequences with Lucien Febvre's sketch of practical Christian life and culture of the sixteenth century. A remarkable fact of the Christian religion of the first half of the sixteenth century is that, according to Febvre's interpretation in his study on Marguerite of Navarre, Christianity was then more a manner of everyday conduct and less a dogmatic set of theories and beliefs. It was thus practically more encompassing and yet theoretically much more flexible and tolerant than the later variants of Christian religion in the age of a "quest for certainty". According to Febvre, it was still possible in the early sixteenth century for a Christian culture to adapt to beliefs and attitudes of a non-Christian origin, whereas a post-Tridentine form of religion:

> a dû se limiter en se définissant [...], se détacher successivement d'une multitude de faits et d'actions à quoi jadis il se mêlait étroitement. [...] Nous ne nous en rendons plus un compte exact – mais il faut bien voir, tout de même, quel libre océan c'était que le christianisme médiéval. Et de combien de courants larges, puissant, tantôt coulant côte à côte, tantôt se contrariant et s'affrontant, il était sillonné.[31]

In contrast to an earlier and more practical form of Christian religion, this post-Tridentine form of Christianity was primarily interested in theological consistency. It purified its dogmatic foundations by attempting to neglect all heterodox or pagan influences, sources or relics of an earlier time.

I will now very briefly mention a *third* trend that Theodore Rabb once happily referred to as the early modern "struggle for stability". How did the "quest for certainty" in scientific, philosophical and religious matters and the theological desire for a providential necessity interact with a "struggle for stability" operating mainly on a political level? How could not only the solitary scientist or the individual believer, but also society or culture as a whole domesticate the whimsical anarchy of Fortuna and thus, to quote Rabb, "attain assurance, control, and a common acceptance of *some* structure where none seemed within reach?"[32] According to Rabb, the period of acute crisis in the early seventeenth

---
[31] Febvre, Lucien, *Amour sacré, amour profane. Autour de l'Heptaméron*, Paris 1971 (1944), 364, 366.
[32] Rabb, Theodore K., *The Struggle for Stability in Early Modern Europe*, New York 1975, 33.

century was succeeded by a renewal of political stability in the late seventeenth century. On a national level, the final result of this political stabilisation was, according to Rabb, the concept of the modern state. On an international level, the most important historical embodiment of the resolution of the European theatre of war in the mid-seventeenth century was evidently the Westphalian settlement that introduced not only a new system of States, but also a new policy for Church-State relations.

However, the so-called "struggle for stability" can be seen at work not only on a national and international political level, but also on a more cultural level: Roland Mousnier, in his book *Les XVI et XVII siècles*, interpreted French literature's return to classicism in the mid-seventeenth century as a kind of struggle for semantic stability against what he called "l'anarchie baroque".[33] According to its founding statutes of 1635, the *Academie française* had to extinguish all expressions of literary ambiguity in order to praise more efficiently the glory of the absolute sovereign. This semantic search for order was understood as the cultural equivalent of the politics of absolutism. In a significant parallel, the literature of French classicism, the literature of Racine or Corneille, according to Mousnier, "fuit les ambiguïtés, les ellipses, les inversions, les vocables rares ou obscurs, les archaïsmes, les termes trop techniques. [...] Le classique veut une langue nette, un mot pour une idée, un seul sens pour un mot. Il simplifie, unifie, fixe le sens des termes, les structures des phrases."[34]

In the context of this cultural struggle for stability in the French literature of the mid-seventeenth century, it is quite significant and eye-opening that Michel Foucault, despite arguing from an entirely different historical and methodological position than Mousnier, interpreted the genesis of what he called the "grammaire générale" of the seventeenth century as one of the three cornerstones of the so-called *episteme* of the "âge classique", and thus as one of the central factors dividing this "classical age", starting, according to Foucault, around 1650, from an earlier Renaissance understanding of knowledge and language.[35]

A *fourth* trend which must be considered when explaining the continuous expulsion of Fortuna from any serious intellectual discourse in the course of the seventeenth century might be termed the "Counter-Renaissance". Even if one refutes, as I have done above, Skinner's and Gilbert's claim that Fortuna could

---

[33] Mousnier, Roland, *Les XVI et les XVII siècles. La grande mutation intellectuelle de l'humanité. L'avènement de la science moderne et l'expansion de l'Europe*, Paris 1953, 228.
[34] Id., *Les XVI et les XVII siècles. Les Progrès de la civilization européenne et le déclin de l'orient 1492–1715*, Paris 1954, 216–217.
[35] See Foucault, Michel, *Die Ordnung der Dinge. Eine Archäologie der Humanwissenschaften*, Frankfurt a. M. 1971 (1966), 118–131.

exist and flourish only in the context of the Renaissance republicanism of the *quattrocento*, it is still legitimate to ask, as Skinner and Gilbert indeed do, whether a so-called "Counter-Renaissance", understood as a broader cultural and political movement occurring several decades after the decline of early modern republicanism, was a very influential factor not only for a fundamentally revised understanding of Fortuna, but also for the final death of Fortuna.

The term and concept of a "Counter-Renaissance" was created by Hiram Haydn, who used it to characterise the main literary and intellectual changes in seventeenth-century England. Haydn was especially interested in the work of John Donne, interpreting his *Anatomy of the World* (1611) as a typical expression of the "major heresies and subversive doctrines of the Counter-Renaissance".[36] Indeed, if one compares Donne's most famous phrase "Tis all in pieces, all coherence gone" with Francis Bacon's essay "Of Fortune", published only one year later in the context of an updated version of Bacon's *Essayes*, it becomes apparent how fundamental the cultural change of mentality was that had taken place during these first decades of the seventeenth century.

Bacon insisted in his essay of 1612 that "chiefly, the Mould of a man's Fortune, is in his owne hands."[37] By learning a number of precepts, Bacon presupposed, one could sketch some kind of rulebook for a successful everyday life, just as Cicero had formulated rules for the orator, Machiavelli for the prince, or Castiglione for the courtier. In the era of a "Counter-Renaissance", according to Haydn, Bacon's final articulation of the typically Renaissance belief in a superiority of human action and virtue over Fortuna was replaced by a constant lamenting of the transiency and decay of all things under the sun, no longer giving humankind the theoretical and practical room for moulding "a man's Fortune" (Bacon).

But the so-called "Counter-Renaissance" of the early seventeenth century not only helped to provoke the continuous cultural decline of the optimistic belief in human superiority over Fortuna in the English literature of this period. A political "Counter-Renaissance" can also be seen at work in the early seventeenth century, and this political tendency delegitimised not only the Renaissance belief in the malleability of Fortuna by human virtue, but indeed the entire Renaissance understanding of human history based on a dichotomy of human virtue and Fortuna itself. This can best be illustrated by an episode in Venetian history in the very first years of the seventeenth century.

---

36 Haydn, Hiram, *The Counter-Renaissance*, Gloucester, Mass. 1966 (1950), 2.
37 Bacon, Francis, "Of Fortune" (1612), in: id., *The Essayes or Counsels, Civill and Morall*, Michael Kiernan (ed.), Cambridge, Mass. 1985, 122.

In his book *Venice and the Defense of Republican Liberty. Renaissance Values in the Age of the Counter Reformation,* William Bouwsma described how in the first two decades after the victory of Lepanto in 1572, a new political generation had come to dominate the political circles and cultural elites of the Venetian city-republic. On a practical level, these *giovani*, as Bouwsma called them, defined Venice as a commercial and tolerant community, immune against any political alliances with larger empires or the papacy. On a theoretical level, this new generation of political leaders argued against any over-simplified generalisation in political theory and in historiography in the name of a more empirical and historical understanding of mundane reality.

For Paolo Paruta, who started a very successful diplomatic career for the *Serenissima* in his early twenties and even became the official historian of Venice in 1580, "all earthly experience", Bouwsma summarises, presented "itself as a chaos of unrelated and unstable impression" which was "absolutely beyond man's intellectual grasp."[38] Indeed, in his *Discorsi Politici*, published posthumously, Paruta wrote: "Ma gli accidenti che ponno ocorrere, sono tanti, che non è possibile comprendere ogni particolare sotto una medesima regola."[39] This affirmation of historical chance, however, of "gli accidenti", and the resulting interpretation of history as the never-ending realm of instability and of historical change as an inescapable dimension of human life and history, was precisely one of the convictions loathed with particular anger by the Roman Church in the context of the great Venetian interdict of 1606–1607 and the resulting pamphlet wars and intense diplomatic quarrels.

What was intellectually and politically at stake in this conflict? According to Bouwsma, the Venetian interdict must be interpreted as a conflict between two fundamentally different understandings of intellectual and political order. "On its deepest level", Bouwsma concludes, "the Venetian interdict may be seen as nothing less than a struggle over the nature of order in the entire structure of reality."[40] A small and declining republic, convinced of the finitude of all mundane existence, accepted the entity of Fortuna as the epitome of disorder, attempted to stabilise its existence under conditions of permanent and irrefutable disorder, and thus accepted Fortuna as the legitimate opponent of the attempt to chart one's own political course. Consequently, the menacing danger of political disorder could only be overcome by the permanently unstable attempt at political self-determination. However, according to this understanding

---

38 Bouwsma, William, *Venice and the Defense of Republican Liberty. Renaissance Values in the Age of the Counter Reformation,* Berkeley 1968, 275.
39 Paruta, Paolo, *Opere politiche,* Cirillo Monzani (ed.), Firenze 1852, 335–336.
40 Bouwsma, *Venice,* 420, 431.

of human history, the conflict between the political attempt at self-determination and the irrefutable existence of Fortuna could never be transcended. The Roman Curia, on the other hand, attempted to erase all forms of disorder by imposing a universally valid spiritual and legal order, thereby also disqualifying the Venetian understanding of history and politics as the never-ceasing conflict between human virtue and Fortuna.

A *fifth* historical trend that is of relevance for our question might be called, to borrow a phrase from the American sociologist Philip Gorski, the "disciplinary revolution".[41] According to the work of Gerhard Oestreich, the political genesis of the early modern state was erected not only on a legal or constitutional basis, but also on a much broader social and cultural foundation constitutive for early modern history in a most general way. Oestreich invented the terminology of "social disciplining" (*Sozialdisziplinierung*) for describing this process.[42] Bureaucracy, absolutism, militarism and mercantilism were all seen by Oestreich as aspects of this one over-arching and most basic process of early modern history influencing the daily routines not only of political institutions, but also of public and social life in general: from the daily ceremonies at the absolutist court or the new mental drill in the practices of the new standing armies, from the creation of standing armies themselves to the police ordinances formulating guidelines for public behaviour, street-cleaning and fire prevention.

According to Oestreich, the intellectual movement of Neostoicism, and particularly the work of Justus Lipsius in the Netherlands, functioned as a broad intellectual foundation for this process of social disciplining. In this sense, Lipsius became, according to Oestreich, the "philosophical father of the early modern state."[43] The process of social disciplining required an individual capable of self-discipline, an individual being able to calculate rationally his or her relationship to the external world. To take the world but as the world, namely as a stage, as the Merchant of Venice once melancholically exclaimed, or even to take the world as the result of the incalculable arbitrariness of Fortuna, this kind of acceptance of ambiguity and uncertainty, still so constitutive for the textual and visual representations of Fortuna in the early seventeenth century, was precisely the mentality that the process of social disciplining despised.

---

41 Gorski, Philip S., *The Disciplinary Revolution. Calvinism and the Rise of the State in Early Modern Europe*, Chicago / London 2003.
42 Especially important in this context: Oestreich, Gerhard, "The Structure of the Absolute State", in: id., *Neostoicism and the Early Modern State*, Brigitta Oestreich / Helmut G. Koenigsberger (eds), Cambridge 1982, 258–273.
43 Oestreich, Gerhard, "Political Neostoicism", in: ibid., 57–75, here 71.

3 The Death of Fortuna and Two Different Versions of Modernity

I now come to my conclusion: In the second section, I described *five* historical trends which preferred certainty, necessity, stability, order and discipline in philosophy, science, religion, politics, culture and society, and thus rejected any attempt to understand human life as a never-ending conflict with uncertainty, chance, instability, disorder and ambiguity. All *five* historical trends that I have discussed reached their historical peak, as we have seen, in the first third or half of the seventeenth century, and thus roughly coincide with the watershed dividing Fortuna's late blossoming from the beginning of its decline, dividing the penultimate from the ultimate chapter of its life.

Hence, the final rise and fall of Fortuna, which must be explained using references to *five* historical trends and tendencies of early modernity, might also be used as a helpful hermeneutic key to distinguish between two different forms of modernity: one which accepted uncertainty, ambiguity and chance as intrinsic elements of human life, and a later one which pushed this earlier version aside because this acceptance of uncertainty, ambiguity and chance was seen precisely as the obsolete embodiment of a pre-modern mentality.

Thus, I wish to offer the following suggestion: the history of the late blossoming and of the subsequent decline of Fortuna allows us to distinguish between two different versions of modernity. A first and earlier version of modernity accepted chance, ambiguity and uncertainty as part and parcel of the human condition, and thus was still vexed by the existence of Fortuna. To live with Fortuna and to be modern was not seen as self-contradictory. This version of modernity, however, progressively lost its cultural and intellectual reputation in the course of the seventeenth century, whereas a second and later version of modernity, haunted by the quest for certainty, necessity, stability, order and discipline, became increasingly influential. This later and quite different version of modernity interpreted any acceptance of Fortuna's relevance for human affairs as an obsolete element of a pre-modern mentality, representing precisely the theoretical and practical deficits which modernity had to overcome. To put it bluntly: to become truly modern, the proponents of this quite different version of modernity either explicitly argued – or the cultural and intellectual tendencies of this kind of modernity implicitly presupposed – that Fortuna had to die.

Needless to say, my interpretation of the visual and textual representations of Fortuna, my suggestion for dating her late blossoming, her subsequent decline and her final death in the first part, my attempt to bring together the death of Fortuna with various historical trends and tendencies in the second part, and my systematic distinction between two different versions of modernity in this third part are all painted with very broad brushstrokes. In order to complete and also to confirm indirectly my provisional attempt to combine the rather peculiar topic of the final stages of the life of Fortuna with a more general historical and systematic perspective, it might therefore be useful to ask if and when this process of a continuous eradication of Fortuna finally accomplished its goal.

Even if it is conceded that the *five* historical tendencies discussed above contributed to the decline and death of Fortuna, the question still remains as to how human beings coped with the experience of chance after the decline and death of Fortuna. Did a version of modernity which was haunted by the quest for certainty, stability, necessity, order and discipline find or even create a new way to handle the experience of uncertainty, ambiguity and chance, a way better suited to its fundamental ambitions and theoretical presuppositions? In other words, can we at the end of the seventeenth century discover some kind of substitute or "functional equivalent" for a declining or even dead Fortuna following the accomplishments of the *five* trends described above, which had already reached their historical peak in the early and mid-seventeenth century?

This question leads us to the concept of probability: I take the concept and the idea of probability, which emerged, as Ian Hacking showed, in the 1660s, as a new way to handle the same old questions of brute chance and unexpected coincidences in an era in which Fortuna had lost all intellectual credibility. The concept of probability operated, from the beginning of the last third of the seventeenth century onwards, as a kind of "functional equivalent" of Fortuna which allowed human beings to think in a radically altered way about the timeless experience of chance in human life. Chance in human life could no longer be embodied as a pagan deity, presumably governing, whether subordinated to a Christian God or not, the coincidental dimensions of human life. A calculation of probabilities seemed to offer a new and much more rational way to cope with precisely the dimension of human life which, for centuries, seemed to escape any rational thought. Since this "emergence of probability" (Hacking) in the late seventeenth century, it has become increasingly common in our contemporary "risk society" [44], as it was once called by Ulrich Beck, to cope with the experience of chance by calculating probabilities, instead of opposing virtue to Fortuna, stoically accepting the supremacy of an autonomous Fortuna, or subordinating Fortuna to Christian providence.

---

[44] See Beck, Ulrich, *Risikogesellschaft. Auf dem Weg in eine andere Moderne*, Frankfurt a. M. 1986.

According to Hacking, the very first symptoms of this so-called "emergence of probability" emerged in the decade around 1660, when Pascal, first in his famous wager, began to use the means of decision theory to solve a religious or an existential dilemma under conditions of uncertainty. But Pascal did not speak explicitly about "probability". It was rather Pascal's colleagues at Port-Royal "who first spoke of measuring something they actually called probability"[45] in the context of the famous *Logic* of Port-Royal, first published in 1662 and written by several authors, mainly by Pierre Nicole and Antoine Arnauld.

Calculations of probability were used in the *Logic* of Port-Royal, especially in its last chapter on the *futuribus contingentibus*, a subject of classical dignity since the days of Aristotle's metaphysics. The most fundamental questions of any biography, the dimensions of life and death, for which aspects of quantitative frequency had been completely irrelevant for centuries, now became a matter of probabilistic calculation. In this sense, it is quite revealing to read the following reasoning in the very last chapter of the *Logic* of Port-Royal about the probability of perishing in a thunderstorm:

> There are [...] many people who are excessively terrified when they hear thunder [...] if it is only the danger of death that fills them with their extraordinary fear, it is easy to show that this is unreasonable. It would be an exaggeration to say that one in two million people is killed by a thunderstorm; there is scarcely any kind of violent death less common. Fear of harm ought to be proportional not merely to the gravity of the harm, but also to the probability of the event, and since there is scarcely any kind of death more rare than death by thunderstorm, there is hardly any which ought to occasion less fear. [...] We ought to fear or hope for an event not solely in proportion to the advantage or disadvantage but also with some consideration of the likelihood of the occurrence.[46]

This plea for probabilistic calculations in the most fundamental biographical matters of life and death must be seen in the context of the Jansenist theology of Port-Royal. Due to the extreme Augustinianism of Port-Royal, the world was interpreted as fundamentally corrupt and necessarily evil. This theological position strengthened the attitude of using nothing but purely human rationality for practical matters and mundane affairs. To live our lives in this evil world and thus to come to terms with the experience of chance, we do not need to tame Fortuna or to see Fortuna as a means of Christian providence, because a Christian is not interested in this evil world anyway. In religious matters, we rather have to stay focused exclusively on a supramundane transcendence. Regarding the sphere of immanence, however, all we need is a pure form of rationality.

---

[45] Hacking, Ian, *The Emergence of Probability. A Philosophical Study of Early Ideas about Probability Induction and Statistical Inference*, Cambridge 2006 (1975), 70.
[46] Quoted from ibid., 77.

Therefore, the Jansenist strain of Christianity de-sacralised mundane affairs and legitimised the emergence of a new form of practical rationality for mundane affairs based on a calculation of probabilities.

From this theological perspective of Jansenism and the corresponding "emergence of probability", any kind of reflection on the relationship between a Godly providence and a realm of worldly chance, between God's grace and Fortuna's incalculability, became obsolete, whereas a form of Christianity which not only accepts the doctrine of a *creatio ex nihilo*, but also is still convinced of a *creatio continua*, necessarily has to find an answer to the question of how this *creatio continua* can still be held theologically valid in the face of the brute fact of chance.

Let us at the very end, and for the sake of my general argument, compare the position of the *Logic* of Port-Royal with Boethius's late ancient melancholy about his tragic imprisonment in his cell: can one imagine that Dame Philosophy consoled Boethius by assuming that, unfortunately, there is a probability of a Christian Roman Senator in late antiquity with the wrong political alliances becoming a victim of intrigues, and that approximately "one in two million people is killed" not only by a thunderstorm, as the *Logic* assumed, but also by fatal intrigues at the imperial court? Certainly not. To Shakespeare and Gracián, to Gryphius and Lipsius, or, to speak more generally, to the "fortune-obsessed inhabitants of early modern Europe"[47], as Werner Gundersheimer once called them, the idea of discussing the most fundamental questions of life and death using mathematical and probabilistic calculations would have seemed absurd.

However, whether we still wish to appreciate these "fortune-obsessed inhabitants of early modern Europe" as the most valid intellectual companions for our own time is, though a very good question, no longer a matter of historical expertise. I have thus reached an appropriate point to end my discussion of the late stages of the life of Fortuna in early modernity, my attempt to contextualise and explain the decline and death of Fortuna, and my suggestion of distinguishing between two different versions of modernity.

---

[47] Gundersheimer, Werner, "Foreword", in: Leslie Thomson (ed.), *Fortune: 'All is but Fortune'*, Washington D. C. 2000, 7.

Franziska Rehlinghaus
Farewell to Fortuna – Turning towards Fatum

The Transformation of Fate Conceptions in the Seventeenth and Eighteenth Centuries

1 Introduction

Fortuna, like other figures, changed her face in the early modern period. Scholars have observed a resurgence, but also a transformation, of concepts of Fortuna in the sixteenth and seventeenth centuries, a resolute rejection of the *virtù vince fortuna* idea of the Renaissance, and a greater emphasis on the features of *mala fortuna*.[1] As a result, Baroque evocations of Fortuna were dominated by her unpredictability and invincibility, which degraded man to an object of supra-mundane forces which could be controlled neither by volition nor by virtues. Only death could overcome Fortuna's authority. This semantic transformation has been tied to the radical religious, political and social changes in the sixteenth and early seventeenth centuries, such as the Reformation and the Thirty Years' War, the political strengthening of the princely courts and the decline of the republicanism of the Italian city-states.[2] People's experiences corresponded with a world ruled by Fortuna, in which the future seemed increasingly unpredictable, and in which the place of the Christian God had also become precarious.

This semantic shift, however, is seen as Fortuna's last gasp before her final decline from the mid-seventeenth century onwards.[3] Her loss in plausibility has been extensively discussed. But in searching for the reasons, scholars have so far mainly concentrated on the changes in the concept or motif of Fortuna herself.[4] A different perspective arises if we ask – in the Blumenbergian sense –

---

[1] Kirchner, Gottfried, *Fortuna in Dichtung und Emblematik des Barock: Tradition und Bedeutungswandel eines Motivs*, Stuttgart 1970, 164; Tanzer, Ulrike, *Fortuna, Idylle, Augenblick. Aspekte des Glücks in der Literatur*, Würzburg 2011, 82.
[2] Forster, Leonard W., *The temper of seventeenth century German literature*, London 1952, 8–9; Kirchner, *Fortuna*, 114; Vogt, Peter, *Kontingenz und Zufall: Eine Ideen- und Begriffsgeschichte*, Berlin 2011, 597.
[3] Vogt, *Kontingenz*, 607.
[4] For example: Meyer-Landrut, Ehrengard, *Fortuna: Die Göttin des Glücks im Wandel der Zeiten*, Munich 1997, 178. Scholars who interpreted Fortuna and Fatum in an interconnected his-

what gap Fortuna actually left behind in the early Enlightenment, and how this gap was filled.[5] If we embed Fortuna in a semantic field of terms dealing with questions about the determination of human life, the rules governing the course of the world and the scope for individual decision and action, we find a remarkable coincidence in terminological and conceptual history: the agony of Fortuna was accompanied by the rise of different forms of the concept of Fatum, which provided new answers to similar questions. After numerous debates about the several manifestations of Fatum, the term *fatum christianum* became a common notion for the interpretation of the world around 1700.[6] I would argue that these coincidences can be interpreted as different aspects of the same process. The decline of Fortuna, the advancement of different Fata and the establishment of the *fatum christianum* were products of mechanistic philosophy that started its triumph in the second half of the seventeenth century.

The aim of the present article is to elucidate the interconnected history of Fortuna and Fatum, in which the position of man was renegotiated in a world that was perceived as predetermined. The central thesis is that the two concepts belong to the same frame of reference and could only be shaped and defined with regard to and in contrast to one another. I argue that the seventeenth century must be understood as a pivotal period in the early modern understanding of fate. I thereby share Heinz Dieter Kittsteiner's view that this development reflects a process of social stabilisation.[7] The concept of Fatum can thus be regarded as the missing link between a genuinely early modern interpretation of the world and a modern one.

I will illustrate the most important stages of Fatum's rise and Fortuna's decadence[8] by first presenting Boethius's attempt, in his *Consolatio philosophiae*, to integrate Fatum and Fortuna into a common Christian world view as intermediaries of providential influence – an attempt that had a great impact on the early modern period (2). The next section analyses several images that demon-

---

tory are fairly rare. See for example: Fichte, Joerg O., "Providentia – Fatum – Fortuna", *Das Mittelalter* 1 (1996), 5–20; Konst, Johannes W. H., *Fortuna, fatum and providentia Dei in de Nederlandse tragedie 1600–1720*, Hilversum 2003.

5 Blumenberg, Hans, *Säkularisierung und Selbstbehauptung*. 2nd ed., Frankfurt 1983, 77.

6 With this assumption, the article contradicts the view asserted in several encyclopaedias that the concept of destiny loses relevance in the eighteenth century. For example, with reference to Kant: Ahn, Gregor / Bergmeier, Roland / Klaer, Ingo / Schulz, Heiko, Art. "Schicksal", *Religion in Geschichte und Gegenwart. Handwörterbuch für Theologie und Religionswissenschaft* 30 (1999), 118; Kranz, Margarita, Art. "Schicksal", *Historisches Wörterbuch der Philosophie* 8 (1992), 1282.

7 Kittsteiner, Heinz-Dieter, *Die Stabilisierungsmoderne: Deutschland und Europa 1618–1715*, Munich 2010.

8 There is a focus on German-speaking sources.

strate how Fortuna broke out from the common religious system (3). The following section discusses how the Neostoicism of Justus Lipsius prepared the ground for a deeper engagement with Fatum, which initially entailed a reinterpretation of Fortuna (4). In part four, Fortuna's disappearance is attributed to the new epistemic principles of the mechanistic philosophers of the seventeenth century, who developed a world view that postulated a universal causal determination, thus leaving no room for chance (5). The final section shows how Gottfried Wilhelm Leibniz and Christian Wolff restricted the concept of Fatum to the area of divine providence (6). This marked the transition to a more or less consensual understanding of Fatum in the Enlightenment, which no longer relied on the concept of Fortuna.

2 Boethius: Fatum and Fortuna as Parts of Divine Providence

It was Boethius who, in his *Consolatio philosophiae* at the beginning of the sixth century, put forward an influential vision of the world, in which Fortuna and Fatum were integrated as self-evident parts of divine providence. For centuries, this model provided the adaptation of ancient philosophy to Christian doctrine.[9] Boethius defined *providentia* as the supra-temporal order of God's salvation plan, which was in itself reasonable and free of contradiction. Fatum, on the other hand, represented the concrete execution of providence in the changeable and physical order of being. According to this understanding, providence and Fatum became two different modes of action of the same divine guidance of the world, with providence giving the orders and Fatum carrying them out.[10] Fortuna was the tool for the fulfilment of providence, God's scope of influence on human actions. By subjecting man to the influence of chance, Fortuna deliberately tested him, thereby leading him to an understanding of the divine order. "The vicissitude of all things earthly is thus a programmatic element of God's

---

9 Boethius, Anicius Manlius Severinus, *Consolatio philosophiae: Lateinisch-deutsch. Trost der Philosophie*, Dusseldorf/Zurich 2004.
10 "Providenz verhält sich zu Fatum wie Sein zu Werden, wie göttliche Einsicht zu unserem menschlichen Denken, wie Ewigkeit zum Zeitablauf in Gegenwart, Vergangenheit und Zukunft", Sanders, Willy, *Glück: Zur Herkunft und Bedeutungsentwicklung eines mittelalterlichen Schicksalsbegriffs*, Vienna/Cologne/Weimar 1965, 65.

plan of salvation".[11] In these manifestations, Fortuna and Fatum were no longer autonomous deities in an ancient pantheon[12] who were susceptible to the influence of humans, but rather helpers of God, modes of the decree of providence. In this hierarchical form,[13] they were neither in competition with the Christian God nor with each other. This also made them compatible with the medieval vision of the world,[14] although the risks of absorbing originally heathen concepts into a Christian language were certainly known and discussed.[15]

In the German-speaking world, Boethius's influence was still evident in sixteenth-century lexicons and dictionaries: Fatum was, almost without exception, still associated with divine providence. In articles in which the terms "Schickung", "Geschick" and later "Schicksal"[16] are given as the appropriate translations of the Latin *fatum*, these were always linked with the attribute of divinity. In 1561, Josua Maaler thus equated "Ein Schickung oder heissung Gottes" with the term *fatum*, while in 1568, Johannes Fries explained *fatum* with the words "Was eim von Gott erachtet ist und seyn muß / ein notzwang und volg oder ordnung Gottes / Ein Schickung oder heissung Gottes". In 1596, Petrus Dasypodius translated "Schickung Gottes" into Latin simply as *fatum*, and in 1620, Johannes Starck conversely translated *fatum* as "Gottes Ordnung".[17] In 1595, Basilius Faber described *fatum* as a concept which the theologians called providence or

---

11 "Die Unbeständigkeit alles Irdischen gehört also programmatisch zum göttlichen Heilsplan." Haug, Walter, "O Fortuna. Eine historisch-semantische Skizze zur Einführung", in: Walter Haug / Burghart Wachinger (eds.), *Fortuna*, Tübingen 1995, 6.
12 The hybrid position of the ancient Fatum between principle and deity has been analysed by Pötscher, Walter, "Das römische Fatum. Begriff und Verwendung", in: Wolfgang Haase / Hildegard Temporini (eds.), *Aufstieg und Niedergang der römischen Welt*. Vol. 16, Berlin 1978, 393–424.
13 Fichte, Providentia, 5.
14 For the medieval reception see: Frakes, Jerold C., *The Fate of Fortune in the Early Middle Ages: The Boethian Tradition*, Leiden/New York/Copenhagen 1988; Haug / Wachinger, Fortuna.
15 For example: Aquinas, Thomas, *Summe gegen die Heiden*. Vol. 3,2, Darmstadt 1996, 58–59.
16 The probable first use of "schicksel" is found in: Kilian, Cornelis, *Etymologicvm Tevtonicæ Lingvæ: Sive Dictionarivm Tevtonico-Latinvm, Præcipvas Tevtonicæ Lingvæ dictiones et phrases Latinè interpretatas, & cum aliis nonnullis linguis obiter collatas complectens*. 3d ed., Antwerp 1599, 464.
17 Maaler, Josua, *Die Teutsch Spraach: Alle wörter namen vn[d] arten zu reden in Hochteutscher spraach dem ABC nach ordentlich gestellt vnnd mit gutem Latein gantz fleissig vnnd eigentlich vertolmetscht dergleychen bißhär nie gesehen [...]*, Zurich 1561, 351; Fries, Johann, *Dictionarium Latinogermanicum: Ad usum literatae juventutis ordine alphabetico ex probatis Autoribus quampulcherrime digestum*, Zurich 1568, 547; Dasypodius, Petrus, *Dictionarium latino-Germanicum: Et vice versa Germanicolatinum, ex optimis Latinae linguae scriptoribus concinnatum [...]*, Augsburg 1596, N iiir; Starck, Johannes, *Lexicon latino-germanicum, originale novum*, Lüneburg/Goslar 1620, 64.

predestination, "Die versehung".[18] He was referring here to the debates about the reformed doctrine of predestination, which was repeatedly associated with the concept of Fatum, especially in sixteenth-century religious writings.[19]

At that time, Fortuna had long since escaped from the cosmological framework which she had shared with providence and Fatum.[20] Since the Renaissance, she had first evolved from an *ancilla dei* into an autonomous force and, true to the topos *Virtù vince Fortuna*, seemed to be malleable. But by the sixteenth century, she was acting in a more unruly manner, reflecting the feeling which many people shared that it was impossible to command one's own life.

3 Fatum and Fortuna in Images

This development is also reflected in images. In iconographic terms, it had been unproblematic for Fortuna and Fatum to share tasks as long as Fortuna was represented as a goddess with a wheel, which had especially been the case in mediaeval times. The wheel itself, on which the changing lives of individuals were depicted, showed not just the impermanence of individual fortune in life, but also the regularity of change, and thus Fortuna's attachment to a higher order.[21] In an eleventh-century image in the Montecassino Abbey – one of its earliest medieval images – the wheel is accompanied by *Necessitas*,[22] which in many writings coincides semantically with Fatum. On a woodcut by Albrecht Dürer from Sebastian Brant's *Narrenschiff* of 1494, we see how the hand of God itself drives the wheel of Fortuna.[23]

We also find similar depictions in the modern period. On a single-sheet woodcut from 1630, for example, the wheel of the "Welt-Uhr" of the "Roman Empire" is driven on the right-hand side by the weight of Fatum (fig. 1).[24]

---

18 Faber, Basilius, *Thesauri Eruditionis Scholasticae Epitome*, Leipzig 1595, Q 3r.
19 Calvin himself, in the *Institutio*, protested against the view that Reformed predestination was the same as the Stoic fate: Calvin, Johannes, *Institutio Christianae Religionis nunc vere demum suo titulo respondens*, Strasbourg 1543, 368.
20 Vogt, *Kontingenz*, 571.
21 Alfred Doren, "Fortuna im Mittelalter und in der Renaissance", in: Ernst Cassirer / Fritz Saxl (eds.), *Vorträge der Bibliothek Warburg 2*, Leipzig 1922/23, 83–84.
22 See: Vollmer, Matthias, *Fortuna diagrammatica. Das Rad der Fortuna als bildhafte Verschlüsselung der Schrift "De consolatione philosophiae" des Boethius*, Frankfurt 2009, 142–151.
23 Brant, Sebastian, *Das Narrenschyff*, Basel 1494, picture 38, F 6v.
24 Deß Römischen Reichs Grosse Welt Uhr (ca. 1631), in: Wolfgang Harms (ed.), *Deutsche illustrierte Flugblätter des 16. und 17. Jahrhunderts. Die Sammlung der Herzog-August-Bibliothek in Wolfenbüttel*. Vol. 2, Munich 1980, 219.

Fig. 1: Deß Römischen Reichs Grosse Welt Uhr, engraving, ca. 1630, SLUB Dresden, no. Hist.Germ.C.16,misc.23 – © SLUB Dresden.

Gottfried Kirchner shows an *impresa* by Cardinal Johannes Toledanus from the beginning of the seventeenth century, in which under the Virgilian quote "Fata obstant", Fortuna's wheel is chained to a rectangular plate which stops the *Rota Fortunae* from turning (fig. 2).[25] This image can also be interpreted as an attempt to demonstrate both the impotence of Fortuna and the power of Fatum. Perhaps we find here an anticipation of semantic developments which actually occurred later in the century.

---

25 Kirchner, *Fortuna in Dichtung*, 113.

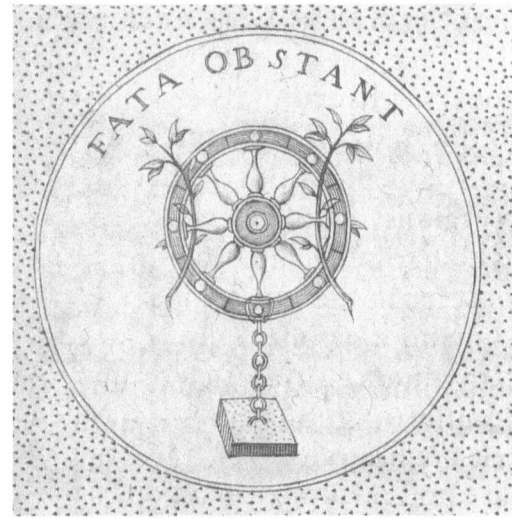

Fig. 2: Fata obstant, engraving in Octavius de Strada, *Symbola varia Diversorum Principum Sacrosanc Ecclesiae & Sacri Imperii Romani*, Vol. 2, plate 49, 1652 – © Herzog August Bibliothek Wolfenbüttel, 28.4 Quod. 2° (1a).

However, images that represent Fortuna and Fatum together are fairly rare. In contrast to Fortuna, Fate seems barely able to be represented in iconographic form. This may also be the reason why the wheel of Fortuna often does not require any reference to Fatum.

The removal of Fortuna from the cosmological system, and thus the detachment of Fortuna from Fatum, appeared iconographically around 1500, when the sphere became another central attribute of the goddess besides the wheel.[26] On top of the sphere, Fortuna stood on insecure, unsteady ground; she wandered around aimlessly and unpredictably; humans were powerless to influence her movements.[27] In these representations, the connection with Fatum and hence with the divine order was cut.[28] Even in 1556, on the title page of *The Castle of Knowledge*, Fortuna appeared as a blind deity balancing on a sphere. The

---

26 Kirchner, *Fortuna in Dichtung*, 19.
27 See: Holländer, Hans, "Die Kugel der Fortuna", *Das Mittelalter* 1 (1996), 149–167; Meyer-Landrut, *Fortuna*, 157–164.
28 "Fortuna scheint aus dem theologisch-philosophischen Bereich, in dem sie [...] einen Platz in einer streng geordneten Hierarchie von Himmelsmächten innehatte, wie auf einer Kugel rollend in die Welt hinausgefahren zu sein. [...] so erscheint aus menschlicher Perspektive betrachtet die providentielle Ordnung oft undurchsichtig, bizarr und unverständlich. Im irdischen Bereich offenbart sie sich als unzuverlässige und wechselhafte Fortuna-Welt," Fichte, Providentia, 19.

book was a work of astronomy by the English mathematician and medical doctor Robert Recorde.[29] (fig. 3).

Fig. 3: Engraving in Robert Recorde, *The castle of knowledge*, London 1556, frontispiece – © The Bodleian Libraries, The University of Oxford, K 4.8 Art, title page.

---

29 Recorde, Robert, *The castle of knowledge*, London 1556.

Standing on the right-hand side of the picture, Fortuna dominates the *Sphaera Fortunae*, additionally symbolised by a wheel hovering in the air, which is connected by a rope to heaven and to the goddess on the earth. According to the inscription, "The wheele of Fortune" is governed by ignorance and not by fate. Fatum stands on the opposite side of Fortuna, on the left-hand side of the picture. The *Sphaera Fati* is directly opposed to the *Sphaera Fortunae*: a female figure with a set of compasses, probably Urania, balances a mechanical globe, "The Sphere of Destiny", which is, according to the inscription, governed by knowledge. What we see here is undoubtedly a representation of the so-called *fatum mathematicum*, describing the calculable connection of the celestial bodies to the earth. The image refers to a long tradition which can be traced back, in the Christian context, all the way to Augustine.[30] The *fatum mathematicum* was a subject studied by seventeenth-century astrologists, but became one of several semantic manifestations of Fatum, which was criticised in the light of scientific rationalism and ultimately succumbed to this criticism in the eighteenth century.[31] In 1556, however, it still met the requirements of scientism and was thus a notion contained within scientific language. Klaus Reichert's interpretation is therefore plausible when he claims that this representation can also be understood as the expression of the early-Enlightenment optimism, the hope that mathematical models might allow a rational understanding of the realm of fate.[32] Particularly noteworthy is the fact that Robert Recorde associated the enthronement of Fatum with the rejection of Fortuna.[33] In a sense, he anticipated the developments to which Fatum and Fortuna would be subjected during the seventeenth century.

---

30 Augustinus, Aurelius, *Der Gottesstaat. De civitate dei.* Vol. 1, Paderborn 1979, 308–309.
31 See: Clark, William, "Der Untergang der Astrologie in der deutschen Barockzeit", in: Hartmut Lehmann / Anne-Charlott Trepp (eds.), *Im Zeichen der Krise: Religiosität im Europa des 17. Jahrhunderts*, Göttingen 1999, 433–472; Rehlinghaus, Franziska, *Die Semantik des Schicksals: Zur Relevanz des Unverfügbaren zwischen Aufklärung und Erstem Weltkrieg*, Göttingen 2015, 52–72.
32 Reichert, Klaus, *Fortuna oder die Beständigkeit des Wechsels*, Frankfurt 1985, 203–204.
33 Recorde's representation was copied. A visual quote is found in the gallery of the English manor house Little Moreton Hall, in two plaster figures of *fortune* and *destiny*, which also reproduce the relevant inscriptions. See: Johnston, Stephen, "The castle of knowledge: Astronomy and the sphere", in: Gareth Roberts / Fenny Smith, *Robert Recorde. The Life and Times of a Tudor Mathematician*, Cardiff 2012, 73–92.

4 The Quest for Stability: Neostoicism and the Fatum

With the rise of Neostoicism in the late sixteenth and seventeenth centuries, the concept of Fatum attracted new attention and became the centre of reconciliation between Christian faith and ancient Stoic philosophy in a neo-Stoic guise. Justus Lipsius explored the concept of Fatum, which he had acquired from the philosophy of the Stoa, in his influential treatise about constancy, and thus integrated the concept into his moral doctrine. In *De constantia*, Lipsius developed a set of moral and practical guidelines which were designed to allow political, religious and moral survival in situations of social upheaval and individual suffering. Regarding the relationship between Fortuna and Fatum, the importance of the work lies in the clear distinction between the Fatum discourse and the Fortuna discourse. As in Recorde's work, a process of detachment is evident here.[34]

In *De constantia*, Lipsius uses the Stoic writings to distil a concept of Fatum which he can implement in good faith within the Christian doctrine of providence. This *fatum verum*, as "immobile Providentiae decretum, quod singula suo ordine, loco, tempore, firmiter reddit",[35] resembles Boethius's conception in that it does not coincide with providence, but rather describes the spatial and temporal effect of providence in things. According to Lipsius, it is through Fatum that the chain of causality is activated; it is Fatum that makes events necessary. This does not, however, limit the omnipotence of God, who can interrupt the chain of necessity with miracles, nor does it compromise free will (since it allows the influence of secondary causes), nor make God responsible for human sins. Here, Lipsius is attempting to refute the most common objections to Stoic philosophy and its concept of Fatum. To sharpen his idea, he not only distinguishes *fatum verum* from concepts of fate which tie the course of events to the influence of the stars (*fatum mathematicum*) or merely describe the sequence of natural causes (*fatum naturalis*), but also justifies his specific transformation and partial adaptation of the Stoic concept of Fatum, which (he argues) has been discredited by conceptual ambiguities, precisely by the fact that he demonstrates the Stoics' rejection of Fortuna as an example of their good intentions: "Illud quidem elogium serio Stoicorum genti do, non aliam sectam maiestatem suam & providentiam deo magis adseruisse: non aliam homines ad aetherea illa

---

[34] Mout, Nicolette, "Trost im Unglück? Justus Lipsius und Fortuna", in: Walter Haug (ed.), *Fortuna*, Tübingen 1995, 295–310.
[35] Lipsius, Justus, *De constantia libri duo. Qui alloquium praecipue continent in publicis malis.* 3rd ed., Antwerp 1584, 61.

& aeterna traxisse magis. Et in fatalis huius stadii decursu siquid lapsi: a laudabili bonoque studio fuit, caecos mortales a caeca Dea revocandi. Fortunam inquio, cuius non solum numen ab iis fortiter explosum, sed & nomen."[36]

The acceptance of Fatum thus always entailed a permanent struggle against Fortuna. And it is precisely here, according to Lipsius, that human free will manifests itself: "Postremo, voluntati vim illi intulisse visi violentam. Abest hoc a nobis, qui & fatum ponimus, & in gratiam tamen reducimus cum arbitrii libertate. Ita enim Fortunae & Casus fallacem ventum fugimus, ut navim hanc ad Necessitatis scopulum non allidamus."[37] With this phrase, Fortuna is banished from the system of divine providence, or indeed presented as its reverse side.[38] Peter Vogt has referred to the argumentative mechanism behind this as "Fortunathematisierung à contrecoeur",[39] and has argued that in Lipsius's model, the place Boethius had accorded to Fortuna as *ancilla dei* is fully occupied by Fatum. The former realm of Fortuna – the vicissitudes of life, the misfortunes of the world – is now ascribed to Fatum and therefore to divine providence.[40] It is precisely from this insight, from the certainty that humans will not be able to change the course of events, because it is no longer possible to act with Fortuna, that Lipsius legitimises the mental attitude of *constantia*. By awarding Fatum a central position, Lipsius thus prepared the ground for an element of stabilisation in an age of crisis, specified as a fixed, unchangeable world order, determined throughout all eternity. This world order seemed unfathomable to the individual, but it placed individual suffering in a larger, coherent context.

Neostoicism was the starting point, from the beginning of the seventeenth century, for a new and enlarged discussion of the concept of Fatum, which was now treated as an antonym of the concept of Fortuna. In 1666, the Nuremberg preacher Daniel Wülfer (1617–1685) published a biting critique of the heathen belief in Fortuna entitled *Fatum, das ist: das vertheidigte Gottes-Geschick und vernichtete Heyden-Glück*. It is not obvious from the title alone that Wülfer is primarily concerned with elaborating the Christian doctrine of providence, in which heathen ideas of Fortuna have no place. The emblematic Fortuna statue of the frontispiece is therefore not struck and toppled from its pedestal by Fatum, but rather by the thunder and lightning of divine providence.[41] The con-

---

36 Lipsius, *De Constantia*, 60.
37 Ibid., 66.
38 Mout, Trost im Unglück?, 297.
39 Vogt, *Kontingenz*, 614.
40 Lipsius, *De Constantia*, 42.
41 The explanatory comment reads: "Diß Buch / das Glücke / Dich im Himmel suchen lehret; Diß Buch / der Donner ist / der dieses Bild zerstört. [...] Laß Deine Augen sehen / auf Gottes Aug und Hand / so alles heißt geschehen." Wülfer, Daniel, *Fatum, das ist: das vertheidigte*

cept of Fatum is addressed only in a short section concerned with the Stoa's concept of luck.[42] Without citing Lipsius directly, Wülfer shares the Stoic conception, since it comes much closer to the real Christian view than, for example, astrological ideas about the determination of human life. He is thus able to adapt the ancient concept of Fatum smoothly to the Christian world system.

In lexical contexts as well, the seventeenth century saw the establishment of an elaborate scheme of different concepts of Fatum, which adopted Lipsius's categorisations, systematised them further, and added supplementary categories to them. Rudolph Goclenius, for example, in his *Lexicon philosophicum* of 1613, distinguished between different kinds of Fatum, subordinated to the categories of *verum* or *ementitum*. Here, true fate included divine providence and astrological fate, as long as it only referred to the physical world (*fatum physicum*). False fate, on the other hand, included the Stoic concept of fate and that of astrology if it extended to the human soul.[43] In 1653, Johannes Micraelius made similar distinctions between *fatum physicum, fatum chaldaicum* and *fatum stoicum*. In contrast to Goclenius, however, *fatum physicum* here was not related to the influence of the stars, but to the order of the secondary causes, according to the decree of divine providence.[44] Overall, the fourfold differentiation of the concept of fate (*stoicum, physicum, astrologicum/mathematicum/chaldaicum, divinum/verum/christianum*) was established in European knowledge in the second half of the seventeenth century, grew ever more complex, and gained an unexpected relevance for modern issues.[45]

Gottes-Geschick und vernichtete Heyden-Glück: Aus Heiliger Göttlicher Schrift, den alten Kirchenvättern, Geist und weltlichen Schriften und Zeitgeschichten vorgewiesen, Nuremberg 1666, cover.
42 The Stoics, Wülfer states, knew "auch das / was wir das Glück heißen / in ihrer Sprach / zu Latein / fatum, teutsch zu geben / Gottes Vorsorg / Gottes Rathschluß / ja Gott Selbsten genennet / der unfehlbar alle Ding gesehen und geordnet habe / wie Sie künftig ergehen sollen." Ibid., 160–161.
43 Goclenius, Rudolph, *Lexicon philosophicum quo tanquam clave philosophiae aperiuntur*, Frankfurt 1613, 571–574.
44 Micraelius, Johannes, *Lexicon philosophicum*, Jena 1653, 426–427.
45 An overview of numerous treatises from the seventeenth century and earlier dealing exclusively with the complex of Fatum, providence and Fortuna was provided in 1712 by: Arpe, Peter Friedrich, *Theatrum fati, sive notitia scriptorum de providentia, fortuna et fato*, Rotterdam 1712. In addition to the concepts of Fatum mentioned, there were also *fatum turcicum* and *fatum spinozisticum*.

5 Fortuna, Fatum and Providence in the Scientific World View

Lipsius's quest for stability was a reaction to the loss of a common confession in sixteenth-century Europe. The focus on Stoic ethics, however, only provided moral guidelines, which did not offer any new certainty. To the same extent in which faith had lost its universal validity as a final authority,[46] the "light of reason" was able to become a guide to knowledge, and thus constituted the basis from which the question of what was certain could be answered.[47] At the same time, this meant renouncing the traditional authorities, and with them the scholastic method. René Descartes perhaps took this step most radically, resolving in his new doctrine of reason "de ne chercher plus d'autre science, que celle qui se pourroit trouver en moy-meme, oubien dans la grand livre du monde".[48] The ambition he articulated was to explain order and regularity in nature,[49] indeed to allow a universal understanding of the world, in which specific elements, cases and events were arranged and subordinated.[50] The scientific method was based on mathematics as the discipline which produced the most reliable and valid results, and was therefore expected to provide orientation for understanding the world as a whole. And this orientation had the goal of eliminating chance and therefore Fortuna: "se soustraire à l'empire de la fortune".[51]

This had crucial effects on the world view of the scholars and philosophers of the seventeenth century. If the world could best be understood with the aid of reason and *more geometrico*, then the world itself also obeyed solely mathematical laws. The insights of mechanics into the size, shape, position and movements of matter became the leading science, and were now also applied to

---

[46] Schneider, Martin, *Das Weltbild des 17. Jahrhunderts: Philosophisches Denken zwischen Reformation und Aufklärung*, Darmstadt 2004, 16.
[47] Ibid., 16–22.
[48] Descartes, René, *Discours de la méthode pour bien conduire sa raison et chercher la verité dans les sciences*, Leiden 1637, 11.
[49] Hüttemann, Andreas, "Einleitung", in: Andreas Hüttemann (ed.), *Kausalität und Naturgesetz in der frühen Neuzeit*, Stuttgart 2001, 7.
[50] Sanders, Hans, *Lebenswelten: Imaginationsräume der europäischen Literatur*, Berlin/Boston 2013, 189.
[51] Descartes, *Discours*, 27. And in 1649, in his treatise *Les passions de l'âme*, Descartes had rejected the popular view "qu'il y a hors de nous une fortune, qui fait que les choses arrivent ou n'arrivent pas, selon son plaisir." Instead, he ascribed everything that happened to divine providence, whose decisions were eternal and unchangeable, so that nothing happened, "qui ne soit necessaire & comme fatal". Admittedly, Descartes excluded those things that were subject to human free will. Descartes, René, *Die Leidenschaften der Seele: Französisch-deutsch*. 2d ed., Hamburg 1996, 266–267.

those phenomena that could not be perceived by the human senses.[52] Conversely, the occult or animistic forces were banished from matter, at least for the scientific approach. This had the effect of undermining the fourfold Aristotelian understanding of causes for inanimate nature.[53] If there were no longer any hidden forces controlling matter, the relation between two bodies could no longer be explained by anything but efficient causes, which could in turn be described mathematically. All physical events in the world were thus interpreted as links in a causal chain, in which every event was the consequence of a preceding cause, and would inevitably become the cause of further events. The most prominent visual representation of this idea was the image of a clock mechanism, working according to the ideas and arrangements of its creator.[54]

This view of the world became problematic as soon as it left the firm ground of physical things and tried to offer answers to metaphysical questions. This critical point was reached once the topic turned to understanding the relationship between human actions and God's involvement in the world. If the world was structured solely according to causal laws of nature, then God had to be the first cause of the chain of events. But could he then still intervene in the sequence of events? Were divine miracles still possible, for example? And if humans were also – in body at least – subject to physical causality, were they still free in their will and actions, and responsible for their deeds?[55] Or did the existence of evil have to be ascribed to God as well?

The assumption of an unbroken causal structure, produced by the effect of mechanistic ontology, promoted a comprehensive determinism which challenged the Christian world view. In the public discourse about the *mechanicos*, especially religious, often pietist writers associated this determinism with the

---

52 Dijksterhuis, Eduard Jan, *Die Mechanisierung des Weltbildes*, 2nd ed., Berlin 2002; Maier, Anneliese, *Die Mechanisierung des Weltbilds im 17. Jahrhundert*, Leipzig 1938.
53 Artuk, Simone, *Das Problem der Kausalität in der Philosophie des 17. und 18. Jahrhunderts: Zur Frage nach der Anwendbarkeit und der Reichweite des Satzes vom zureichenden Grund*, Istanbul 1982, 17; Hecht, Hartmut, "Causae finales und Physik der Bewegung", in: Veit Elm / Günther Lottes / Vanessa de Senarclens (eds.), *Die Antike der Moderne: Vom Umgang mit der Antike im Europa des 18. Jahrhunderts*, Hanover 2009, 32–33.
54 Mayr, Otto, "Die Uhr als Symbol für Ordnung, Autorität und Determinsimus", in: Klaus Maurice / Otto Mayr (eds.), *Die Welt als Uhr. Deutsche Uhren und Automaten (1555–1650)*, Munich 1980, 1–9; Albus, Vanessa, *Weltbild und Metapher*, Würzburg/Bochum 2001, 131–144, 193–205; Westfall, Richard S., *Science and Religion in Seventeenth-Century England*, New Haven 1973, 73–74; Mager, Kurt, "Mensch und Welt im Spiegel der Uhrenmetapher", *Perspektiven der Philosophie. Neues Jahrbuch* 35 (2009), 244–245; and many more.
55 Hobbes, for example, examined the problem of free will at length in: Hobbes, Thomas, *The questions concerning liberty, necessity, and chance clearly stated and debated between Dr. Bramhall, Bishop of Derry, and Thomas Hobbes of Malmesbury*, London 1656.

concept of Fatum, frequently with polemic intentions and without any differentiation. The linkage of determinism and fatalism served for the demonstration that mechanistic philosophy was the result of a pagan interpretation of the world.

Most scholars and philosophers of the seventeenth century were aware of this danger. Consequently, the writings of the relevant proponents of the "scientific revolution"[56] show their will to avoid or even disavow the concept of Fatum,[57] and to include the possibility of contingency in their understanding of the world as a corrective to necessity. The inclusion of contingency marked the difference between an absolute and a conditioned necessity and was intended to guarantee the freedom of God and thus save his omnipotence.

This led to a wide range of different solutions: For Descartes, for instance, God was the *ens necessarium*, the only being that required no cause and was therefore necessary, while the things which he had created had to be understood as contingent.[58] Spinoza, on the other hand, with his pantheistic conflation of God and nature, had radically excluded the possibility of contingency.[59] According to this concept, God was the immanent cause of all things. Everything that happened in reality was therefore not an act of divine creation, which could be distinguished from the creator himself, but a necessary product of divinity itself.[60] For this reason, human acts were not free in the proper sense, but determined by the necessity of the divine nature. Although Spinoza himself, in his letters and writings, always protested against the mixing of his concept of God with the concept of Fatum,[61] the *fatum spinozisticum* as a fifth category of

---

[56] For the problems associated with this expression see, for example: Hampe, Michael, "Revolution, Epoche und Gesetz. Zur Entwicklung der wissenschaftlichen Terminologie in der Frühen Neuzeit", in: Andreas Hüttemann (ed.), *Kausalität und Naturgesetz in der frühen Neuzeit*, Stuttgart 2001, 225–231; Osler, Margaret J., *Rethinking the scientific revolution*, Cambridge 2000; Shapin, Steven, *The scientific revolution*, Chicago 2004.

[57] Newton, in the second edition of his *Philosophia naturalis*, thus argued against explaining the development of the world purely from natural laws and causal-mechanical necessity. "Deus sine dominio, providentia, et causis finalibus nihil aliud est quam Fatum et Natura." Newton, Isaac, *Philosophae naturalis principia mathematica*. 2d ed., Cambridge 1713, 483.

[58] For a detailed discussion see: Goldstein, Jürgen, *Kontingenz und Rationalität bei Descartes. Eine Studie zur Genese des Cartesianismus*, Hamburg 2007.

[59] Dierken, Jörg, "Kontingenz bei Spinoza, Hegel und Troeltsch. Ein Umformungsfaktor im Verhältnis von Gott, Welt und Mensch", in: Ingolf U. Dalferth / Philipp Stoellger (eds.), *Vernunft, Kontingenz und Gott. Konstellationen eines offenen Problems*, Tübingen 2000, 215–217.

[60] Spinoza, Baruch, *Tractatus theologico-politicus*, Amsterdam 1670, 69.

[61] Ibid., 44; Spinoza, Baruch, *Opera posthuma. Quorum series post praefationem exhibetur*, Amsterdam 1677, 453.

fate[62] became established in the European debate about his work, especially after the publication of his *Opera posthuma* of 1677. Initially, this fifth category was always equated with the teachings of the Stoics,[63] but soon it came to be seen as an independent category: Fatum here meant the absolute identification of God and nature, and therefore the pure immanence of God which made everything that happened necessary. The Spinozistic concept of Fatum thus developed into the epitome of godlessness, which was equally dangerous for both public morality and the interpretive authority of the church. The complex debates in the history of Spinoza's reception cannot be discussed here;[64] what is important is that the engagement with Spinoza meant a new, radicalised stage in the debates about Fatum. His opponents, however, saw it as merely the culmination point of a whole series of dangerous writings.

At the beginning of the eighteenth century, for example, the pietist theologian Johann Conrad Dippel, in his work *Fatum Fatuum*, subsumed all the proponents of the new philosophy under the concept of Fatum and condemned them

---

[62] The term was probably coined by the French mysticist and philosopher Pierre Poiret. He speaks of the *Fatum Spinozae* or *Spinoziam Fatum*: Poiret, Pierre, *Cogitationum rationalium de Deo, anima, et malo: libri quatuor. In quibus quid de hisce Cartesius, ejusque sequaces, boni aut secus senserint, omnisque philosophiae certiora fundamenta, atque in primis tota metaphysica verior, continentur; nec non Benedicti de Spinoza atheismus & exitiales errores funditus exstirpantur*, Amsterdam 1685, 463, 825.

[63] Wittich, Christoph, *Anti-Spinoza sive Examen ethices Benedicti de Spinoza et commentarius de Deo et ejus attributis*, Amsterdam 1690, Praefatio, *2r–**2v; Heidegger, Johann Heinrich, *Corpus Theologiae Christianae, exhibens doctrinam Veritatis quae secundum pietatem est, eamque contra Adversarios quoscunque ita asserens, ut simul Historiae Ecclesiasticae V. et N.T. contineat diatyposin, adeoque sit plenissimum Theologiae Didacticae, Elenchticae, Moralis, et Historicae Systema*, Zurich 1700, 247.

[64] For the history of his reception see: Israel, Jonathan I., *Radical enlightenment. Philosophy and the making of modernity 1650–1750*, Oxford 2001; Schürmann, Eva, *Spinoza im Deutschland des achtzehnten Jahrhunderts. Zur Erinnerung an Hans-Christian Lucas*, Stuttgart 2002; Delf von Wolzogen, Hanna, *Spinoza in der europäischen Geistesgeschichte*, Berlin 1994; Wulf, Jan-Hendrik, *Spinoza in der jüdischen Aufklärung. Baruch Spinoza als diskursive Grenzfigur des Jüdischen und Nichtjüdischen in den Texten der Haskala von Moses Mendelssohn bis Salomon Rubin und in frühen zionistischen Zeugnissen*, Berlin 2012; Pätzold, Detlev, *Spinoza – Aufklärung – Idealismus: Die Substanz der Moderne*. 2nd ed., Assen 2002; Schröder, Winfried, *Spinoza in der deutschen Frühaufklärung*, Würzburg 1987; Otto, Rüdiger, *Studien zur Spinozarezeption in Deutschland im 18. Jahrhundert*, Frankfurt 1994; Walther, Manfred, "Spinozissimus ille Spinoza oder wie Spinoza zum Klassiker wurde. Zur Etikettierungs-, Rezeptions- und Wirkungsgeschichte Spinozas im europäischen Vergleich", in: Helmut Reinalter (ed.), *Beobachter und Lebenswelt. Studien zur Natur-, Geistes- und Sozialwissenschaft*, Vienna/Munich 1996, 183–238; Waibel, Violetta L. / Brinnich, Max, *Affektenlehre und amor Dei intellectualis. Die Rezeption Spinozas im deutschen Idealismus, in der Frühromantik und in der Gegenwart*, Hamburg 2012; and many more.

jointly. The work, published in 1708, targeted Descartes, Hobbes, Spinoza and Malebranche with equal vehemence. Dippel saw their teachings as merging into a single pathological syndrome.[65] He did acknowledge the differences between the philosophical systems, but reduced them to the assertion of a "töhrigte[..] Notwendigkeit" which deprived not only humans but also God of freedom. He saw the origin of such false doctrine in the attempt to understand matters of faith with rational methods, and in the inability to admit the supernatural in God's actions. Under these circumstances, "fatal" seemed to Dippel to be the same as "natural":

> And who would not recognise here the inhumane blindness of our atheist bats? For they consider, as the basis of their philosophy, everything that occurs in the world to be natural and a result of fate. And in doing so, they even rob the nature of God Himself of the freedom to act in ways other than those predetermined by the fatal laws of His own nature.[66]

Twenty-one years later, he added another thinker to the ranks of the "Fledermäuse": "the new fatal system of our time, namely [...] Mr Leibnitz' philosophy".[67]

6 The Rehabilitation of Fatum by Leibniz

Without Gottfried Wilhelm Leibniz's systematic examination of Fatum, the term would not have been rehabilitated. In his *Theodizee*, he attempted to reconcile the new scientific world view completely with the Christian world view. Like others, Leibniz's conception of the world was strictly determined by the causal mechanism. In his view, the assumption that Fortuna ruled the world, indeed

---

65 Lorenz, Stefan, *De mundo optimo. Studien zu Leibniz' Theodizee und ihrer Rezeption in Deutschland (1710–1791)*, Stuttgart 1997, 136.
66 "Und wer muß allhier nicht die unmenschliche Blindheit unserer Atheistischen Fleder-Mäusen betasten können, da sie in den ersten Unterstellungen ihrer Philosophie, alles, was auff der Welt geschieht, ganz fatal und natürlich machen, ja dem Wesen Gottes selbst die Freyheit nehmen, etwas, als nach denen fatalen Gesetzen seiner eigenen Natur würcken zu können." Dippel, Christianus, *Fatum Fatuum. Das ist: Die thörige Nothwendigkeit [...]*, Amsterdam 1709, 202.
67 "[...] das neue fatale Systema unserer Zeit, nemlich [...] des Hrn von Leibnitz Philosophie." Dippel, Christianus, *Analysis Cramatis Harmonici Hyper-Metaphysico-Logico-Mathematica. Das ist: Chymischer Versuch zu destilliren per descensum, per ascensum et per latus [...] die drey harmonischen Systemata der heutigen Philosophie, nemlich des Cartesii, Spinosæ und Leibnitzens [...]*, sine loco 1729, 15.

that there could be such a thing as chance, sprang from the inability to discern the real causes of events. "Tous les sages conviennent, que le hazard n'est qu'une chose apparente, comme la fortune: c'est l'ignorance des causes qui le fait".[68] In essence, the exclusion of chance was a reformulation of the principle of sufficient reason. This was, alongside the principle of consistency, the second basic principle of rational knowledge, and stated, "c'est que jamais rien n'arrive, sans qu'il y ai une cause ou du moins une raison determinante".[69] The contraposition of chance and causal determinism seemed at first glance to be absolute and exclusive. But Leibniz did not equate causality and necessity. By integrating the concept of contingency into his determined world view, he created room for the non-necessity of the world and therefore a possibility for God to act freely in his creation. Leibniz used the term "contingent" to refer to things that had become real, but could also have happened differently. It was thus not associated with the realm of the possible, but with the realm of reality.[70] The existence of God, with his attributes of perfection, wisdom, justice and graciousness, was the explanation for how existing, contingent reality could emerge from the multitude of possible realities.[71] On the basis of these attributes, he had created the best of all possible worlds. And this also implied the existence of evil. The cause of the existence of this specific world thus sprang from a purpose-oriented cause, which had determined the world according to the laws of necessity. For this very reason, God did not have to exert any further influence on the course of the world after its creation. God the architect (the efficient cause of being) had already arranged everything for God the lawgiver (the final cause of being).[72]

The concept of Fatum which Leibniz introduced as an interpretive category implied this form of contingency, and thus no longer had anything in common with an insurmountable necessity.[73] In terms of its effect, knowledge of the *fatum christianum* freed people from worrying about the coming day, because

---

68 Leibniz, Gottfried Wilhelm, *Essais de Theodicée: Sur La Bonté De Dieu, La Liberté De L'Homme, Et L'Origine Du Mal*, Amsterdam 1710, 493.
69 Ibid., 156.
70 Stoellger, Philipp, "Die Vernunft der Kontingenz und die Kontingenz der Vernunft. Leibniz' theologische Kontingenzwahrung und Kontingenzsteigerung", in: Ingolf U. Dalferth / Philipp Stoellger (eds.), *Vernunft, Kontingenz und Gott, Konstellation eines offenen Problems*, Tübingen 2000, 87.
71 Leibniz, *Essais*, 114–115.
72 Leibniz, Gottfried Wilhelm, *Lehr-Sätze über die Monadologie, ingleichen von Gott und seiner Existentz [...], wie auch dessen letzte Vertheidigung seines Systematis harmoniae praestabilitae wider die Einwürffe des Herrn Bayle*, Frankfurt/Leipzig 1720, 44–45.
73 "Et comme une necessité insurmontable ouvriroit la Porte à l'impieté [...] il est important de marquer les differens degrés de la necessité." Leibniz, *Essais*, Preface, **6v.

they could be confident that God would guide all things to the best conclusion.[74] For Fatum was nothing other than God's own nature, his own reason, which set rules for his wisdom and goodness. Leibniz therefore referred to this Fatum as "heureuse necessité", the precondition for God's graciousness and wisdom.[75] In this way, Leibniz made providence dependent on God's own attributes, but by the devious route of contingency, he was able to regard it as free.

With this conception of Fatum, Leibniz went beyond the previously accepted doctrines of the *fatum christianum/divinum/verum*. For him, the *fatum christianum* was not just another term for God's providence. It made the doctrine of providence compatible with the understanding of nature held by the new sciences, by re-subordinating natural laws to the initial final cause of the divine will.[76] At the same time, however, he freed the traditional doctrine of providence from God's direct intervention into his creation, thus removing the basis for the theological belief in miracles and asserting the absolute and universal validity of the laws of nature. He saw the consistency of his system as an expression of the harmony of the world. And so he was able to write, in his *Confessio Philosophi* in 1672/73, that it was the same thing if something happened through Fatum or on the basis of universal harmony.[77]

Christian Wolff went on to systematise this theory, and subsequently fought probably the hardest battle that had ever been fought over the concept of Fatum. The dispute with his pietistic adversaries at the University of Halle, in particular with the theologian Joachim Lange, which ultimately lasted fifteen years,[78] was not just about the assertion of the new world view, but also about

---

74 Ibid.
75 Ibid., 361.
76 Bernhardt, Reinhold, *Was heißt 'Handeln Gottes'? Eine Rekonstruktion der Lehre von der Vorsehung*, Gütersloh 1999, 154.
77 Leibniz, Gottfried Wilhelm, *Philosophische Schriften*. Vol. 3, Berlin 2006, 136.
78 For the controversy see: Beutel, Albrecht, "Causa Wolffiana. Die Vertreibung Christian Wolffs aus Preußen 1723 als Kulminationspunkt des theologisch-politischen Konflikts zwischen halleschem Pietismus und Aufklärungsphilosophie", in: Ulrich Köpf (ed.), *Wissenschaftliche Theologie und Kirchenleitung. Beiträge zur Geschichte einer spannungsreichen Beziehung für Rolf Schäfer zum 70. Geburtstag*, Tübingen 2001, 159–202; Bianco, Bruno, "Freiheit gegen Fatalismus. Zu Joachim Langes Kritik an Wolff", in: Norbert Hinske (ed.), *Halle, Aufklärung und Pietismus*, Heidelberg 1989, 111–155; Gerlach, Hans-Martin, "Streit in der Aufklärung: Halle – ein Ort der deutschen Frühaufklärung und drei philosophische Konzeptionen im Kampf. (Thomasius, Wolff, Lange)", in: Karol Bal (ed.), *Philosophie und Regionalität*, Wrocław 1999, 79–93; Gerlach, Hans-Martin, "Christian Wolff – seine Schule und seine Gegner", *Aufklärung* 12 (2000), 3–8; Gerlach, Hans-Martin / Bartsch E., *Christian Wolff, oder von der 'Freyheit zu philosophiren' und ihre Folgen. Dokumente über Vertreibung und Wiederkehr eines Philosophen*, Halle (Saale) 1992; Goubet, Jean-Francois, "Wolffs systematische Denkweise auf dem Prüfstand der theologischen Kontroverse", *Aufklärung* 23 (2011), 175–188; Hinske, Norbert, "Die Philoso-

the scope of the concept of Fatum. This concept was also the reason for Wolff's expulsion from Prussia in 1723.[79] The controversy generated countless texts[80] on the philosophy of science, the perception of God and human ethics. Surprisingly, all the participants were first on the side of those who rejected the concept of Fatum, because, after Spinoza, it was considered the epitome of atheism. Christian Wolff himself, as a final response to these objections, offered a detailed discussion of the concept of the "fatalist" in the second volume of his *Natürliche Gottesgelahrtheit* in 1742, to show that any form of belief in Fatum was wrong.[81]

Despite this rejection by Wolff himself, the ongoing debates during the 1730s made the concept of Fatum or – in German – "Schicksal" increasingly popular in the current language. It was Leibniz's conceptual groundwork that allowed the concept of Fatum, in the form of a "Christian" and later "rational" Fatum,[82] to become an established notion in common usage. After Wolff's rehabilitation in the 1740s, when the Leibniz-Wolffian philosophy was regarded as innocuous and became the leading German philosophy, the concept of Fatum,

---

phie Christian Wolffs und ihre Langfristfolge", in: Heiner F. Klemme (ed.), *Aufklärung und Interpretation: Studien zu Kants Philosophie und ihrem Umkreis*, Würzburg 1999, 29–38; Holloran, John, "Wolff in Halle. Banishment and Return", in: Jürgen Stolzenberg / Oliver-Pierre Rudolph (eds.), *Christian Wolff und die europäische Aufklärung. Akten des 1. Internationalen Christian-Wolff-Kongresses*, Hildesheim 2010, 365–375; Kühnel, Martin (ed.), *Joachim Lange (1670–1744), der 'Hällische Feind' oder: Ein anderes Gesicht der Aufklärung. Ausgewählte Texte und Dokumente zum Streit über Freiheit – Determinismus*, Halle (Saale) 1996; Schmidt-Biggemann, Wilhelm, "Praktische Philosophie als Provokation. Christian Wolffs Philosophie in der Ideenpolitik der Frühaufklärung", *Aufklärung* 21 (2009), 147–160; Wermes, Peter, "Aufklärung im Streit oder Streit in der Aufklärung? Bemerkungen zum Verhältnis von Pietismus und Wolffianismus", in: Hans-Martin Gerlach (ed.), *Christian Wolff als Philosoph der Aufklärung in Deutschland. Hallesches Wolff-Kolloquium 1979 anläßlich der 300. Wiederkehr seines Geburtstages*, Halle (Saale) 1980, 111–117; and many more.

79 In his own description of his life, Wolff reports that officers accused him in front of the Prussian King, Frederick William I, of ascribing the possible desertion of soldiers to the necessity of Fatum: Wolff, Christian, *Christian Wolffs eigene Lebensbeschreibung*, Leipzig 1841, 195–196.

80 Ludovici, Carl Günther, *Sammlung und Auszüge der sämmtlichen Streitschrifften wegen der Wolffischen Philosophie zur Erläuterung der bestrittenen Leibnitzischen und Wolffischen Lehrsätze*, Leipzig 1737; Ludovici, Carl Günther, *Neueste Merckwürdigkeiten der Leibnitz-Wolffischen Weltweisheit*, Frankfurt, 1738.

81 Wolff, Christian, *Natürliche Gottesgelahrtheit nach beweisender Lehrart abgefasset*, Halle (Saale) 1742.

82 Art. "Fatum", *Brockhaus Conversations-Lexicon* 3 (1820), 617–618; Korth, Johann D., Art. "Schicksal", *Oeconomische Encyklopädie oder allgemeines System der Land-, Haus- und Staatswirthschaft* 142 (1826), 251; Art. "Schicksal (fatum)", *Allgemeines Handwörterbuch der philosophischen Wissenschaften nebst ihrer Literatur und Geschichte* 3 (1828), 543; and many more.

or "Schicksal", was rehabilitated too and lost its explosive nature. Supporters of Wolff confessed themselves to be proponents of the *fatum christianum*,[83] and in homiletics and poetry, the concept advanced to become a common phrase.[84] Christian Fürchtegott Gellert, for instance, defined fate in his poem "Schicksal" of 1748 as continuous connection of cause and effect that came out of divine providence and was always fair but not fully comprehensible for human beings.[85]

The growing acceptance of Fatum was the product of its increasing practical value in recurrent situations of communication.[86] The debates about its definition since the seventeenth century led to a semantic differentiation process in which the meanings of the concept were separated into true and false. When debating the relationship between God, natural laws and human beings, the untenable positions such as *fatum astrologicum*, *fatum stoicum* or *fatum spinozisticum* could be put aside quietly without banishing the concept as such. The *fatum christianum*, in Leibniz's definition, was therefore something like a compromise formula that put mechanistic philosophy and Christian world view, human freedom and providence together.

Hence, the Enlightenment actually only appeared to have condemned Fatum;[87] instead, it accepted fate as the reasonable way of the world in a kind of second order fatalism; one had to go with its flow in order to be sure of doing the right thing.[88] After the major debates about the concept of Fatum in the first third of the eighteenth century, anyone who believed several years later in a "rational" concept of Fatum was in an irrefutable position. The frontispiece of a treatise from the 1770s gives a succinct representation of the Enlightenment understanding of fate: we see the divine hand lifting a board lying on the earth and thus setting a sphere in motion (fig. 4). The rolling sphere passes on its momentum, thereby causing a chain of events, without any need for further inter-

---

83 For example: Fischer, Christian Gabriel, *Vernünftige Gedanken von der Natur*, sine loco 1743, 203.
84 Crusius, Samuel Friedrich, *Fatum non stoicum, sed Christianum: Die Göttliche Schickung, Welche [...] Christian Zscherp [...] In Seinem fatalen Leben wohl erkannt [...]*, Dresden 1739; Gottsched, Johann Christoph, "Daß Gott der Menschen Schicksal von Ewigkeit bestimmt habe", in: Johann Christoph Gottsched (ed.), *Gedichte*. 2nd ed., Leipzig 1751, 595.
85 Gellert, Christian Fürchtegott, *Fabeln und Erzählungen*, Leipzig 1748, 116.
86 This is, according to Willibald Steinmetz, one of the possible causes for semantical change: Steinmetz, Willibald, "40 Jahre Begriffsgeschichte – The State of the Art", in: Heidrun Kämper / Ludwig M. Eichinger (eds.), *Sprache – Kognition – Kultur*, Berlin 2008, 188–189.
87 Raulff, Ulrich / Sloterdijk, Peter, "Schicksalsfragen. Ein Roman vom Denken", in: *Marbacher Magazin, Schicksal: Sieben mal sieben unhintergehbare Dinge*, Marbach am Neckar 2011, 27.
88 Ibid., 29.

vention from God.[89] God initiates freely the first motion, he defines the direction, he foresees the way of the world, but he confines himself to this first act. Even the sphere itself cannot resolve its direction. The author Karl Ferdinand Hommel wanted to show that everything, matter as well as mind, was part of fate. This fate, understood as causal necessity, was part of the omniscient providence that never revised its decisions and therefore did not need something like chance or Fortuna. Chance, Hommel stated, was nothing other than the product of insufficient knowledge.[90] And this impossibility of chance was the precondition for the effectiveness of moral laws. The Enlightenment understanding of fate stated exactly this: the embedding of Fatum in the divine order, the freedom of God to choose between different possible worlds, the impossibility to intervene in providence and the absence of Fortuna or chance. On the frontispiece, Fortuna had accordingly lost her sphere and thus her dominance over the world in the eighteenth century.

Fig. 4: Engraving in Karl Ferdinand Hommel [Alexander von Joch] , *Über Belohnung und Strafe nach türkischen Gesezen*, 2nd ed. Bayreuth/Leipzig 1772, frontispiece – © Bayerische Staatsbibliothek München. Sign. Ph. pr. 658.

---

89 Hommel, Karl Ferdinand [Alexander von Joch], *Über Belohnung und Strafe nach türkischen Gesezen*. 2nd ed., Bayreuth/Leipzig 1772, frontispiece.
90 Joch, *Belohnung*, 9.

7 Conclusion

If we understand the history of Fortuna and Fatum as an integrated history of modern ideas of fate, it becomes clear that the decline of Fortuna in the middle of the seventeenth century is connected with the rise of different concepts of Fatum. The stage was set for this development when Fortuna dropped out of the cosmological system of divine providence. Initially, this gave her a new independence, but in a time in which the quest for certainty pointed to the ultimately causal structuring of the world, she became an absurdity. Inevitably, Fortuna had to lose her place in a world that was no longer structured by anything but natural laws. Under the influence of the new world view, the isolated cases of individual destiny symbolised by Fortuna became links in the universal chain of mechanical events, as represented by Fatum.

In the course of this process, however, Fortuna was not re-embedded in the world system, as in Boethius's concept. As the very symbol of causeless chance, she was banished from the cosmological system. In the Enlightenment, the unsteady, uncertain position of humans in the Baroque world had been replaced by the certainty that the world in heaven and on earth obeyed the same eternal laws, and that humanity was part of this. The frightening idea that this bond to natural laws made an absurdity not only of human freedom, but also of divine omnipotence, was softened by the new concept of the *Fatum christianum* which integrated contingency as a corrective to necessity. This contingency, in a certain sense, took the place of chance, which had previously been occupied by Fortuna, and transformed it. From the moment when Leibniz placed Fatum under the primacy of divine graciousness, and Wolffianism became established as the dominant school of philosophy at German universities, Fatum was able to play a successful role in the vocabulary of the Enlightenment.

In the extensive debates over the concept of Fatum beginning in the last third of the seventeenth century, the same questions were discussed which had been relevant in dealing with Fortuna. Besides the universal question of how the world as a whole was structured, and what laws it obeyed, the concepts of Fortuna and Fatum were used to debate individuals' freedom and scope for action, the causes of good and bad luck, or of good and evil in the world, and the relationship between humans and God. In keeping with the new view of the world, the answers that emerged were highly varied, as shown above. The transition from a Fortuna-dominated world to a world of Fatum thus shows, paradigmatically, that modernity did indeed begin with a "quest for certainty"[91] or a search

---

[91] Dewey, John, *The Quest for certainty. A study of the relation of knowledge and action*. 3d ed., New York 1929.

for stability,[92] for which a new space of contingency had to be created in order to be compatible with the Enlightenment's own view of human and divine liberty.

---

[92] Kittsteiner, *Stabilisierungsmoderne*.

Kristiina Savin
Fortuna in Early Modern Sweden
The Heyday and Decline of a Commonplace Concept

Why did Fortuna – a key concept of the pre-modern world, deeply rooted in literary and artistic imagery – lose its central position at the beginning of modernity? This question is even more intriguing when taking into account the crucial role of Fortuna within philosophical, historical and biographical discourses, where it functioned as a fundamental category structuring analyses of worldly happenings and human actions, viewed through the prism of classical taxonomies *natura-ars-fortuna* and *fortuna-virtus*. Today, nature and art are still crucial notions, but the latter has undergone a remarkable change of meaning. The somewhat old-fashioned concept of virtue was revived in the moral philosophy of the late twentieth century. But what about Fortuna? She does not seem to make a comeback. When and why was she consigned to history?

Several attempts to explain the end of Fortuna have been made. The most influential of these suggests that with the emergence of mathematical probability, Fortuna was replaced by new scientific notions of contingency, particularly the concept of risk. In contemporary sociological research, it has become commonplace to illustrate the fundamental difference between modern and pre-modern attitudes and world views by opposing fortune to risk. The British sociologist Anthony Giddens has maintained that the rise of the concept of risk marked a historical turning point at which people came to recognise that unanticipated events could be viewed as the results of their own actions: "'Risk' largely replaces what was previously thought of as fortuna (fortune or fate) and becomes separated from cosmologies."[1] Giddens's interpretation is mirrored in other surveys of the history of risk which hold that pre-industrial societies viewed all worldly happenings as emanations of God's will or other forces lying beyond human control. Instead of risk, people tended to reason in terms of fate, divine providence, fortune and luck – concepts that appear to give expression to an underlying determinism inhibiting freedom and responsibility.[2]

---

[1] Giddens, Anthony, *The Consequences of Modernity*, Cambridge 1990, 30.
[2] Cf. Lupton, Deborah, "Introduction: Risk and Sociocultural Theory", in: Deborah Lupton (ed.), *Risk and Sociocultural Theory. New Directions and Perspectives*, Cambridge 1999, 4; Reith, Gerda, "Uncertain Times. The Notion of 'Risk' and the Development of Modernity", *Time & Society* 13 (2004), 386.

https://doi.org/10.1515/9783110455045-009

At first glance, this seems to be a highly plausible explanation. However, scrutinising the multiple meanings and functions of the concept of *fortuna* and its vernacular counterparts, and considering the vast multitude of literary configurations in pre- and early modern sources, it becomes clear that this explanation must be amended and nuanced. The aim of the following article is to provide some hypotheses suggesting a range of possible causes of the decline of Fortuna. It begins by mapping out some of the most common outlooks on Fortuna in early modern Swedish sources. It then provides a short diachronic overview of possible factors influencing the destiny of Fortuna during the eighteenth century, pointing to the breakthrough of the mechanical world view, the decline of orality, vernacularisation and secularisation. The sources examined were all written or at least read in early modern Sweden, but the conclusions are probably applicable in all Lutheran nations, and to a certain extent in the rest of Western world as well.[3]

1 Background: Transfer of a Continental Concept

Until the seventeenth century, Sweden is usually described as an intellectual periphery, receiving, rather than exporting, ideas, concepts and other kinds of cultural inventions. The first centuries of Swedish intellectual history thus first and foremost tend to be a history of reception, interpretation and adaptation. Like other learned concepts, the Latin notion of *fortuna* arrived in Sweden as a continental import, already embedded in a package of tensions between classical, Augustinian, Boethian and other interpretations.

One of the earliest and most eminent Swedish medieval authors, master Mathias of Linköping (d. ca. 1350), writes in his *Homo conditus*, a theological treatise commenting on the creation and condition of man, that fortune and fate, *fortuna* and *fatum*, are "the worst of idols" (*ydola pessima*), contradicting the first of the Ten Commandments. Mathias is not explicit about to whom his criticism is addressed, but his interpretation of the concept of *fortuna* and the theoretical orientation of his Latin treatise might indicate that it was directed against the kind of determinism that was spread among the late-thirteenth-cen-

---

[3] Large parts of this paper are based on the author's doctoral thesis: Savin, Kristiina, *Fortunas klädnader. Lycka, olycka och risk i det tidigmoderna Sverige*, Lund 2011. The dissertation, however, does not discuss the causes of the end of Fortuna explicitly.

tury Averroist theologians in Paris, where Mathias had conducted his theological studies.[4]

But it is also possible that the condemnation is intended as a warning to his Swedish countrymen embracing superstitious ideas, as is the case in the *Revelations* by Saint Bridget of Vadstena (1303–1373), the most famous pupil of Mathias. In a vision, Saint Bridget meets Christ, who admonishes her to chastise a man believing in the power of *fortuna*, or *lyckia* as it translates in the medieval Swedish version. Being preserved both in Latin and Swedish translations, the visions of Saint Bridget testify to the existence of an established translation. From the fourteenth to the nineteenth century, the Latin *fortuna* is almost without exception translated as *lycka*. The superstitious ritual described in the vision seems be rooted in local folk belief: the sinner, who is said to believe "that everything is governed by fate, that is by chance and fortune" (*omnia fato regi, id est casu et fortuna*), is using incantations while fishing in order to increase the catch. Unwilling to listen to the warnings of Saint Bridget, he is killed by the devil shortly thereafter.[5]

Making no clear distinction between chance, fate and fortune, Mathias and Saint Bridget represent an outlook that is in line with the Augustinian rejection of fortune as a pagan idea dangerously misleading man from his path to salvation. Saint Bridget also sheds light upon the central significance of the Swedish concept of *lycka* in the pre-Christian magical world view, in which a wide range of rituals, charms and incantations were thought to bring luck and good fortune or to avoid the opposite. The church's struggle against such pagan superstitions peaked during the heyday of Lutheran orthodoxy in the second half of the seventeenth century, but the ideas and magical practices maintained their importance in Swedish folk culture until the end of the nineteenth century.[6]

In the late fourteenth century, a Boethian outlook on fortune as an instrument of divine providence seems to have become established, bringing with it the motif of a wheel-toting personification, an allegory found in both written and visual sources. The highest concentration of visual representations has

---

[4] Lincopensis, Mathias, *Magistri Mathiae canonici Lincopensis opus sub nomine Homo conditus vulgatum*, Stockholm 1984, 57–58. Mathias's attitude towards Averroism is discussed in: Strömberg, Bengt, "Magister Mathias' ställning till tidens heretiska strömningar", *Svensk teologisk kvartaltidskrift* 19 (1943), 301–321.

[5] Birgitta, Heliga, *Revelationes*. Vol. 2, ed. Birger Bergh, Stockholm 1991, ch. 6:76.

[6] Swedish folk belief has been mapped by Schön, Ebbe, *Folktro om ödet och lyckan*, Stockholm 2002; Bringéus, Nils-Arvid, *Lyckan kommer – lyckan går. Tankar, ord och föreställningar om lyckan*, Stockholm 2004; Östling, Per-Anders, *Blåkulla, magi och trolldomsprocesser. En folkloristisk studie av folkliga trosföreställningar och av trolldomsprocesserna inom Svea hovrätts jurisdiktion 1597–1720*, Uppsala 2002.

been found in the churches of the province of Uppland, where the wheel of fortune, alternatively called the wheel of life, occurs in the wall paintings of 28 churches.[7]

Fig. 1: Albertus Pictor, Wheel of Fortune, wall painting in Härkeberga church, Uppland – © Photo: Bengt A. Lundberg, Riksantikvarieämbetet.

During the fourteenth and fifteenth centuries, the bonds between Sweden and continental Europe tightened, loading the Latin *fortuna* and its Swedish counterpart *lycka* with multiple meanings and functions in different genres, such as translations of medieval romances, historical chronicles and business contracts.[8] In the latter, the Latin word *fortuna* occurs as a *terminus technicus*. A merchant exporting copper from Stockholm to Lübeck (1331) writes that the transaction will be carried out *sub amborum eventu et fortuna*.[9] Somewhat later, the phrase is established in Swedish as "på någons lycka och äventyr" ("on someone's fortune and adventure"). In theoretical and practical approaches to

---

[7] The motif of the wheel in wall paintings is scrutinised in Nilsén, Anna, *Program och funktion i senmedeltida kalkmåleri. Kyrkmålningar i Mälarlandskapen och Finland 1400–1534*, Stockholm 1986, 40, 419–421.
[8] Cf. Söderwall, K. F., *Ordbok öfver svenska medeltids-språket*, Vol. 1, Lund 1884–1918, 790.
[9] Koppe, Wilhelm, *Lübeck-Stockholmer Handelsgeschichte im 14. Jahrhundert*, Neumünster 1933, 98.

mining, the terms *fortuna* and *lycka* signify the uncertainty of profitable returns on investments.[10]

For the educated Swedes of the fifteenth and sixteenth century, Fortuna was first and foremost not the name of an ancient goddess or a higher "power" to be manipulated by means of magic, but rather a concept used to denote the external circumstances and occurrences that befall human beings irrespective of their own intention. In Aristotelian physics, which formed a part of Swedish school curricula until the end of the seventeenth century, *fortuna* was placed in the category of accidental causes (*causa per accidens*), where it was contrasted with chance (*casus*) and necessity (*necessitas*). During the sixteenth century, this view was incorporated into Lutheran cosmology and anthropology.

2 Confessionalization of Fortuna

Due to their connection to several crucial theological issues of the Protestant Reformation – such as free will, predestination and the workings of divine grace – the questions of contingency abide at the very epicentre of religious turmoil. In the mid-sixteenth century, a division emerges, sorting the multitude of competing philosophical and religious outlooks on fortune along confessional and geographic lines.

The Swedish Lutheran clergy largely seems to have adopted a Boethian-Aristotelian line, ascribing accidental events and worldly vicissitudes to the workings of providence and the inscrutability of divine grace. This was also what was taught in German and Swedish schools. Passages explaining the relation between fortune and providence were a standard ingredient in sixteenth- and seventeenth-century physics textbooks. To give just one example: In his *Physica peripatetica* (1597), written for the students of the university of Marburg, Johannes Magirus comments on Aristotle's *Physics* (2.5): "But more rightly, for Christians, fortune (*fortuna*) is a small part of the divine providence. With God foreseeing and permitting, and nothing happening by chance, as the Scripture teaches us."[11]

---

10 Savin, *Fortunas klädnader*, 326–328.
11 Magirus, Johannes, *Physica peripatetica ex Aristotele, eiusque interpretibus collecta*, Francofurti 1597, 12: "Rectius autem Christianis fortuna est particula diuinae providentiae. Deo enim prouidente et permittente, & nihil fortuito fieri sacrae nos docent literae." Magirus had a great influence on the first work on physics in Swedish, Sigfrid Aron Forsius's *Physica* (1611), see Sigfrid Aron Forsius, *Physica*, ed. Johan Nordström, Uppsala 1954. For other similar explanations in school textbooks, see e.g. Sperling, Johann, *Synopsis physica*, Wittenberg 1649, 49.

In his new translation of the Bible (1534), Martin Luther uses the German word *Glück* ("fortune", "happiness"): "Es kompt alles von Gott, Glück und Vnglück, leben vnd tod, armut vnd reichtum."[12] ("Everything comes of God, fortune and misfortune, life and death, poverty and riches"). A search in the electronic edition of Luther's Bible yields 40 instances of the word *Glück*, and 162 of the word *Unglück*.[13] This number is remarkable and unexpected, as it lacks a counterpart in earlier Bible translations. Instead, the quoted phrase from the apocryphal book of Ecclesiastes, also known as the Book of Sirach, translates: "bona et mala" ("good and evil"). The terms *fortuna* and *infortunium* do not occur in the Latin Vulgate, except for a critical remark in Isaiah (65:16) mentioning people who have abandoned the Lord in order to worship Fortuna.[14]

Entering the Bible, notions of *Glück* and *Unglück* gained an authoritative significance in the Lutheran theology, articulating an inherent quality of contingency of worldly events. The first Swedish Bible to be published (the Bible of Gustavus Vasa, 1541) follows Luther's translation closely, applying the Swedish word *lycka* where Luther uses *Glück*.[15] Since the two words have a common etymology, this is not surprising. However, a similar development can also be observed in other, non-Germanic vernaculars of early modern Sweden: the first Finnish translation refers to *onni*, while the Estonian clergymen spoke of *õnn*, both concepts meaning fortune, luck and happiness, and fitting nicely with the German *Glück*. This, of course, is no coincidence, as Lutheran clergymen were educated in German Lutheran universities. Considering the Danish biblical translation *lycke* as well,[16] we could speak of a Lutheran conceptual community sharing a theologically sanctioned framework of contingency, where the vicissitudes of fortune were surprisingly un-problematically subordinated to the will of God and harmonised with the workings of divine providence.

In this regard, the Lutheran translations diverge significantly from those used by other confessions. In the Geneva Bible (1539), which had an immense impact on the cultural imagery of Tudor and Elizabethan England, the notions "fortune", "misfortune" and "luck" never appear.[17] Instead, Coverdale's translation and later the King James Version, formulate fortune and misfortune in

---

12 Ecclesiastes 11:14, in: *Biblia, das ist die gantze Heilige Schrifft Deudsch*. Facsimile of the edition from 1534, Köln 2002.
13 Search on www.biblegateway.com (Luther Bible 1545) (15.01.2016).
14 Search on www.biblegateway.com (Biblia Sacra Vulgata) (15.01.2016).
15 Cf e.g. *Biblia, Thet är, All then Helgha Scrifft, på Swensko*, Uppsala 1541.
16 For Finnish, see *Biblia: Se on: Coco Pyhä Ramattu Suomexi*. Stockholm 1642, and for Estonian *Johannes Gutslaffi piiblitõlge (1647–1657)*, Tallinn 2013. For Danish, see *Biblia, det er den gantske hellige scrifft, vdsæt paa Danske*, Copenhagen 1550.
17 Search on www.kingjamesbibleonline.org (15.01.2016).

terms of *prosperity, adversity, success, peace* and other similar expressions. While the King James Version exclaims "God save the king!", the Swedish Bible translates "Lycka skee konungenom" ("Let good fortune happen to the kings!").[18]

The discourse on *lycka* flourished in the pastoral care of souls, reaching every Swedish inhabitant. It constantly cropped up in sermons, hymnals and a vast number of prayer books. But *lycka* was also a political concept, frequently used in state communication. The annual royal letters of intercession – the most important instrument for state communication, read in all Swedish churches – established a nationwide rhetoric based on the ideas and vocabulary of the Old Testament. Here, the duties of the Swedish subjects towards God and each other were defined and related to the prosperity, success and good fortune (*lycka*) of the Swedish power, its kings and armies. During the seventeenth century, the concept of *lycka* became an instrument for establishing national unity, social solidarity and moral order.[19]

In Roman Catholic theology, the Augustinian position seems to have prevailed during the sixteenth century. The Roman cardinal Carlo Borromeo (1538–1584) warns Catholic clergymen against using the words *fortuna* and *infortunium*.[20] The Swedish priests, too, were particular in choosing their words. Among the expressions rarely uttered from the pulpit were *öde* (fate) and *slump* (chance). Polemical Lutheran writers connected these notions with two groups of heretics: Calvinists accepting the stoic fate and Epicureans believing in chance.[21]

Early modern Swedish subjects were not to be led to believe that their lives were governed by fate (*öde*). Moreover, this belief was strictly prohibited, at least if by fate one meant a latent power that cannot be swayed, governing all events in the world. The notion of an ineluctable fate contradicts the idea of divine providence as laid out in Lutheran theology. To be sure, God maintains, governs and foresees everything that happens on earth, but that does not imply

---

18 1 Sam 10:24; 2 Sam 16:16; 1 Kings 1:25, 1:31; 2 Kings 11:12.
19 Savin, *Fortunas klädnader*, 35–36; Östlund, Joachim, *Lyckolandet. Maktens legitimering i officiell retorik från stormaktstid till demokratins genombrott*, Lund 2007.
20 Borromeo, Carlo, *Instructiones pastorum ad concionandum, confessionisque et eucharistiae sacramenta ministrandum utilissimae. [...] Editio novissima*, Augsburg 1758, 83. For other Catholic critics, see Alain Legros, "Montaigne Between Fortune and Providence", in: Lyons, John D./Wine, Kathleen (ed.), *Chance, Literature, and Culture in Early Modern France*, Farnham 2009, 17–30.
21 Hafenreffer, Matthias, *Compendium doctrinae coelestis*, Skara 2010, For contemporary translations of Swedish concepts, cf. Hafenreffer, Matthias, *Compendium theologiae, Ex D. Matthiae Hafenrefferi Locis Communibus Collectum, Thet är, Then Christelige Religionens Läro-Stycker*, Stockholm 1693, 23.

that all events are predetermined.²² At this point, Lutheran authors are prone to place Stoicism and Calvinism in the same category: like the Stoics, the Calvinists are said to dispute the possibility of freedom, since everything is a matter of necessity. This view has important implications for how one regards the free will of human beings and the rule of God over his creation: both will be constrained by a predetermined and immutable fate (*fatum*). From a Lutheran point of view, there is no such immutable necessity. This was emphasised by a theology textbook read in all Swedish schools, the *Compendium theologiae ex locis communibus* (1611) by Matthias Hafenreffer, professor of theology in Tübingen.²³

Notwithstanding the polemical nature of the account in the manuals of dogmatics, which makes it impossible to consider them as objective descriptions of the competitors of Lutheranism, it is justified to draw parallels between Calvinism and Stoicism. Jean Calvin showed great interest in Stoicism, particularly in Seneca. Nevertheless, in his *Institutiones* he explicitly claims that Christian providence differs from the fate of the Stoics.²⁴ But, as the German and Swedish material demonstrates, he failed to convince his Lutheran critics. Other sources confirm that the concept of *fatum* was more current in Calvinist than in Lutheran circles. Justus Lipsius, for example, put *fatum* on an equal footing with the eternal decree of God and with divine providence. Whoever honours God and religion should do likewise to fate, he writes in *Monita et exempla politica*, a Latin collection of exempla for young people (1605).²⁵

Until the turn of the eighteenth century, fortune was a philosophical concept defined with scholastic precision, a concept whose position in relation to other affiliated concepts carried extensive theological and confessional implications. Fortune was not the same thing as blind chance (*casus*) and was similarly divorced from the necessity of fate (*fatum*). These distinctions revert to the descriptions of efficient causes called *týche* (translated into Latin as *fortuna*), *automaton* (*casus*) and *ananke* (*necessitas*) in Aristotle's *Physics* (2.4–6).²⁶ For Aristotle and his early modern students fortune and chance designated unexpected outcomes not intended by deliberate actions of humans or processes of nature. Fortune refers to unintended and unexpected changes in agents capable of deliberation – for example a peasant who finds a treasure while digging his field. Chance befalls non-deliberating agents: animals, plants, inanimate things

---

22 Hafenreffer, *Compendium*, 58–71.
23 Ibid., 60–71.
24 Cf. Battles, F.L. & Hugo, A.M., *Calvin's Commentary on Seneca's De Clementia*, Leiden 1969, 46; Strohm, Christoph, *Ethik im frühen Calvinismus*, Berlin 1996, 116–118.
25 Lipsius, Justus, *Monita et exempla politica. Libri duo, qui virtutes et vitia principum spectant*, Leiden 1630, 44.
26 Aristotle, *Physics*, ed. W.D. Ross, Oxford 1936, 5.197a–197b.

and humans incapable of deliberation. Indeed, events of chance are rare. The most of natural processes are subordinated necessity (*necessitas*), also called *fatum*, fate, in some textbooks.[27]

Around 1700, the Aristotelian-scholastic philosophy of causes was gradually being replaced by the mechanical philosophy of René Descartes, fixed in Sweden through the mandatory literature imposed in the ordinance of 1724.[28] From now on, fortune and chance ceased to function as scientific concepts. They were eliminated from physics, with the hitherto meticulously observed definitions being dissolved.

At this time, the Swedish *öde* and the Latin *fatum* were increasingly appearing in Swedish documents. The many examples provided by Andreas Hellerstedt in his survey of the concept of fate in early-eighteenth-century Sweden indicate that fate often served the purpose that had previously been covered by fortune.[29] The emerging popularity of *öde* and *fatum* can be interpreted as evidence of the changes that took place within physics and theology during the final decades of the seventeenth century. If fortune represented sudden, unforeseeable and irregular courses of events, the notion of fate, in contrast, implied a regularity that fitted more smoothly with the mechanical view of the world and of nature that took hold around 1700.

3 The Rhetorical Repertoire of Fortuna

Realising that fortune was a concept with important theological and philosophical implications does not immediately help us to understand its significance in everyday practices and documents. How did the concept of fortune relate to early modern genres and typical rhetorical situations of the time? Let us examine some representative examples.

The Swedish noblewoman Agneta Horn (1629–1672) presented her life in her autobiography as a series of pendulum swings between fortune and misfortune, with an emphasis on the latter, which is already indicated in the title *A description of my miserable and laborious wandering, all my great misfortunes*

---

27 Sperling, *Synopsis physica*, 47–53, 60–64. Cf. Magirus, *Physica peripatetica*, 9–12.
28 In 1724, the new school ordinance recommends the first cartesian physics textbook printed in Sweden: Svicerus, Joannes Henricus, *Erotematicum Physicae Aristotelico-Cartesianae compendium*, Linköping 1725. Cf. the 1724 school ordinance in Hall (ed.), *Sveriges allmänna läroverksstadgar*. Vol. 5, 49.
29 Hellerstedt, Andreas, *Ödets teater. Ödesföreställningar i Sverige vid 1700-talets början*, Lund 2009.

and heavy sorrows of the heart and adversity that has been heaped upon me from my first childhood, and of how God has always helped me to endure all my adversities with good patience.[30] Fortune vacillates: the death of her mother and brother, complicated relations with her stepmother and bad servants are contrasted with the few happy periods of the author's life. Fortune (*lycka*), which is said to come from God, is in some cases personified as "a fish playing with the hook", lifting her up and dropping her again. The author's virtue of patience stands out in strong relief against the many adversities.[31] Similar narratives can be found in many other early modern Swedish biographical accounts, where the vicissitudes of fortune act as a structuring principle for personal experiences.[32]

The motif of a miserable victim of fortune regularly occurs in apologies and written defences. The autobiography of Agneta Horn was probably written to vindicate her position in a conflict with her stepmother over her father's inheritance.[33] A poem written by the poet Lars Wivallius (1605–1669) while in jail having been convicted of passport forgery – he had assumed a false identity in order to marry a noblewoman – complains that fortune has been cruel to him and thrown him off her wheel.[34] Complaints of this kind are common in broadside ballads attributed to prisoners sentenced to death. Several of these ballads depict the crime in question as a consequence of hapless circumstances, a misfortune that befell the perpetrator against his own will. One good example is a ballad composed on the occasion of the execution of the student Josephus Lundebergius from Uppsala in 1629. He had been convicted of manslaughter, but the ballad portrays him as the victim of a bad spin on the wheel of fortune. The idea of man's vulnerability to the vagaries of fortune functions in this case both as a means of consolation and as an apologetic argument, connected to the ju-

---

30 Horn, Agneta, *Beskrivning över min vandringstid*, ed. G. Holm, Stockholm 1959, 3: "Beskrifningh öfwer min älända och mÿket wederwärtiga wandringestidh samt alla mina mÿket stora olÿker och hiärtans hårda sårger och wederwärtighet, som migh ther wnder hopetal har mött altifrån min första barndom, och huru gudh altidh har hulpit migh mädh et gåt tålamodh igönomgå alla mina wederwärtighet."
31 Horn, *Beskrivning*, 19, 22: "som en fisk med kroken".
32 Savin, *Fortunas klädnader*, 64–70. Cf. Dömling, Anna Katharina, "Billigen kand ieg med Job sige. Selbstbilder und Selbstinszenierung in den autobiographischen Texten von Leonora Christina Ulfeldt (1693), Agneta Horn (1657) und Christina Regina von Birchenbaum (1651) ", *Skandinavistik* 31 (2001), 24–40.
33 Hættner Aurelius, Eva, *Inför lagen. Kvinnliga svenska självbiografier från Agneta Horn till Fredrika Bremer*, Lund 1996, 71–111.
34 Wivallius, Lars, *Självbiografi. Brev och prosastycken*, Uppsala 1957, 29.

ridical praxis of the time, where *fortuna* was the Latin term for chance, a mitigating circumstance.[35]

The most important discipline regulating the practical uses of *fortuna* was rhetoric, "the most comprehensive academic subject in all western culture for two thousand years," as Walter J. Ong has put it.[36] Rhetoric was an essential part of the pedagogical programme of Swedish as well as of other European schools, and a crucial tool shaping early modern habits of writing, thinking, memorising and organising arguments, commonplace phrases and tropes in a casuistic repertoire adaptable to a wide range of communicative situations.

In handbooks of rhetoric, *fortuna* serves different functions on different levels of texts: first of all, it was a biographical topos – *locus a persona*, which could be exploited for descriptions of people's lives. Classical rhetoric looked upon man from three points of view: *bona animi* (the goods of the soul) – *bona corporis* (the goods of the body) – *bona fortunae* (the goods of the fortune).[37] Greatest attention was paid to the category of *bona animi*, comprising talents and virtues, and being in contrast to *bona fortunae*. In epideictic rhetoric in particular, the virtues were discussed and given a status as "seats" of argument (*loci, topoi*). This was also the origin of the influential opposition between fortune and virtue (*fortuna-virtus*).[38]

Such a division into the goods of the soul, of the body and of fortune was already common in ancient philosophy and rhetoric. A series of writing exercises, the so-called *Progymnasmata* by Aphthonius and Theon (ca. 400 CE), which was mandatory in early modern Swedish schools, and re-edited in 1670 by Johannes Schefferus, a professor at the University of Uppsala, specifies that when eulogising a person, one can describe, in addition to the qualities of the body and the soul, "the goods of fortune" (gr. *agathá týches*, lat. *fortunae bona*), such as birth, native country, parents, education, friends, reputation, charges, wealth, well-mannered children and an honourable death.[39] One of the most widespread textbooks of the early modern Swedish schools, Gerhard Johann Vossius's *Elementa rhetorica*, recommends that in their descriptions of persons,

---

35 Savin, *Fortunas klädnader*, 274.
36 Ong, Walter J., *Orality and Literacy: The Technologizing of the Word*, London 2002, 9.
37 Aphthonius, *Aphthonii sophistae progymnasmata ... Item Theonis sophistae progymnasmata*, Uppsala 1680, 31, 100. Cf. Lausberg, Heinrich, *Handbuch der literarischen Rhetorik*, Munich 1960, 133–134.
38 Moss, Ann, *Printed Commonplace-Books and the Structuring of Renaissance Thought*, Oxford 1996, 7. Cf. Cicero, *De oratore*, II.XV.49.
39 Aphthonius, *Aphthonii sophistae progymnasmata ... Item Theonis sophistae progymnasmata*, 30–31, cf. 100. For the importance of *progymnasmata* in early modern Swedish context, see Hansson, Stina (ed.), *Progymnasmata. Retorikens bortglömda tankeform*, Åstorp 2003.

the pupils should also mention "fortune, or success, which comprises riches, honours, and the like."[40]

In epideictic rhetoric, *fortuna* was consequently a topos for praise and blame, in judicial rhetoric it structured arguments of accusation and defence, and in deliberative rhetoric it served adhortations and consolations – all of which had their own typical arguments adjusted to various occasions, highlighting different aspects of life. The topos of *fortuna*, however, could serve to stress either that man had a personal responsibility for his actions or to demonstrate the opposite. The genre and the concrete rhetorical situation determined which option was put to use. The same type of occurrence could be given very different – even contradictory – interpretations. Whereas funeral sermons emphasised the vanity and fickleness of fortune and the idleness of human aspirations, court minutes focused their attention on worldly causes and personal responsibility.

Even the use of proverbs and words of wisdom obeys the rules of genre and social situation. In congratulations and eulogies, genres in which it is essential to point out that an individual is deservedly fortunate, the ideas that fortune favours the brave (*fortuna fortes adiuvat*), or that every man is the architect of his own fortune (*faber quisque fortunae suae*), often appear. Writings addressed to unfortunate persons, on the other hand, console them with virtually the opposite thought, namely that fortune despises the best, or that fortune is blind (*fortuna caeca est*) and distributes her favours unfairly – thoughts which would hardly be possible to cite when congratulating a victorious general or a newly appointed professor.

Therefore, statements about fortune in everyday documents should not be generalised as statements about a specifically early modern cosmology or anthropology, but rather as arguments expressing subjective experiences of particular situations which served different rhetorical purposes. The fact that modern researchers have often portrayed the people of earlier times as fatalistic and resigned is a result of their neglect to take into account the rhetorical situations in which the ideas were applied.

Questions of causality were continuously debated according to the interests and perspectives of differing actors. The image of man exposed to the vagaries of fortune was very common, but it was not employed in all situations. Juridical sources are probably the ones that demonstrate most conclusively which forms of testimony were taken as decisive in the practical questions of the time. The accused forger Wivallius and the murderer Lundebergius, who both complained that they were victims of fortune's disfavour, failed to win the sympathy of the

---

40 Vossius, Gerhardus Johannes, *Elementa rhetorica*, Stockholm 1697, 9.

court. Similarly, despite the fact that shipwrecks could be used in other contexts to illustrate divine intervention and man's vulnerability to the whims of fortune, the question of responsibility was rigorously analysed in official examination registers in the case of accidents and shipwrecks such as the wreck of the famous man-of-war Vasa (1626).[41]

4 The Decline of Orality

When discussing the end of Fortuna, we should scrutinise the changes of its practical uses in the different contexts in which the notion played a role. Given the multitude of genres and rhetorical situations, this is a complicated task. Developments differ within autobiographies, history writing, funeral sermons, apologies and congratulation poems, and various broadside ballad genres, for example, demanding separate diachronic studies. Some broad remarks, however, should be made concerning the general characteristics of the particularities of early modern media. What happened to the early modern genres and discourses that sustained the popularity of Fortuna?

As noted above, Fortuna functioned as a topos, a source of arguments, of which many were extremely famous, even proverbial. But rhetoric became secondary to logic with the rise of Ramist rhetoric in the sixteenth century, which separated rhetoric from dialectic, downgrading rhetoric to a matter of ornament. These tendencies became manifest in late-seventeenth- and early-eighteenth-century rhetoric textbooks that concentrated increasingly on *elocutio* rather than *inventio*, gradually leaving out the topoi of argumentation.

This, however, raises the question of Fortuna's declining value as a figure of speech. As we know, Fortuna was often represented as a personification, connected to different metaphors such as the wheel, the globe or the sea. To modern readers, the stylistic device of personification appears old-fashioned. A Swedish university textbook on literary theory and stylistics from 1970 exemplifies the "dry and conventional" images of classicist literary aesthetics with the personifications of Fortuna and Fama.[42] This feeling of distance, alienation and aesthetic disengagement affected many allegorical figures that had been enormously popular during the early modern era. They ceased to appeal to aesthetic taste and artistic imagination with the breakthrough of romanticism around 1800.

---

41 Savin, *Fortunas klädnader*, 264–270, 368–370, 377–379.
42 Hallberg, Peter, *Litterär teori och stilistik*, Göteborg 1972 [1970], 93: "torra och konventionella".

A cultural shift contributing to – or perhaps even causing – this development was the gradual move from orality to literacy. Until the eighteenth century, the public communication culture of early modern Sweden was marked by residual orality. Due to the classical rhetoric, oral traits were conserved and sustained in the majority of written genres.[43] As a Roman deity and personification of prosperity, Fortuna originated from cultural settings dominated by oral traits. According to the scholars of orality and literacy, personifications are particularly characteristic for oral cultures. Human intentions, feelings and experiences are projected outside the self, where they appear as objective realities, "powers" of the world.[44] In contrast, Fortuna and a wide range of other classical Graeco-Roman personifications would probably be perceived as strange or comically pretentious in a modern text of highly literate culture.[45]

In general terms, one could argue that the classical dichotomy *fortune-misfortune* belongs to the polarised universe of the oral world view, whose agonistic structure is made up of binary oppositions such as good and evil or virtue and vice. Such dualisms are effective in oral communication, but may appear as old-fashioned, aesthetically too simple and unappealing in written texts.

As several scholars have pointed out, the conceptions of contingency are expressed in different levels of texts: the notions and tropes, the structuring principles of the plot, time-space relations and cause-effect development.[46] Today, the literary representations of early modern romance and chapbook heroes such as Fortunatus or Griseldis may appear "psychologically unsatisfying", as not much is said about the feelings and the inner life of these heroes[47] whose main task is to stay unchangeable and to preserve their virtues during their numerous adventures and trials in the midst of an unpredictable world. The transformation of literary genres and the emergence of the modern novel during the seventeenth century rejects these earlier and aesthetically quite representative stories about Fortuna.

---

[43] Hansson, Stina, "Talandets mimesis", *Tidskrift för litteraturvetenskap* 1 (1986), 67–69. Cf. Ong, *Orality and Literacy*, 44.
[44] Lindhardt, Jan, *Tale og skrift. To kulturer*, Copenhagen 1989, 43–44.
[45] Ong, *Orality and Literacy*, 45.
[46] Cf. Lyons, John D. / Wine, Kathleen (eds.), *Chance, Literature, and Culture in Early Modern France*, 65–122; Witmore, Michael, *The Culture of Accidents. Unexpected Knowledges in Early Modern England*, Stanford 2001, 62–81.
[47] Burman, Lars, "Om folkbokens vackra Grisilla. Bokhistoria, dygdemoral och erotik", *Tidskrift för litteraturvetenskap* 36 (2006), 49. Literary historian Lars Burman describes the narrative of the chapbook editions of the story of Griseldis as "psykologiskt otillfedsställande".

5 Vernacularisation and Secularisation

An interesting issue in need of additional research concerns the complex interplay of Latin and vernacular concepts in early modern thought. The strong position of the Swedish *lycka* (and probably of the German *Glück* as well) depended on the fluid character of the concept, containing multiple meanings stretching from success, prosperity and happiness to luck, worldly insecurity and fickleness of fortune. Simultaneously folkish and learned, religious and philosophic, classical and Christian, it was capable of merging multiple functions in a single word, a possibility that did not exist in all European vernaculars.

In its vernacular version, Fortuna gained immense popularity. But after having been separated from its classical framework, where its denotations and connotations were fixed through the unchanging Graeco-Roman literary canon, it also became exposed to the ephemeral influences of continually changing semantic fields of vernaculars, which were undergoing a fundamental transformation from the mid-eighteenth century onwards. It is probably no coincidence that the end of Fortuna falls in the period labelled *Sattelzeit* or *Schwellenzeit*, a transition from early modern to modern society with extensive significance for the vocabularies of European nations.

In her study of the Swedish broadside ballads, historian Anna Nilsson Hammar shows how the Swedish concept of *lycka* underwent a considerable change during the period 1750–1850. Having a clearly defined and fixed place in Lutheran cosmology at the beginning of the period, its definition and position was destabilised around 1800, as the cosmology and anthropology of Lutheran orthodoxy were replaced by a less homogeneous world view. In the new, gradually de-Christianised, settings, *lycka* lost its dangerous and negative aspects of fickleness and became synonymous with "well-being" – expressing the subjective emotional state of an individual rather than an accidental happening rooted in a cosmological framework.[48]

Given that Fortuna was a classical concept rooted in pre-Christian literature, the connection between the secularisation process and the destinies of Fortuna is perhaps not obvious, but in the Swedish and other Lutheran contexts, it cannot be ignored. As shown above, the idea of fortune and its Swedish equivalent *lycka* were deeply influenced by the developments within Lutheranism. Later, during the eighteenth century, developments in physico-theology and rationalistic theology moved the centre of interest from the inscrutable effects of divine grace, which had been of great importance to Luther, to the regu-

---

[48] Nilsson, Anna, *Lyckans betydelse. Sekularisering, sensibilisering och individualisering i svenska skillingtryck 1750–1850*, Malmö 2012.

lar workings of providence. In the second half of the eighteenth century, the presence of expressions including *lycka* decreases in almost all genres. During the eighteenth century, expressions connecting *lycka* to God, for example "om Gud ger lycka" ("if God gives good fortune"), earlier omnipresent in both official and private documents, gradually disappear. A measurement of the frequency of such expressions would probably provide a good picture of the paradigmatic shift that could indicate gradual secularisation.

For centuries, the Latin *fortuna* was almost without exception translated as *lycka*. In modern Swedish, the Latin word *fortuna* lacks an adequate equivalent, being translated in different ways, sometimes as *tur* (a word for "luck" dating back to the nineteenth century), *öde* (fate), or more seldom as *lycka*.

6 Conclusion

Paradoxically, Fortuna was flung down from its eminent position by the very same mechanisms that had once contributed to its promotion. After having been ascribed the status of a scientific category in Aristotelian physics, it was abandoned along with Aristotelianism. Christianisation and confessionalisation gave it a crucial position in Lutheran cosmology, but the theological discourse turned out to be changeable, and consequently fortuna was subjected to secularisation – despite originally being an ancient pagan concept. At first, vernacularisation lent it new force and instilled the classical interpretation of Fortuna in broad segments of the population, but in the long run, it led to a fragmentation of the conceptual field which was its original source and continuing support. Rhetoric and residual orality, upholding the classical Graeco-Roman tropes, also helped to pull the concept down when it was toppled by the new aesthetics of romanticism.

An intriguing question is the relation between ideas and the changing forms of social life. In this respect, a plausible hypothesis might be that the concept of fortune was closely intertwined with the social, economic, political and material conditions of pre-modern societies from which it once emerged. Since these conditions radically changed from the second half of the eighteenth century onwards, the concept became gradually inadequate and superfluous. It lacks the capacity to describe the realities of the modern welfare state, whose primary concern has been the emancipation of individuals from the structures of inequality and diminishing the insecurity and unpredictability of life through different kinds of juridical, social and economic measures – from laws, progressive taxes, social benefits and gender quotas to health insurance and mass vaccinations.

On the other hand, the emergence of the concepts of risk and probability only had a very limited effect on the expressions once catalogued in the vast rhetorical repertoire of Fortuna. People are still wishing each other good luck, they keep excusing themselves by referring to unanticipated events and accidents, they still complain about not being treated in accordance with their merits, and they find solace in arguments that contravene personal responsibility. They fear the ups and downs of the stock exchange, the irregularities of economic conjunctures, the insecurity of investments, the uncertainties of the labour market, the unpredictability of political developments, the changeableness of relations and the unpredictability of love and family life.

The most crucial difference between modern and pre-modern views on contingency is probably the absence of a consolidating topos capable of shaping a coherent cluster of mental images, rhetorical devices and literary configurations in our time. In this respect, Fortuna still is unrivalled in history.

Florence Buttay
La Fortune victime des Lumières ?

Remarques sur les transformations de Fortune aux XVIIe et XVIIIe siècles

A l'issue de nos riches journées de travail, un échange passionnant – et vif – s'est déroulé entre nous sur la disparition ou non de la Fortune, entre le milieu du XVIIe et le début du siècle suivant. Il ne me semblait pas possible de parler de disparition, ni dans les images ni dans les textes, mais plutôt de transformation, une fois de plus, dans ses usages. Tout en étant loin de mes terres de spécialité (les XVe et XVIe siècles), je me risquerai ici à quelques remarques et à quelques hypothèses sur l'allégorie de la Fortune aux XVIIe et XVIIIe siècles. Il me semble que l'on peut observer un effacement apparent de l'allégorie dans le discours sur les rapports entre les hommes et Dieu, où elle est concurrencée par la Nature, au cours du XVIIe siècle. Cependant, Fortune reste une figure opérationnelle pour parler du monde des hommes et de ses règles, du jeu social, et notamment de la place grandissante (moralement condamnable, mais aussi source d'espérance) de l'argent dans la définition de la hiérarchie sociale. On analysera à la fois le glissement sémantique qui s'opère, en français en particulier, dans l'usage du mot fortune et de ses dérivés, qui en fait de plus en plus l'équivalent de richesse, de patrimoine, et les images liant Fortune et argent, notamment dans l'iconographie de la loterie.

1 Les images de la Fortune entre XVIIe et XVIIIe siècles

Un sondage dans l'iconothèque de l'Institut Warburg est une bonne piste pour tenter de répondre à la question de la possible "fin de la Fortune" au cours du XVIIe siècle. En feuilletant les différents fichiers relatifs à *Fortuna*, on peut noter sa persistance, tout au long siècle, sur tous les supports où elle apparaissait précédemment (médaille, décor éphémère ou non, mais aussi peinture avec en particulier le succès du modèle de Guido Reni, qui se trouve fréquemment reproduit par la gravure ou le dessin.¹ On remarque également la persistance de différents types iconographiques. L'image renaissante de la Fortune-Occasion,² souvent proche de la Fortune-Vénus marine, reste très présente; c'est celle choisie par Rubens vers 1636–1638.³ On voit aussi des Fortunes aveugles.⁴ Il semble qu'on puisse noter un regain de faveur du thème de la roue et de la Fortune à la roue qui, sans avoir disparu, n'était plus le plus courant à la fin du XVIᵉ siècle.⁵ Mais cette Fortune à la roue est volontiers nue et attirante comme la Fortune-Occasion. Ainsi, Fortune-Occasion, dressée sur une roue, semble devenir l'iconographie dominante. On reviendra plus bas sur cette importance de la roue.

2 *Conflation* de Fortuna et Natura?

Une autre caractéristique me semble le rôle joué, à la fin du XVIIᵉ siècle, par la Nature là où Fortune avait jusqu'alors toute sa place, c'est-à-dire dans les discours sur les relations entre monde céleste et monde terrestre, entre Dieu et sa créature. D'un côté, on observe des images de la Fortune assimilée à la Nature et, de l'autre, la façon dont on parle de la Nature est bien proche des discours traditionnels sur la Fortune (on insiste volontiers sur sa versatilité, sur une Nature joueuse et imprévisible). Sans être complètement une nouveauté, ces traits semblent plus marqués dans cette période, ce qui pourrait conduire à penser qu'on a affaire à une deuxième *conflation*, selon le terme utilisé par Frederick Kiefer pour caractériser l'assimilation de la Fortune à l'Occasion à la Renaissance: une *conflation* qui signerait pour le coup, entre XVIIᵉ et XVIIIᵉ siècle, la

---

1 Voir: Mahon, Denis / Pepper, Stephen, "Guido Reni's 'Fortuna With a Purse' Rediscovered", *The Burlington Magazine* 141 (1999), 156–163.
2 Aby Warburg est le premier à avoir repéré les transformations iconographiques de la déesse dans un article justement célèbre "Les dernières volontés de Francesco Sassetti". Voir: Buttay, Florence, *Fortuna. Usages politiques d'une allégorie morale à la Renaissance*, Paris 2008, 89–90.
3 Rubens, Pierre Paul, *Fortune*, 1636–1638, huile sur toile, 182,3x100,5 cm, Madrid, Museo del Prado. On voit Fortune avançant sur les flots, un pied sur une boule transparente, tendant derrière elle une draperie gonflée de vent.
4 Ainsi la Fortune aux yeux bandés recevant des trésors de Jupiter, Pluton et Neptune, connue par la gravure de Pierre Brébiette (1624), voir : Galactéros de Boissier, Lucie / Giraud, Yves, *Fortune*. Catalogue de l'exposition du Musée de l'Elysée, 2 octobre 1981–3 mars 1982, Lausanne, Musée de l'Elysée 1982, n°95, 75.
5 Ainsi, dans son "Encyclopédie de la Fortune", datée de 1568, Imbert d'Anlézy notait que la représentation qu'on dirait aujourd'hui de la Fortune-Occasion est le type le plus couramment peint par les artistes de son temps. Voir: Buttay, *Fortuna*, 352.

rencontre entre Fortune et Nature.⁶ Comme Frederick Kiefer le notait pour l'assimilation entre Fortune et Occasion, l'immixtion de la Fortune à la Nature se remarque à la fois dans les textes et les images.

Remarquons d'abord la place grandissante prise à cette période par la Nature dans les discours sur l'organisation de la sphère terrestre et dans ses relations avec la divinité. La philosophie naturelle lie le problème de la Providence à la Nature.⁷ Pour parler de l'ici-bas, pour débattre de la liberté humaine et de l'intervention de Dieu dans la marche du monde et le cours des actions humaines, la figure de la Nature devient essentielle. Alors que la Fortune et le Monde pouvaient être assimilés à la Renaissance,⁸ Nature en vient à désigner le monde créé dans son ensemble, voire l'œuvre créatrice de Dieu, jusqu'à prendre l'extension même de Dieu.⁹ On repère que la "Ministre de Dieu", comme Dante appelait la Fortune, devient la Nature sous la plume de Robert Fludd.¹⁰ On note également l'assimilation de Nature à Isis, dont était aussi souvent rapprochée la Fortune: dans les deux cas, il s'agit de désigner et de réfléchir sur le mystère de la causalité ici-bas.¹¹ On peut repérer des images précoces du rapprochement entre Nature et Fortune, comme le dessin de Johannes Ebelmann (actif entre 1598 et 1624). Il montre une Fortune nue, voguant sur la mer sur une boule ailée, tenant un voile gonflé de vent. Mais cette iconographie bien connue intègre un trait propre à l'image de la Nature: de ses seins partent des jets de lait.¹² La Fortune peut aussi apparaître dans un contexte agraire où on attendrait Nature. Ainsi, au frontispice du *Tractatus de transactionibus* de Manuel Román Valerón

---

6 Kiefer, Frederick, "The Conflation of Fortuna and Occasio in Renaissance Thought and Iconography", *Journal of Medieval and Renaissance Studies* 9 (1979), 1–27.
7 Voir : Par exemple Ehrard, Jean, *L'idée de nature en France dans la première moitié du XVIIIe siècle*, Paris 1963.
8 Buttay, *Fortuna*, 150.
9 Tocanne, Bernard, *L'idée de nature en France dans la deuxième moitié du XVIIe siècle. Contribution à l'histoire de la pensée classique*, Paris 1978, 12, cite le chimiste anglais Boyle, qui s'exclame en 1686: "qu'y a-t-il de plus confus que les notions ordinaires que l'on se forme de la Nature ? Quel mot est plus souvent prononcé que celui-là en plusieurs significations différentes ?". Le *Dictionnaire* de Furetière ne donne pas moins de 9 sens, dont les deux premiers sont :
1. "La masse du monde, l'assemblage de tous les êtres".
2. "L'action de la Providence, ce qui agit en tous les corps et qui leur donne certaines propriétés que les philosophes appellent causes secondes. Nature se dit aussi en parlant de ce qui est ordinaire, qui arrive tous les jours".
10 "Natura, non Dea, sed proxima Dei ministra"; cité dans Kemp, Wolfgang, *Natura, Ikonographische Studien zur Geschichte und Verbreitung einer Allegorie*, Bamberg 1973, 91.
11 Hadot, Pierre, *Le voile d'Isis. Essai sur l'histoire de l'idée de Nature*, Paris 2004.
12 Johannes Ebelmann, dessin passé en vente chez Sotheby's, Amsterdam, le 19 mai 2004.

(fig. 1),[13] on voit une Fortune ensemençant un champ que laboure une charrue conduite par la Vertu et traînée par le Temps. La déesse nue, dressée sur sa boule, cheveux et pagne au vent, tirée de son univers marin, roule assez curieusement sur la terre creusée de sillons.

Fig. 1: Semina fortunae geminat cum tempore virtus, engraving in Manuel Román Valerón, *Tractatus de transactionibus [...] nunc primum in lucem prodit*, Lyon 1665, frontispiece – © Bibliothèque nationale de France.

Alors qu'au XVIe siècle les relations entre Nature et Fortune, relations d'opposition ou de complémentarité, selon les auteurs, étaient fondées sur l'idée que la Nature désigne les règles immuables de l'univers et la Fortune les interventions divines qui s'exercent hors de ces règles, ce partage semble se brouiller. La description de la nature par Diderot ressemble de manière frappante aux discours sur la variable et trompeuse Fortune, qu'on peine à suivre :

> Il semble que la nature se soit plus à varier le même mécanisme d'une infinité de manières différentes. Elle n'abandonne un genre de productions qu'après en avoir multiplié les individus sous toutes les faces possibles [...]. C'est une femme qui aime à se travestir, et dont les différents déguisements, laissant échapper tantôt une partie, tantôt une autre,

---

13 Román Valerón, Manuel, *Tractatus de transactionibus... nunc primum in lucem prodit*, Lyon, Philippe Borde, 1665. La gravure est encadrée par le *motto* suivant: "Semina fortunae geminat cum tempore virtus".

> donne quelque espérance à ceux qui la suivent avec assiduité de connaître un jour toute sa personne.[14]

Certes, il ne s'agit pas d'un thème complètement nouveau. Si Aristote voyait dans la Nature une bonne ménagère économe, les stoïciens ne la pensaient pas toujours raisonnable; Chrysippe en voulait pour preuve la queue du paon, pur caprice de la nature; Sénèque estimait que sa production se caractérisait par la variété (*ipsa varietate se jactat*); Pline soulignait sa folie (*lascivia*), et son caractère joueur (*varie ludens*), tous termes qui ont été largement appliqués au domaine de la Fortune.[15] Mais Pierre Hadot note combien "cette métaphore de la Nature joueuse aura un rôle important, à partir du XVIIIe siècle, dans l'essor de l'idée d'évolutionnisme".

Entre XVIIe et XVIIIe siècles, il semble bien que les usages de la Fortune changent, ce dont témoignent certaines innovations iconographiques. L'évolution du sens du mot «fortune», en français, est significative du contexte dans lequel on retrouve de plus en plus l'image de Fortune, celui de la description des bienfaits et des méfaits de l'accumulation de richesses.

3 Un tournant sémantique significatif: il n'est de fortune que de richesse

3.1 Le sens des mots: une progressive assimilation de la Fortune à la richesse

Si l'on concentre l'attention sur la France, on note un glissement sémantique sensible du mot "fortune" et de ses dérivés. On le vérifiera dans un deuxième temps par l'examen d'images de la même période.

Fortune commence en effet au XVIIe siècle son assimilation à la richesse (pécuniaire et patrimoniale). En français, de "malheureux", "frappé par le sort", au XVe siècle, le "fortuné" désigne plus souvent l'homme "heureux" au cours du XVIe siècle, avant de devenir un synonyme de "riche". Le *Nouveau dictionnaire étymologique et historique* d'Albert Dauzat, Jean Dubois et Henri Mitterand (1964)[16] fait remonter au XVIIe siècle le sens de "riche" pour "fortuné". Cepen-

---

14 *De l'interprétation de la nature*, cité par Pierre Hadot, 206.
15 *Ibid.*
16 Dauzat, Albert / Dubois, Jean / Mitterand, Henri (eds.), *Nouveau dictionnaire étymologique et historique*, Paris 1964, 316.

dant, ce sens tarde à faire son apparition dans les dictionnaires. Entre l'édition de 1694 et celle de 1799, le *Dictionnaire de l'Académie française* conserve exactement le même texte à l'entrée "Fortune". Prenons l'édition de la fin de la période :[17]

FORTUNE, s. f. Cas fortuit, hasard. *Bonne fortune. Mauvaise fortune.* [...] *Il court fortune d'être quelque jour un grand Seigneur* [...]. Il se prend quelquefois pour Bonheur. *Il est en fortune, il gagne tout ce qu'il veut.* Il se prend aussi pour Malheur, péril, danger, risque: *Dieu vous préserve de mal et de fortune* [...]. On appelle *Fortune de mer*, Les fâcheux accidens qui arrivent à ceux qui naviguent sur mer, comme de faire naufrage, d'échouer, etc.

FORTUNE, se prend aussi pour Tout ce qui peut arriver de bien ou de mal à un homme. *Courir la fortune de quelqu'un. Nous courons tous deux même fortune* [...]. On dit familièrement, *Courir la fortune du pot*, pour dire, S'exposer à faire mauvaise chère en allant dîner dans une maison où l'on n'est point attendu.

FORTUNE, se prend aussi pour l'avancement et l'établissement dans les biens, dans les charges, dans les honneurs. Grande fortune. *Belle fortune. Médiocre fortune. Sa fortune est digne d'envie. Faire fortune. Faire la fortune de quelqu'un. Etablir, affermir sa fortune. Ruiner sa fortune. Perdre sa fortune par sa mauvaise conduite. Ménager bien sa fortune. Parvenir à une haute fortune. S'il vit, il poussera, il portera sa fortune bien loin. Vous êtes en bon chemin, poussez votre fortune. N'abusez pas de votre fortune. Sa fortune est encore chancelante. Il semble que sa fortune diminue, qu'elle baisse. Ses envieux tâchent de traverser, d'ébranler sa fortune. Tenir sa fortune de quelqu'un. Il doit sa fortune à un tel. Il ne doit sa fortune qu'à son propre mérite. On a vu des fortunes bien étonnantes depuis vingt ans. Les fortunes subites sont rarement durables. N'avoir point de fortune.* Il se prend aussi pour L'état, la condition où l'on est. *Se contenter de sa fortune. Il s'est toujours tenu dans sa première fortune. Il n'a point changé sa fortune.* On appelle *Biens de la fortune*, Les richesses, les honneurs, les charges. *Les biens de la fortune ne sont pas les vrais biens. Le Sage ne recherche pas ardemment les biens de la fortune.* On appelle *Homme de fortune*, Un homme qui, d'un fort petit commencement, est parvenu à de grands biens; et, *Soldat de fortune*, Un homme de guerre qui, sans naissance, et sans autre recommandation que son mérite, est parvenu des derniers rangs aux grades les plus élevés. On appelle de même, *Officier de fortune*, Un soldat devenu officier par son seul mérite. On dit proverbialement et figurément, que *Chacun est artisan de sa fortune*, pour dire, que, Généralement parlant, chacun peut se rendre heureux dans son état, que notre bonheur dépend de notre conduite. Et on dit proverbialement, *Busquer fortune*, pour dire, Chercher à faire fortune. On le dit aussi, pour dire, Chercher une bonne rencontre.

BONNE FORTUNE, se dit en termes de Galanterie, pour signifier, Les bonnes grâces d'une femme. [...]

FORTUNE, selon les Païens, étoit une Déesse qui faisoit le bonheur et le malheur, tous les bons et les mauvais succès. *Le Temple de la Fortune.* [...] Aujourd'hui que nous reconnais-

---

[17] *Dictionnaire de l'académie française*, 5ᵉ édition, vol. 1, An VII de la République, 605–607.

sons que la *Fortune* n'est rien par elle-même, on ne laisse pas néanmoins de se servir de la plupart des phrases dont les Anciens se servoient; et alors elles sont figurées. Ainsi on dit: *La Fortune est aveugle, inconstante, légère, variable, contraire, favorable, cruelle, bizarre, capricieuse, changeante, volage.* [...] *La Fortune lui rit. La Fortune lui en veut* ; ce qui se dit également en bonne et en mauvaise part. *La Fortune lui a tourné le dos. La Fortune élève les uns, abaisse les autres.* [...] On appelle Tous les grands changemens qui arrivent aux hommes ou aux Etats, et qui les élèvent ou les abaissent, *Des jeux, des coups, des caprices de la Fortune.* On dit figurém. et proverb. *Attacher un clou à la roue de la Fortune,* pour dire, Trouver un moyen de la fixer. On dit, *Adorer, encenser la Fortune, sacrifier à la Fortune,* pour dire, S'attacher à ceux qui sont en faveur, en crédit.

FORTUNE, EE. adject. Heureux. *Prince fortuné. Amans fortunés. Siècle fortuné.*

En 1832 le *Dictionnaire universel de la langue française (rédigé d'après le Dictionnaire de l'Académie),*[18] ne comprend toujours pas le sens de "riche" pour "fortuné". Heureux est donné comme son synonyme, avec cette précision: "*Heureux* se dit à l'égard de tous les genres de biens et de bonheur; *fortuné* désigne le bonheur singulier et des grâces signalées. On est *heureux* par les bienfaits de la nature; on est *fortuné* par les événements". Si l'adjectif "fortuné" est désormais bien ancré dans un sens positif, il désigne une abondance de bienfaits inattendus. On retrouve cela dans la définition proposée pour le mot "fortune" lui-même. Il signifie toujours en premier lieu "la suite des événements qui rendent les hommes heureux ou malheureux", puis "Bonheur.- Malheur, mauvais succès.- [...] Hasard. *Tenter fortune.- Bonne fortune,* faveur d'une personne du sexe, qu'on obtient par hasard.- Ce qui peut arriver de bien ou de mal à quelqu'un.- Biens, richesses, état d'opulence.- Charges, grades élevés, dignités, honneurs. *Homme de fortune, soldat de fortune* [...].- Divinité aveugle, bizarre et fantasque, qui, dans le système du paganisme, présidait à tous les événements, et distribuait les biens et les maux selon son caprice". On voit que la notion essentielle est celle de hasard, qui marque même désormais le succès amoureux "qu'on obtient par hasard" ce qui n'était pas le cas dans le *Dictionnaire de l'Académie* précédemment cité, par exemple. Si la richesse arrive au début du XIXe siècle avant les "charges, grades élevés" et autres "dignités", elle n'a pas encore prévalu complètement sur les autres significations.

---

[18] Nodier, Charles / Verger, Victor (eds.), *Dictionnaire universel de la langue française*, Paris 1832, 697.

3.2 Dans les images: Fortune et le pouvoir de l'argent

On sait que les dictionnaires sont en retard sur les usages effectifs des mots qu'ils recensent. Il faut donc se tourner vers les images, pour mieux mesurer cette assimilation progressive de la Fortune à la richesse, et en particulier à la richesse obtenue par hasard. On remarque d'abord, entre le XVIIe et le XVIIIe siècle, la place grandissante prise, parmi les cadeaux distribués par la déesse, des espèces sonnantes et trébuchantes qui ont tendance à prévaloir sur les couronnes et autres signes de dignité. Même si c'est un peu schématique et qu'il faudrait pousser l'investigation, cela me semble remarquable. On peut se demander si ce n'est pas du côté des Pays-Bas que ce trait est devenu prépondérant. Précocement, la gravure de Peter Warnersoen fait de la bourse déliée déversant ses écus la métonymie de la Fortune, l'enjeu de la roue.[19] En tout cas, dans la gravure populaire,[20] où Fortune est très présente, elle est de plus en plus liée au thème de l'argent et de ses méfaits sur la bonne marche de la société: on peut prendre pour exemple les apparitions de la déesse dans la collection Bertarelli[21]. Si la Fortune sert souvent à condamner ce pouvoir de l'argent, elle peut aussi permettre de célébrer les bienfaits de la prospérité. D'ailleurs, à la même période naît une représentation de la richesse, *Divitiae*, qui prend ses attributs de la Fortune.[22]

L'ascension et la chute de John Law dont la banque, après quelques mois de spéculation insensée, s'effondre en 1720 dans un crash qui marque longtemps les esprits, marque peut-être un tournant pour l'allégorie de la Fortune. Au niveau européen, la banqueroute de Law a suscité une grande production iconographique dans laquelle la Fortune tient le premier rôle. Elle y est associée aux valeurs monétaires décrédibilisées (le papier monnaie) et, plus traditionnellement, aux bulles symboles d'espoirs fragiles. Le vocabulaire contemporain

---

19 De Meyer, Maurits, *Stampe popolari dei Paesi Bassi*, Milan 1960–69, n°92: *Die Stat en Beloop der Werldt*, gravure sur bois, vers 1560, 355x218 mm, Amsterdam, Rijksmuseum, Prentenkabinet.
20 Comme le rappelle Maurits de Meyer, "il termine *populaire* indica in primo luogo la destinazione delle stampe in questione e non concerne che in via secondaria il carattere specifico di queste immagini", *ibid.*, 5.
21 Mori, Giovanna/Salsi, Claudio (eds.), *Rappresentazioni del destino. Immagini della vita e della morte dal XV al XIX secolo nelle stampe della Raccolta Bertarelli*, Milan 2001.
22 Vasselin, Martine, «Entre opulence et avarice, le cheminement périlleux des riches. Observations sur les thématiques liées à la richesse dans l'iconographie du XVIe siècle européen», dans Huchard, Cécile / Roig-Miranda (eds.), *Réalités et représentations de la richesse*, Nancy 2010, 11–50. Dans le même volume, Jacqueline Ferreras montre que la richesse évoque souvent davantage le patrimoine que le numéraire («Représentation de la richesse dans le dialogue humaniste espagnol», 93–120).

des crises boursières (la "bulle spéculative" et son "éclatement") est directement issu de ces variations sur l'allégorie de la Fortune. En particulier, en décembre 1720, un groupe d'éditeurs d'Amsterdam forme un recueil de textes et d'images qui ont circulé aux Pays-Bas pendant la période de gloire et depuis la chute du banquier écossais. Le volume, anonyme, s'intitule *Le Grand miroir de la folie (Het Groote tafereel der dvaasheid)*.[23] La page de titre proclame que ces pièces doivent servir à garder mémoire de la catastrophe financière et à en prévenir la tentation pour les générations futures, ce qui ne laisse pas de sonner

Fig. 2: Bernard Picart, Monument consacré à la postérité en mémoire de la folie incroyable de la XX. année du XVIII. siècle, engraving, 1720, London, Bibliothèque nationale de France, département Estampes et photographie, no. RESERVE FOL-QB-201 (89) – © Bibliothèque nationale de France.

étrangement en ce début du XXIe siècle. Le succès est énorme: trois versions de la première édition sont publiées en quelques semaines. Il y aura deux autres éditions dans les années suivantes et une dernière en 1780. Catherine Labio note que "le Miroir est un phénomène européen qui repose sur l'existence d'un

---

23 Voir: La très belle édition commentée: Goetzmann, William N. et al. (eds.), *The Great Mirror of Folly. Finance, culture and the Crash of 1720*, Londres/New Haven 2013.

marché européen de l'estampe satirique", d'ailleurs plusieurs planches sont bilingues. Beaucoup d'entre elles ont connu des versions pirates en Angleterre, en France, en Allemagne.[24] La plus célèbre des gravures du recueil est le *Monument consacré à la postérité en mémoire de la folie incroyable de la XX. année du XVIII. siecle*, par Bernard Picart, qui montre la Fortune des actions sur son char conduit par la Folie (fig. 2). Mais l'image de la roue de Fortune revient, comme le disent les auteurs de la récente réédition, tel un motif obsessionnel, dans tout le recueil.

On peut donc dire que dans ce premier tiers du XVIIIe siècle, la Fortune se trouve étroitement liée aux expériences financières et aux ascensions sociales plus ou moins condamnables qu'elles promettent. La dimension hasardeuse du profit est importante. Sans être du tout nouveau, ce lien entre Fortune et jeu de hasard devient un des usages essentiels de l'allégorie au siècle des Lumières. On va s'intéresser au cas particulier de l'image de la Fortune dans l'iconographie des loteries, qui se développent alors dans toute l'Europe et qui, comme la spéculation sur les actions de la compagnie du Mississippi, sont une innovation financière de la période.

3.3 Fortuna ludens: *jeu et loterie*

Fortune personnifie les espoirs d'enrichissement par la loterie, à la fois jeu et mode de circulation des biens qui connaît un succès sans précédent au XVIIe et plus encore au XVIIIe siècle. C'est son iconographie qui guide la mise en scène des loteries, surtout à partir de la fin du XVIIe siècle.[25] Auparavant, on remarque que, dans les peintures flamandes représentant des loteries de kermesses, le tirage ne se fait pas à partir d'une roue, mais dans des sacs ou des jarres.[26] Dans les affiches publicisant la tenue prochaine d'une loterie, on montre l'étagement des lots à gagner, les linéaires de vaisselles et autres biens, et non le tirage au

---

24 Labio, Catherine: "Staging folly in the Dutch Republic, England, and France", dans: William N. Goetzmann et al. (eds.): *The Great Mirror*, 145. Hogarth s'en inspire dans sa gravure *South Sea Scheme* (1721).

25 Voir: Loterie National (ed.): *Loteries en Europe. Cinq siècles d'histoire*, Bruxelles 1994, et, pour la France, Terrier, Max / Vanier, Henriette / Goineau, Fraçoise, *La Loterie racontée par l'image. Histoire abrégée des Blanques, Tontines et Loteries faites en France de 1539 à 1933 et propre à servir de guide à l'Exposition ouverte du mois de Mars au mois de Juin 1936 au Musée Carnavalet*, Paris 1936.

26 Par exemple le tableau d'après David Vinckboons (1576–1632), Kermesse de village, huile sur bois, 110x167 cm, Anvers, Koninklijk Museum voor Schone Kunsten, reproduit dans Muchembled, Robert, "La roue de fortune. Loteries et modernité en Europe du XVe au XVIIe siècle", dans: Loterie National (ed.): *Loteries en Europe*, 17–54.

sort ou le principe du sort. C'est le cas par exemple de l'affiche pour la loterie en faveur de la Bogaerdenschool à Bruges en 1574.[27]

Dans le courant du XVIIe et surtout au XVIIIe siècle, dans tous les pays européen est adopté le tambour de la roue de la Fortune pour le tirage. C'est l'image de la Fortune-Occasion dressée sur une roue (plutôt que sur une boule) qui va déterminer désormais la scénographie du tirage. Si l'on en croit les auteurs du catalogue de l'exposition du Musée des Arts et Traditions populaires consacrée aux jeux de hasard, en France, la roue de loterie proviendrait du

> jeu du tourniquet, attesté à partir du XVIIe, puis utilisé pour tirer les friandises par le colporteur, le marchand d'oublies, était probablement connu dès le XVe [...]. Le tourniquet comportait une aiguille de fer mobile dans un cercle portant chiffres ou divisions. Selon l'endroit où s'arrêtait l'aiguille, on était gagnant ou perdant. Malgré les similitudes de ce jeu avec nos actuelles roues de loterie, l'on aurait joué pendant plusieurs siècles au tourniquet, sans pour autant considérer qu'il symbolisait un attribut de la Fortune. Aussi, quand la roue de la loterie Saint-Roch est pour la première fois, le 10 novembre 1705, appelée "Fortune", ce n'est pas une pure coïncidence, mais en raison d'une évolution qui rend acceptable, voire évidente, la similitude de fonction entre roue de loterie et roue de fortune. A partir du XVIIIe, la parenté établie entre un jeu et un symbole renouvelle le répertoire des formes et des images associées à la fortune.[28]

En tout cas, il est certain que c'est la loterie royale de 1705 qui, en France, introduit une telle scénographie.[29] Ce sont toujours des enfants qui officient. Ils tirent deux billets de deux roues distinctes: l'un portant le nom du gagnant, extrait de la plus grande roue et l'autre tiré de la plus petite, indiquant le lot gagné. On adopte par la suite le principe de la loterie génoise, où les joueurs misent sur des numéros compris entre 1 et 90.[30] Un point intéressant est que les frontispices des arrêts du conseil d'Etat sur la création ou la suppression des

---

[27] Gravure sur bois coloriée, d'après un dessin de Pierre Pourbus (1571), 27,5x38 cm, Bruges, Stedelijk Museum.

[28] Monestier, Alain et al. (eds.): *Les clefs de la Fortune*, Les dossiers du Musée des ATP, exposition 6 mai–15 juin 1987, Paris 1987, 85. Dans le catalogue de l'exposition *La Loterie racontée par l'image*, 16, les auteurs rappellent que les Almanachs de 1701 et 1706 montrent le tirage de la loterie de Saint-Roch à l'Hôtel de Ville sont "la plus ancienne représentation des 'roues de fortune' qui viennent de remplacer les sacs de cuir ou les boîtes, et qui permettaient de mieux mêler les billets. Deux 'enfants bleus' tirent, l'un de la petite roue le billet indiquant un lot, l'autre, de la grande, le billet du gagnant".

[29] Sur les loteries d'Etat, voir: Legay, Marie-Laure, *Loteries royales dans l'Europe des Lumières 1680–1815*, Lille 2014.

[30] Dans le même catalogue figure une gravure, "Mr Courtaud ou la Mauvaise Avanture", publiée à Paris, chez Noël Frères (taille douce, fin XVIIIe siècle) où l'on voit une enseigne dédiée à la bonne Fortune. Elle montre que l'association de la Fortune et de la loterie se trouvait aussi dans les jeux de foire, *ibid.* 88.

loteries ne mettent jamais en scène l'allégorie de la Fortune mais soit les armes de France, soit surtout une personnification de la loterie elle-même qui,

Tandis qu'au mouvement d'une Roüe agitée,
Cinq nombres incertains agitent mille cœurs,
FRANCE, des coups du fort ne fois point affectée;
LOUIS, à tes besoins consacre ses faveurs.

Fig. 3: Bernard Picart, Institution de la loterie royale par Louis XVI, en 1776, engraving, 1776, Bibliothèque nationale de France, département Estampes et photographie, no. RESERVE FOL-QB-201 (110) – © Bibliothèque nationale de France.

puissance redistributrice, prend de l'argent d'un côté pour le mettre ailleurs, avec l'œil de la raison sur le cœur. On y trouve aussi un Amour ailé au milieu des sacs d'or, tenant la balance de la Justice, comme on le voit sur l'arrêt du Conseil portant création de la loterie royale de 1776.[31] Pourtant, dans une gravure de réclame, cette même création est célébrée par une image de la Fortune proche du *Monument à la postérité* de Picart, avec l'inscription : "Tandis qu'au mouvement d'une roue agitée/ Cinq nombres incertains agitent mille cœurs/ FRANCE, des coups du sort ne sois point affectée/ LOUIS à tes besoins consacre ses faveurs" (fig. 3). On retrouve, dans ce contexte nouveau du jeu patronné par l'Etat, un vieux thème, très en faveur à la Renaissance, mais tiré de l'Antiquité impériale, du prince lui-même Fortune de son peuple.[32]

4 De Fortune à la fortune

Pour Yves Giraud, cette roue de Fortune devenue, au XVIIIe siècle, roue de loterie est le signe de l'épuisement du potentiel signifiant de la figure:

> Dès lors, l'image de la Fortune pâlit et dégénère. Elle avait servi bien des fois, dès le Moyen Age, aux oracles, divinations et prédictions. Elle va présider désormais aux loteries, s'étaler dans les tarots, patronner les jeux d'argent, de l'entreprise de Law aux casinos modernes. Littérairement, le sujet semble presque épuisé et les auteurs qui s'y attachent ne répètent que des lieux communs.[33]

C'est oublier que les jeux de hasard, auxquels elle n'a d'ailleurs jamais cessé d'être liée, occupent une place moins marginale, moins frivole et anecdotique qu'il n'y paraît dans la culture des XVIIe –XVIIIe siècles. En effet, les historiens ont montré que la loterie, comme le papier monnaie ou les actions, fait partie de ces techniques financières inventées alors et qui ont permis l'accumulation de capital et l'investissement (privé et surtout public). Comme la spéculation, la loterie contribue à bouleverser les hiérarchies sociales traditionnelles fondées sur le statut de la personne, l'état (ou ordre) pour lui adjoindre (sinon lui substituer) une hiérarchie fondée sur l'argent.[34] L'argent en effet, "devient un person-

---

31 Par exemple, *Arrêt du Conseil d'Etat portant suppression des loteries de l'Ecole royale militaire, de l'hôtel de ville de Paris [...] et création d'une nouvelle loterie sous le nom de loterie royale de France, 30 juin 1776.*
32 Buttay, *Fortuna*, 167–230.
33 Giraud, Yves dans *Fortune*. Catalogue d'exposition cité, 80.
34 Comme le souligne Robert Muchembled, la loterie "permet des enrichissements que la morale religieuse classique réprouve", 42.

nage de premier plan à l'époque moderne". Il est même, selon Marie Legay, "une des forces génératrices de la modernité". Il devient progressivement le "grand ordonnateur de la vie sociale".[35] Les loteries se multiplient dans toute l'Europe au XVIIIe siècle. Les emprunts-loteries de la monarchie française deviennent de plus en plus fréquents dans la deuxième moitié du siècle: on songe à ceux de Necker, en 1777, restés célèbres. Ceci fait dire à Marie Legay que, "s'il est une institution qui caractérise le siècle des Lumières, c'est bien la loterie royale, qui s'est imposée à cette époque dans toutes les capitales européennes". Il s'agit de la "création d'un instrument financier permanent qui, pour devenir bénéficiaire, dut combiner tout à la fois la science mathématique et la publicité pour atteindre le plus grand nombre [...]. La loterie royale fut, avec la banque, le premier instrument de gestion publique installé dans les régimes politiques anciens".[36] Fortune est donc utilisée pour désigner une réalité économique et financière qui est un marqueur fort des transformations de la société telle qu'elle se dessine avant la Révolution.

D'ailleurs, à lire l'abondante littérature morale sur les loteries et les jeux de hasard parue entre la fin du XVIIe et la première moitié du XVIIIe siècle, il semble que l'enjeu ait été moral, philosophique, voire théologique, autant que social et économique. Le débat sur le libre arbitre n'a jamais été aussi fort au début du XVIIIe siècle.[37] La question du hasard, de la possible absence de causalité, est alors tout aussi décisive pour la théologie que pour les sciences.[38] Dans ce contexte, les jeux de hasard, et singulièrement la loterie, font l'objet d'un examen attentif par les moralistes et les théologiens. En principe les jeux de hasard sont condamnés par les Eglises: provoquer le sort revient à bafouer le Créateur, interrogé en vain.[39] Cependant, des moralistes prennent la plume pour défendre un "bon usage" des loteries. Ainsi le pasteur suisse Jean Leclerc dans ses *Réflexions sur ce qu'on appelle bonheur et malheur en matières de loteries et sur le bon usage qu'on en peut faire* (1696) qui les trouve utiles quand le

---

35 Legay, Marie-Laure, *Histoire de l'argent à l'époque moderne: de la Renaissance à la Révolution*, Paris 2014, 5–7.

36 Legay, Marie-Laure, *Loteries royales*, 9–10.

37 Ehrard, Jean, *L'idée de nature*, 661: "Vers 1715, le vieux problème théologique du libre-arbitre divise plus que jamais la pensée chrétienne. Il faut se résoudre soit à rendre l'homme responsable de ses actes, quitte à rogner la toute puissance de Dieu, soit à proclamer le néant de la créature au risque de rejeter sur l'auteur de l'univers la repsonsabilité du péché".

38 Ceccarelli, Giovanni, *Il gioco e il peccato. Economia e rischio nel Tardo Medioevo*, Mulino 2003, rappelle que dès le Moyen Age "le jeu de hasard le plus simple et commun, le jeu de dés, a offert à la théologie et au droit un champ dans lequel discuter les rapports entre phénomènes casuels et économie".

39 Dunkley, John, *Gambling: A Social and Moral Problem in France 1685–1792*, Oxford 1985, 101: "Theology: gambling as profanation".

profit revient aux pauvres, ou encore Le Père Ménestrier, célèbre emblématiste jésuite, qui propose en 1700 une *Dissertation des loteries*[40] dans laquelle il distingue des sorts licites et illicites, selon la condition des personnes. Il considère la loterie comme une forme de contrat, ce qui sera âprement débattu. La discussion porte autant sur la nature des jeux de hasard que sur leur licéité. Le cœur est toujours la discussion de la Providence et des modes d'intervention de Dieu dans le monde.[41]

L'aube du XVIIIe siècle est particulièrement riche en réflexions sur ce thème, mais les publications continuent par la suite. Pierre de Joncourt, dans ses *Quatre lettres sur les jeux de hazard* (1712), s'insurge contre toute tentative de légitimation de la loterie. En 1742, c'est au tour de Christophe Coudrette, un janséniste français, de répondre à ceux qui croient possible un accommodement moral avec les jeux de hasard et au protestant italien Gregorio Leti (1630–1701), qui partait du principe, dans sa *Critique historique, politique, morale, économique et comique sur les lotteries anciennes et modernes*[42] que le monde entier n'est qu'une loterie: "tout le monde y joue, tout le monde en espère beaucoup".[43] Coudrette écrit donc sous le couvert de l'anonymat une *Dissertation théologique sur les loteries*.[44] Il a été poussé à l'écrire face à ce qu'il appelle ce "débordement de loteries" qui caractérise son époque.[45] Ce dernier est très inquiétant parce qu'il bouleverse la hiérarchie sociale:

> D'un côté tant de familles réduites à la pauvreté, deviennent à charge de la République. [...] D'un autre côté, ces hommes tirés de la poussière & qui ont englouti la subsistance de tant de personnes, vont se placer dans la Noblesse. Leur argent seul, & non le mérite, les élève à des charges & à des emplois qui demandent des talents & des sentimens, qu'on ne reçoit ordinairement que par une éducation honnête. Ils portent dans ces places des moeurs étrangères. Qui pourroit exprimer combien est grande la corruption que ce bouleversement des Etats a coutume d'introduire dans un Royaume?[46]

---

[40] Ménestrier, Claude-François, *Dissertation des lotteries*, Lyon 1700.

[41] Dunkley, John, *Gambling*, 218, conclut de son parcours dans les débats passionnés sur les jeux de hasard: "we saw to what degree thinking about gambling in all its aspects could polarise attitudes between Catholics and Protestants, between Frenchmen in France and religious refugees, and between different shades of protestantism".

[42] De Joncourt, Pierre, *Quatre lettres sur les jeux de hazard*, Amsterdam 1697. Ce polémiste est aussi bien l'auteur d'un panéyrique de Louis XIV (*La Fama gelosa della Fortuna*, Gex, chez l'auteur, 1680) que d'un pamphlet intitulé *Le Puttanisme de Rome* (*Il puttanismo romano, o vero Conclave generale della Corte per l'elettione del nuovo pontefice*, s.l., 1668).

[43] Voir: Bernard, Bruno, "Aspects moraux et sociaux des loteries", dans: Loterie National (ed.), *Loteries en Europe*, 64–65.

[44] Coudrette, Christophe, *Dissertation théologique sur les loteries*, s. l. 1742 (exemplaire consulté: BnF, Arsenal, 8-T-5263).

[45] *Ibid.*, préface.

Dans son chapitre XIV, Coudrette s'attaque à la "Notion des termes de sort, hazard & de fortune". Et il va montrer que "la Loterie est pour une infinité de gens une occasion de superstition et un reste d'idolatrie".[47] En effet, elle pousse les hommes à l'oubli de la Providence.

> Rien n'est plus propre à fomenter cette sorte de Paganisme, que les jeux de hazard & la Loterie en particulier. L'inconstance & la vicissitude qui y régnent, & font passer subitement & alternativement du gain à la perte, répondent parfaitement à la peinture, que les Payens faisoient de la Fortune. Tout le monde sait qu'ils la représentoient ordinairement sous la forme d'une femme aveugle & chauve qui se tenoit debout sur une rouë avec deux aîles au pied. Comme à ces jeux ni le travail, ni l'industrie n'ont aucune part, & qu'on n'apperçoit pas la cause qui fait passer l'argent à celui qui gagne, on soustrait aisément ces événemens à la Divine Providence pour les attribuer à une prétenduë Divinité qui favorise aveuglément & par caprice l'un plûtôt que l'autre. Qu'on jette les yeux sur les Listes des gagnans à la Loterie, on appercevra qu'elles sont pleines de dédicaces à la Fortune: si on pouvoit lire toutes les devises des perdans, on en verroit encore bien plus d'exemples. Presque par tout on ne découvre que des pratiques superstitieuses de la part de ceux qui mettent à la Loterie.[48]

On retrouve donc dans ces ouvrages sur la nature et la légitimité des tirages au sort la Fortune comme outil pour penser et discuter la Providence, la place respective de l'action de Dieu et des hommes dans les événements, rôle dans lequel elle nous semblait s'être quelque peu effacée au profit de la Nature. Il faut dire que la Fortune a toujours été plutôt que employée dans la littérature morale que dans les textes strictement théologiques ou philosophiques.

5 Conclusion

Cette communication a cherché à présenter des remarques et des pistes qu'il faudrait suivre plus attentivement, en distinguant mieux les temps et surtout les lieux. On s'est donné de manière un peu ambitieuse, et sans doute imprudente, le droit de regarder des productions venant de toute l'Europe, dans un voyage de plus de deux siècles. Il conviendrait de les contextualiser davantage. Cependant, il me semble que ce coup d'œil, certes rapide, montre bien la difficulté de poser la pierre tombale de l'allégorie de la Fortune une fois pour toutes. Je crois que cela tient à ce que je montrai pour une période antérieure: Fortune n'est pas un concept, dont le contenu pourrait se périmer, ou ne plus correspon-

---
46 *Ibid.*, 43–44
47 *Ibid.*, 235.
48 *Ibid.*, 233–234.

dre à un état de la société, de la littérature ou de la pensée philosophique. Elle est d'abord et avant tout une forme, dont on se sert pour parler du monde des hommes et des lois que le régissent. Comme les hiérarchies sociales évoluent, comme la conception de la causalité ou de l'absence de causalité se transforme, Fortune est utilisée dans des contextes différents et assume différents visages. En quelque sorte, Fortune ne peut pas mourir puisque Fortune, en elle-même, n'existe pas. Si le mot a disparu du langage philosophique, c'est sûrement parce qu'il n'avait rien de précis, c'est justement parce qu'il manquait de *sens propre*, parce qu'il peinait à être un concept. Mais surtout, si l'image de la déesse a fini

Fig. 4: Jean Dratz, On saisit la Fortune par les cheveux, lithography, 1935, Brussels, Collection Loterie Nationale – © Musée de la Loterie, Brussels.

par s'affaiblir, quoiqu'on la retrouve jusque dans les années 1930 dans les publicités pour la loterie nationale, en Belgique par exemple (fig. 4),[49] c'est parce que, pour parler du monde et des vicissitudes des hommes, on s'est définitivement éloigné du vocabulaire antique, mais aussi chrétien. Fortune était indissociable de ce vocabulaire, indissociable de la question de la Providence, qu'elle se confonde avec elle ou qu'elle s'y oppose, qu'elle la serve ou qu'elle la nie. Elle était liée à une société moderne «pas encore capitaliste, dont les fondements juridiques et idéologiques renvoient à un ordre divin», comme la caractérise Marie-Laure Legay.[50] Le mot "fortune" en revanche ne disparaît pas, au contraire: en français, il est devenu le nom commun de la richesse accumulée, objectif premier (voire unique) de l'activité économique en général et de l'ambition des individus en particulier, dans une société matérialiste. L'éloignement de la référence à Dieu, et au Dieu chrétien en particulier, emporte avec lui Dame Fortune, sa Ministre, son adversaire, son scandale.

---

[49] Dratz, Jean, *On saisit la Fortune par les cheveux*, lithographie, Bruxelles, Archives de la Loterie nationale.
[50] Legay, Marie-Laure, *Histoire de l'argent*, 59.

List of Illustrations

Florence Buttay: La Fortune victime des Lumières ? Remarques sur les transformations de Fortune aux XVIIe et XVIIIe siècles

Figure 1:   Semina fortunae geminat cum tempore virtus, engraving in Manuel Román Valerón, *Tractatus de transactionibus [...] nunc primum in lucem prodit*, Lyon 1665, frontispiece – © Bibliothèque nationale de France.

Figure 2:   Bernard Picart, Monument consacré à la postérité en mémoire de la folie incroyable de la XX. année du XVIII. siècle, engraving, 1720, London, Bibliothèque nationale de France, département Estampes et photographie, no. RESERVE FOL-QB-201 (89) – © Bibliothèque nationale de France.

Figure 3:   Bernard Picart, Institution de la loterie royale par Louis XVI, en 1776, engraving, 1776, Bibliothèque nationale de France, département Estampes et photographie, no. RESERVE FOL-QB-201 (110) – © Bibliothèque nationale de France.

Figure 4:   Jean Dratz, On saisit la Fortune par les cheveux, lithography, 1935, Brussels, Collection Loterie Nationale – © Musée de la Loterie, Brussels.

José M. González García: Fortuna in Seventeenth Century Spain. Literature, Politics and the Visual Arts

Figure 1:   Bernhard Strigel, Portrait of Emperor Maximilian and his Family, oil on lime, after 1515, Kunsthistorisches Museum Vienna, no. GG_832 – © Austrian Archives/ Scala Florence.

Figure 2:   On the right, Prince Charles spins the wheel of fortune in his entrance into the city of Bruges, engraving in Remy Du Puys, *Recueil de chroniques, chartes et autres documents concernant l'histoire et les antiquités de la Flandre-Occidentale. 3,6*, Brussels 1515 (reprint Brussels 1850), after p. 54 – © Private.

Figure 3:   Prince Charles, The Virtues (Prudence, Justice, Fortitude and Temperance) and Fortune, engraving in Remy Du Puys, *Recueil de chroniques, chartes et autres documents concernant l'histoire et les antiquités de la Flandre-Occidentale. 3,6*, Brussels 1515 (reprint Brussels 1850), before p. 33 – © Private.

Figure 4:   Pieter van Aelst, central section of the tapestry *La Fortuna*, ca. 1520. Museo de Tapices del Palacio Real de La Granja de San Ildefonso, Segovia, no. 10026276 – © Patrimonio Nacional, Madrid.

Figure 5:   Maior quam cui possit Fortuna nocere, engraving in Sebastián de Covarrubias, *Moral Emblems*, Madrid 1610, nr. 65 – © Fundación Universitaria Española.

Figure 6:   Fortuna in the iconographic programme of the Palacio del Marqués de Santa Cruz, en Viso del Marqués, Ciudad Real, fresco painted between 1576 and 1586 – © Photo by the author.

Figure 7:   Peter Paul Rubens, Fortuna, oil on canvas, 1636–37, Madrid, Museo del Prado, no. P01674 – © Museo Nacional del Prado.

Figure 8:   In contraria ducet, engraving in Diego de Saavedra Fajardo, *Empresas políticas*, [Milan 1642] – © Editorial Planeta.

Jürgen Müller / Bettina Gruber: Fortuna Revalued. On the Goddess's Sexualisation in the Renaissance

Figure 1: Lady Fortune hands a never empty purse to Fortunatus, woodcut, *Fortunatus*, Augsburg 1509, fol. 23^v – © Bayerische Staatsbibliothek München.

Figure 2: Rise and Fall of the Three Donkeys, woodcut in Sebastian Brant, *Das Narrenschiff*, Basel 1494, fol. 46^v – © Bayerische Staatsbibliothek München.

Figure 3: Leonardo da Vinci, A study for a winged figure, Allegory with Fortune, pen and brown ink, with brown wash, ca. 1480–1485, British Museum, no. 1895,0915.482 – © Trustees of the British Museum.

Figure 4: Mantegna (School), Occasio and Poenitentia, fresco, ca. 1500, Mantua, Museo della Città di Palazzo San Sebastiano – © Museo della Città di Palazzo San Sebastiano, Mantua.

Figure 5: Nicoletto da Modena, Fortune, engraving, 1500–1510, British Museum, no. 1873,0809.695 – © Trustees of the British Museum.

Figure 6: Dirck Vellert, Venus sailing in a scallop shell, engraving and etching, 1524, British Museum, no. E,1.273 – © Trustees of the British Museum.

Figure 7: Albrecht Altdorfer, Fortune, engraving, 1511, British Museum, no. 1863,1114.757 – © Trustees of the British Museum.

Figure 8: Hans Holbein, Fortune and a fool, pen and black ink drawing in *Erasmi Roterdami encomium moriae [...]*, Basel 1515, Kupferstichkabinett, no. 1662.166, fol. S2^v – © Kupferstichkabinett, Basel.

Figure 9: Frontispiece of Carolus Bovillus, Liber de Sapiente, woodcut in Carolus Bovillus, *Que hoc volumina continentur [...]*, Paris 1510, fol. 116^v – © Bayerische Staatsbibliothek München.

Figure 10: Urs Graf, Title-Border with the Triumph of Humanitas, woodcut in Erasmus, *Germaniae decoris, Adagiorum Chiliades tres ac centuriae fere totidem*, Basel 1513 – © Bayerische Staatsbibliothek München.

Figure 11: Urs Graf, Fortune as a prostitute, pen and black ink drawing, ca. 1520, Germanisches Nationalmuseum, Graphische Sammlung, no. Hz 160 – © Germanisches Nationalmuseum, Nuremberg.

Figure 12: Albrecht Dürer, Nemesis (Large Fortune), engraving, 1502, British Museum, no. 1895,0915.346 – © Trustees of the British Museum.

Figure 13: Heinrich Aldegrever, Fortune, 1555, engraving, British Museum, no. 1850,0810.279 – © Trustees of the British Museum.

Figure 14: Marcantonio Raimondi (after Raphael), Galatea, engraving, 1515–1520, British Museum, no. 1980,U.1606 – © Trustees of the British Museum.

Figure 15: Urs Graf, Prostitute washing her leg, etching, 1513, Kupferstichkabinett, no. X.2293 – © Kupferstichkabinett, Basel.

Figure 16: Urs Graf, Foolish Virgin, pen and black ink drawing, 1513, Kupferstichkabinett, no. U.X.46 – © Kupferstichkabinett, Basel.

Figure 17: Urs Graf, Swiss mercenary and prostitute, pen and black ink drawing, ca. 1516, Städel, no. 15673 – © Städel Museum, Frankfurt am Main.

Figure 18: Urs Graf, Prostitute distributing money, pen drawing, 1517, Kupferstichkabinett, no. U.X.80 – © Kupferstichkabinett, Basel.

Franziska Rehlinghaus: Farewell to Fortuna – Turning towards Fatum. The Transformation of Fate Conceptions in the Seventeenth and Eighteenth Centuries

Figure 1:   Deß Römischen Reichs Grosse Welt Uhr, engraving, ca. 1630, SLUB Dresden, no. Hist.Germ.C.16,misc.23 – © SLUB Dresden, http://digital.slub-dresden.de/id334169194.

Figure 2:   Fata obstant, engraving in Octavius de Strada, *Symbola varia Diversorum Principum Sacrosanc Ecclesiae & Sacri Imperii Romani*, Vol. 2, plate 49, 1652 – © Herzog August Bibliothek Wolfenbüttel.

Figure 3:   Engraving in Robert Recorde, *The castle of knowledge*, London 1556, frontispiece – © The Bodleian Libraries, The University of Oxford, K 4.8 Art.

Figure 4:   Engraving in Karl Ferdinand Hommel [Alexander von Joch], *Über Belohnung und Strafe nach türkischen Gesezen*, Leipzig 1772, frontispiece – © Bayerische Staatsbibliothek München, http://www.mdz-nbn-resolving.de/urn/resolver.pl?urn=urn:nbn:de:bvb:12-bsb10040897-0.

Susanne Reichlin: The Relationship between Regularity and Irregularity in Middle High German Poems on Fortune

Figure 1:   Wheel of fortune, pen drawing, 11th century, Archivio Storico di Montecassino, codex 189, fol. 73^r – © Archivio Storico di Montecassino.

Figure 2:   Wheel of fortune, pen drawing, 11th century, Archivio Storico di Montecassino, codex 189, fol. 73^v – © Archivio Storico di Montecassino.

Kristiina Savin: Fortuna in Early Modern Sweden. The Heyday and Decline of a Commonplace Concept

Figure 1:   Albertus Pictor, Wheel of Fortune, wall painting in Härkeberga church, Uppland – © Photo: Bengt A. Lundberg, Riksantikvarieämbetet.

Peter Vogt: The Death of Fortuna and the Rise of Modernity. Prolegomena to any Future Theory of Modernity

Figure 1:   Jost Amman, Eigentliche Abbildung deß ganzen Gewerbs der löblichen Kaufmannschaft samt etlich der nahmhafft und fürnehmsten Handelstädt, woodcut, 1585, Germanisches Nationalmuseum, no. GM-26471-1292 – © Germanisches Nationalmuseum, Nuremberg.

Figure 2:   Jan Harmenszoon Muller, Fortuna verdeelt haar geschenken, engraving, 1590, Amsterdam, Rijksmuseum, no. RP-P-OB-32.213A, RP-P-OB-32.213B – © Rijksmuseum, Amsterdam.

Figure 3:   Utriusque Crepundia Merces, engraving in Francis Quarles, *Emblemes*, 1635, p. 40 – © Penn State University Libraries, Philadelphia.

Figure 4:   Tugendt und Laster Kampff, etching, 1631, Bayerische Staatsbibliothek München, no. Einbl. XI,50 – © Bayerische Staatsbibliothek München.

Figure 5:   Deß Römischen Reichs Grosse Welt Uhr, engraving, ca. 1630, SLUB Dresden, no. Hist.Germ.C.16,misc.23 – © SLUB Dresden, http://digital.slub-dresden.de/id334169194.

Burkhardt Wolf: Fortuna's Sea Change. Renaissance Poetics of Contingency
Figure 1: Fortune's ship, engraving, 1466, British Museum, no. 1845,0825.488 – © British Museum.
Figure 2: Nicoletto da Modena, Fortuna, engraving, 1506, Albertina, no. DG1942/56 – © Albertina, Vienna.
Figure 3: Bernardo Falconi, Fortuna di mare, bronze statue, 1678, Venice – © Photo: Franz Huber/ Florian Runschke.

Index of Persons

Alain de Lille 115
Albert VII, Archduke of Austria 72
Alberti, Leon Battista 4, 50, 57
Albizzi, Piero degli 118
Albrecht von Johansdorf 43
Alciati, Andrea 128
Aldegrever, Heinrich 100
Alexander the Great 73
Alfonso d'Este, Duke of Ferrara 87
Alfonso V (of Aragon) 4
Altdorfer, Albrecht 92–93
Amman, Jost 129–131
Anarcharsis 47
Andersson, Christiane 84, 96
Aphthonius of Antioch 185
Appuhn-Radtke, Sibylle 85
Ariosto, Ludovico 138
Aristotle 48–50, 60–61, 66, 138, 149, 179, 182
Arnauld, Antoine 149
Ausonius, Decimus Magnus 90
Bacon, Francis 144
Baronio, Cesare 67
Bazán, Alonso de 119
Bazán, Álvaro de, Marqués de Santa Cruz 119
Beck, Ulrich 148
Bellarmino, Roberto 67
Bellenger, Yvonne 140
Bellini, Giovanni 90
Bernger von Horheim 44
Beyerlinck, Laurentius 9
Blumenberg, Hans 151
Boccaccio, Giovanni 4, 55–56
Bocchi, Achille 83
Boethius, Anicius Manlius Severinus 1, 15–16, 18–20, 28, 34–36, 40, 48–49, 60, 68, 126, 150, 152–155, 160–161, 173, 176–177, 179
Borromeo, Carlo 181
Bouwsma, William 125, 141, 145
Bovelles, Charles de (Carolus Bovillus) 95
Boyle, Robert 194
Brant, Sebastian 84, 88–89, 155

Brébiette, Pierre 193
Bridget of Sweden 177
Bruder Wernher 37–38
Bruno, Giordano 87
Brunschvicg, Léon 140
Buonarroti, Michelangelo di see Michelangelo
Burckhardt, Jacob 3, 63–64, 85
Burman, Lars 188
Calderón de la Barca, Pedro 6, 108–109
Calvete de Estrella, Juan Cristóbal 110
Cantarini, Simone 132
Cassirer, Ernst 87–88
Castiglione, Baldassare 144
Cervantes de Salazar, Francisco 117
Cervantes Saavedra, Miguel de 12, 108, 123–124
Charles V 11, 110, 115, 117–118
Checa Cremades, Fernando 110, 112
Cicero, Marcus Tullius 2, 48, 50, 64, 88, 96, 144, 185
Coecke van Aelst, Pieter 114, 116
Cooper, Thomas 64
Coriolano, Bartolomeo 132
Corneille, Pierre 143
Cortés, Hernán 117–118
Coudrette, Christophe 206–207
Covarrubias, Sebastián de 118–119
Coverdale, Myles 180
Cuyk, van Hendrik 67
Dante, Alighieri 3, 49–50, 61, 194
Dasypodius, Petrus 154
Dauzat, Albert 196
De Landtsheer, Jeanine 69, 71–72, 77–78, 80
Dekker, Thomas 57
Delmarcel, Guy 114–115
Delrio, Martin 70
Demosthenes 96
Descartes, René 6, 139–140, 163, 165, 167, 183
Dewey, John 139, 173
Diderot, Denis 195
Dietmar der Setzer 23, 25

Index of Persons

Diogenes Laërtius 47
Dippel, Johann Conrad 166–167
Donne, John 144
Doria, Andrea 119
Dratz, Jean 208–209
du Puys, Remy 112
Dubois, Jean 196
Dunkley, John 205–206
Dürer, Albrecht 85, 99–100, 104–106, 155
d'Anlézy, Imbert 193
Ebelmann, Johannes 194
Elizabeth I 65
Elliott, John H. 117–118
Erasmus of Rotterdam 64, 71, 75, 85, 94–97
Faber, Basil 155
Fajardo Saavedra, Diego de 122–123
Falconi, Bernardo 11, 53–54
Febvre, Lucien 142
Ferdinand I 110
Fleming, Paul 6, 127
Fludd, Robert 194
Forsius, Sigfrid Aron 179
Foucault, Michel 143
Frauenlob (Henry of Meissen) 30
Frederick William I (of Prussia) 170
Freud, Sigmund 58
Friedrich, Hugo 140
Friedrich, Susanne 14
Fries, Johannes 154
Galilei, Galileo 6, 139
Gellert, Christian Fürchtegott 171
Giddens, Anthony 12, 175
Gilbert, Felix 5, 126, 143–144
Giraud, Yves 13, 193, 204
Goclenius, Rudolph (the Elder) 162
Gorski, Philip 146
Gottfried von Straßburg 30, 35–36
Gracián, Baltasar 109, 127, 138, 150
Graf, Urs 11, 84, 96–98, 100–106
Gregory IX (Pope) 54
Grimm, Jacob und Wilhelm 85
Gryphius, Andreas 127, 138, 150
Guicciardini, Francesco 5, 126
Gustav II Adolf 137
Hacking, Ian 148–149
Hadot, Pierre 194, 196
Hafenreffer, Matthias 182

Hannibal 73
Haydn, Hiram 144
Heinrich von dem Türlin 16, 29, 39
Heinrich von Morungen 43–44
Hellerstedt, Andreas 183
Herckmans, Elias 129
Herrad of Landsberg 88
Hesiod 11, 47, 93
Hobbes, Thomas 164, 167
Hofmannswaldau, Christian Hoffmann von 127
Hogarth, William 134, 201
Holbein, Hans (the Younger) 94–95
Homer 47, 96
Hommel, Karl Ferdinand 172
Horn, Agneta 183–184
Horsch, Leonard 14
Huber, Franz 14, 53
Hus, Jan 84
Isabella (of Portugal) 114
Jago, Kerry 14
Johann von Ringgenberg 25, 27, 36, 38
Joncourt, Pierre de 206
Kant, Immanuel 152, 170
Kelin 40–42, 44
Kiefer, Frederick 16–17, 33, 193–194
Kirchner, Gottfried 9, 83, 151, 156–157
Kittsteiner, Heinz Dieter 152, 174
Koerner, Joseph Leo 85, 129
Koselleck, Reinhart 84
Labio, Catherine 200–201
Lactantius 48
Laelius Peregrinus 67
Lange, Joachim 169–170
Law, John 199, 204
Leclerc, Jean 205
Legay, Marie-Laure 202, 205, 209
Leibniz, Gottfried Wilhelm 153, 167, 173
Leonardo da Vinci 9, 90
Lessius, Leonardus 70
Leti, Gregorio 206
Leyva, Alonso de 119
Lipsius, Justus 6, 11, 63–81, 146, 150, 153, 160–163, 182
Livy 73–74
Louis II (of Hungary) 79
Louis XVI (of France) 203, 206

Ludwig II (of Hungary) 110
Luhmann, Niklas 83
Lundebergius, Josephus 184, 186
Luther, Martin 85, 180, 189
Maaler, Josua 154
Machiavelli, Niccolò 4–5, 8–9, 50, 58, 72, 84, 114, 118, 126, 138, 144
Magirus, Johannes 179, 183
Makropoulos, Michael 82
Malebranche, Nicolas 167
Manrique, Jorge 108
Mantegna, Andrea 90–91
Manuel I (of Portugal) 78
Maravall, José Antonio 127
Marguerite de Navarre 142
Marlowe, Christopher 6
Mathias von Linköping 176, 183
Maximilian I (emperor) 109–111
Medici, Nannina de' 51
Meissner 35, 42, 44
Mena, Juan de 108
Menander 138
Ménestrier, Claude-François 206
Meyer, Maurits de 199
Michelangelo 85
Micraelius, Johannes 162
Mitterand, Henri 196
Modena, Nicoletto da 52, 91–93
Montaigne, Michel de 140, 181
Mopsus (Lipsius' dog) 81
Mousnier, Roland 143
Muchembled, Robert 201, 204
Muller, Jan Harmenszoon 132–133
Needham, Linda 14
Neuhoff, Bettina 14
Newton, Isaac 165
Nicole, Pierre 149
Nilsson Hammar, Anna 189
Notker 28
Nussbaum, Martha 141
Oestreich, Gerhard 72–73, 146
Ong, Walter J. 185, 188
Opitz, Martin 6, 127
Ovid 20, 118
Pacioli, Luca 57
Panofsky, Erwin 31, 131
Paruta, Paolo 145

Pascal, Blaise 6, 139–140, 149
Petrarca, Francesco 3
Philip I (of Spain, the Fair) 110
Philip II (king of Spain) 69
Philip II (of Spain) 68, 71, 78–79, 114, 119
Philip VI (of Spain) 120
Picart, Bernard 134, 200–201, 203–204
Piccolomini, Enea Silvio 4
Pickering, Frederick P. 16, 18, 37, 137
Pico della Mirandola, Giovanni 85
Pictor, Albertus 178
Pindar 47, 93, 138
Plato 75
Poiret, Pierre 166
Polybius 71, 80
Pompey, Sextus 77
Pontano, Giovanni 56, 65, 138
Pötscher, Walter 154
Pourbus, Pieter 202
Quarles, Francis 133–134, 213
Quevedo, Francisco de 6, 109, 127
Rabb, Theodore K. 142–143
Racine, Jean 143
Raimondi, Marcantonio 101
Raphael 101, 103, 106
Recorde, Robert 158
Reichert, Klaus 51, 59, 61, 159
Reinmar von Hagenau 43
Reinmar von Zweter 25, 34–36
Rembrandt, Harmenszoon van Rijn 127, 129, 138
Reni, Guido 127–128, 132, 138, 192–193
Ripa, Cesare 128
Rojas, Fernando de 108, 117
Rollenhagen, Gabriel 128
Román Valerón, Manuel 194
Rota, Martino 16, 18–19, 23–25, 40, 135, 156
Rubens, Peter Paul 81, 121
Rubens, Philip 81
Rucellai, Bernardo 51
Rudolf von Ems 16, 29, 35, 64
Runschke, Florian 14, 53
Sachs, Hans 85
Sallust 77, 115
Scarsello, Girolamo 132
Schama, Simon 134
Schefferus, Johannes 185

Schut, Cornelis 129
Scipio Africanus, Publius Cornelius 75
Seneca the Younger 2, 48, 50, 63, 76, 78, 81, 142, 182
Servius Tullius 84
Shakespeare, William 6, 50, 57–62, 84, 127, 146, 150
Sieger, Isabel 14
Skinner, Quentin 5, 68, 126, 143–144
Soutschek, Liza 14
Spenser, Edmund 8
Spinoza, Baruch 165–167, 170
Stackmann, Karl 34–35
Starck, Johannes 154
Starobinski, Jean 133
Strigel, Bernhard 109–110
Syrus, Publilius 35–36
Tacitus, Publius Cornelius 79
Tassis y Peralta, Juan de *see* Villamediana, Conde de
Theodosius I 112
Theon of Alexandria 185
Thomas Aquinas 49, 67, 154
Thomas, Keith 65, 140–141
Toledanus, Johannes 156
Toulmin, Stephen 139
Trajan 112
Ulrich von Liechtenstein 35
van Veen, Otto 128
Vega Carpio, Lope de 109
Vélez de Guevara, Luis 108
Vellert, Dirck 92–93
Villamediana, Conde de 108
Virgil 4, 96, 156
Voegelin, Eric 7
Vogt, Peter 161
Vossius, Gerardus 185–186
Walther von der Vogelweide 17, 27, 37, 40, 42–43, 45
Warburg, Aby 52, 128–129, 132, 193
Warnersoen, Peter 199
William I (Prince of Orange) 76
Wirnt von Grafenberg 25
Wivallius, Lars 184, 186
Wolff, Christian 153, 169–171
Woverius, Janus 81
Wülfer, Daniel 161-162
Ziegler, Hannes 14